THE SOUNDS OF SLAVERY

THE SOUNDS OF
SLAVERY

Discovering African American History
Through Songs, Sermons, and Speech

SHANE WHITE AND
GRAHAM WHITE

Beacon Press

BOSTON

Beacon Press
25 Beacon Street
Boston, Massachusetts 02108-2892
www.beacon.org

Beacon Press books
are published under the auspices of
the Unitarian Universalist Association of Congregations.

08 07 06 05   8 7 6 5 4 3 2 1

This book is printed on acid-free paper that meets
the uncoated paper ANSI/NISO specifications
for permanence as revised in 1992.

Composition by Wilsted & Taylor Publishing Services

Library of Congress Cataloging-in-Publication Data

White, Shane.
The sounds of slavery : discovering African American history
through songs, sermons, and speech / Shane White and Graham White.
p. cm.
Includes bibliographical references and index.
ISBN 0-8070-5026-1 (cloth : alk. paper)
1. Slaves—Southern States—Social life and customs. 2. Slaves—Southern States—
Songs and music. 3. Slaves—Southern States—Language. 4. Songs—Southern
States—History. 5. Oral communication—Southern States—History. 6. Plantation
life—Southern States. 7. Southern States—Social life and customs. 8. Slavery—
Social aspects—Southern States—History. 9. African Americans—Southern
States—History. 10. Aural History—Southern States. I. White, Graham J. II. Title.

E443.W59 2005
973'.0496073—dc22   2004021447

For Glenn Hinson and Charles Joyner

CONTENTS

The Lords of Sounds

At day's end the slaves trudged home from their owners' fields. Since sunup they had worked and sweated for the man. Now, for a few hours of darkness, the time was theirs, to the extent that slaves ever owned anything, and they could be something other than brute physical labor. Small groups gathered outside the slave cabins, listening to stories, talking out of earshot of the overseer. Maybe later, particularly if it happened to be a Saturday, there would be singing, and someone might accompany them on a banjo or a fiddle. At a distance, the quarters gave off an industrious hum, reassuring proof to those up in the Big House of the rightness of the plantation order, but from within what the slaves could hear were the invigorating sounds of the reclamation of their humanity. As she often did, Zora Neale Hurston put it best: this was the time of day when blacks "became lords of sounds."[1]

There is something timeless about such a scene. It could be a Virginia tobacco plantation in the 1750s, a South Carolina rice plantation in the 1810s, or a cotton plantation in the Mississippi Delta in the 1850s. Indeed, replace the overseer with the boss man, allow that the blacks did legally own their own time, and this vignette could just as easily be set in the Florida of the 1910s or 1920s that Hurston knew so well. For nearly three centuries of African American history, much of what was distinctive about black culture was to be found in the realm of sound, a characteristic that was particularly clear in the hours in which slaves were not toiling for their owners.

Above all else, slave culture was made to be heard. That was apparent from the moment newly enslaved Africans first arrived in the New World. It is difficult to get at the experiences of the fresh arrivals as they struggled to comprehend their status as slaves in a new and bewildering land. Hardly surprisingly, they left scant records of those experiences; practically all we have are a few descriptions by uncomprehending whites, mostly couched in terms of the impenetrability of the behavior of their newly imported property.[2] But occasionally the incidents whites describe are so striking, the behavior of blacks so apparently strange, that we are afforded some insight into the slaves' reactions to what must have seemed a terrifying and almost impossibly alien world.

In 1786 the brig *Camden* unloaded its cargo of eighty West African males at Edenton Harbor, North Carolina. This was unusual on two counts. Firstly, very few shipments of African slaves had come directly to that colony; most arrived via the Chesapeake or Charleston. Secondly, the importers, Josiah Collins and two partners of the Lake Company, needed the slaves not to work a plantation but to dig the canals that would drain the swamps around Phelps Lake in Washington County on the south of Albemarle Sound. Eventually, these acres, reclaimed by African sweat and blood, would constitute one of the largest plantations in North Carolina, but for that to happen the swamps needed to be emptied, and the principals of the Lake Company believed that Africans, fresh off the boat and unseasoned, were best suited to this arduous task.

Conditions were horrendous. Digging canals was the most dangerous, unhealthy, debilitating, and exhausting work inflicted on American slaves. For much of their waking hours, these "new negroes," as they were called, were waist deep in the muck of the North Carolina swamp, continually chivied by mosquitoes, ticks, and chiggers, always alert for steel-gray cottonmouths, copperheads, and rattlers, toiling in what seemed a never-ending task. Years later, William Trotter, the Lake Company's overseer, recalled that "many of the Africans succumbed under this work." The use of the term "succumbed" here almost shifts the blame for the deaths to the Africans themselves, but Trotter did go on to admit that "when [the company's slaves] were disabled they would be left by the bank of the canal, and the next morning the returning gang would find them dead." As each day drew to a close and fading light made more work impossible, the unfortunate slaves were marched back to cabins on the shore of Phelps Lake for a few hours respite. In his own matter-of-fact way the overseer recounted what had then transpired:

> At night they would begin to sing their native songs, and in a short
> while would become so wrought up that, utterly oblivious to the dan-

ger involved, they would grasp their bundles of personal effects, swing them on their shoulders, and setting their faces towards Africa would march down into the water singing as they marched till recalled to their senses only by the drowning of some of the party.

Apparently, such scenes were witnessed more than once. Confronted by what can fairly be described as a hell on earth, worked to the point of collapse, tormented by strange men barking orders in an incomprehensible language, these Africans, it seems, found some semblance of solace by immersing themselves in the familiar sounds of their homeland. And if, to a group of slaves stranded on the shores of an American lake, the first refrain or two they sang seemed to them absurdly out of place, gradually the resonance of the music's pulse and the reassuring texture of their own words transported them to a place where something other than their appalling conditions mattered. That, looking longingly toward Africa and swayed by the power of their own music, a few desperate Africans chose to fall back on their belief that the dead returned to the country of their birth, and to kill themselves, should come as no surprise. Nor should it shock us that those who controlled the Lake Company, aware that their slaves' desire to spite them was at least a factor in their suicides, quickly picked up on the rudiments of the culture of their property and banned them from their "evening singing."3

If the Lake Company's owners and employees were able to find at least some cultural meaning in the unfamiliar sounds of their slaves' music, others were less comprehending. While out walking in New Orleans on a Sunday afternoon in 1819, the architect and engineer Benjamin Latrobe suddenly heard a "most extraordinary noise, which I supposed to proceed from some horse Mill, the horses trampling on a wooden floor." Following the sound to its source, Latrobe came upon an area of open ground adjacent to the city, on which some five or six hundred blacks were "formed into circular groupes in the midst of four of which . . . was a ring." Within these rings, slave instrumentalists were playing while African Louisianans danced. The sounds emanating from the dancing rings at Congo Square, as this open area near the city had become known, evoked in Latrobe an overwhelming sense of cultural alienation. The drumming was "abominably loud";

the singing "uncouth" and "detestable." "I have never," the traveler announced, "seen any thing more brutally savage, and at the same time dull and stupid than this whole exhibition."[4]

For all of, or perhaps because of, Latrobe's revulsion, Congo Square was an extraordinary place, a site where the sheer din of several hundred sensuous black bodies moving to an unforgiving beat compelled even the most unthinking white onlooker to acknowledge that the people they casually thought of as slaves had an African past. Some four decades later another sojourner in New Orleans strolled through Congo Square on a fine Sunday afternoon, watching and listening to the performances. What caught James R. Creecy's ear was the sheer variety of sounds, from the harsh through to the dulcet, produced by the slave and free black musicians and dancers. Not only were "banjos, tom-toms, violins, jawbones, triangles, and various other instruments" all being played at once, but it was also the case that the bells and shells attached to the dancers arms and legs jingled "a second or counter to the music most sweetly." Music and dance had bled into one another to the point where they were inseparable. "In all their movements, gyrations and attitudenizing exhibitions, the most perfect time is kept, making the beats with the feet, heads or hands, or all, as correctly as a well-regulated metronome!" For most onlookers, this was a rather different conception of how music was made, and Creecy was well aware of the educative function of the performances at the "celebrated Congo Square." By the time of the Civil War, the spectacle was sufficiently familiar and sufficiently well anticipated not to shock, as it had Latrobe, but still strange enough "to amuse and astonish, interest and excite, the risibles and wonder" of those, particularly travelers, who were "unskilled in Creole or African manners and customs."[5]

It is important to realize, though, that the sounds of slavery were hardly confined to music, and that the distinctive aural features of African American culture permeated everyday life in British mainland North America and later the United States. In the years before the Civil War, Americans, especially those living in the South, continually heard, or overheard, the voices of Africans and African Americans talking. To be sure, in some extreme cases nervous whites did wish to silence slaves, at times quite literally. A Dr. C. G. Parsons, touring southern plantations in the mid-1850s, described for his readers a device made of pieces of iron and leather that, when fitted, rendered its wearer dumb. Parsons had seen this gag on a slave preacher, who, despite all manner of threats and punishments, had continued to preach at night in the woods, causing great religious excitement among the slaves. Finally, the errant slave had been taken to the local blacksmith and gagged, after which procedure "he could not speak a word."[6] In another instance, in Adams County, Mississippi, in December 1857, when three slaves were about to be put to death for the murder of an overseer, a local dignitary worried about the details of the hanging. On the one hand, it was essential that local slaves knew that their compatriots were dead, that they had not been quietly sold away. On the other hand, the official wanted to avoid a situation in which the slaves were "brought out in public to be hung and they get up and talk out that they are prepared to die—that they have got religion, and are ready to go home to heaven &c &c." Wary of the verbal prowess of the malefactors, the white Mississippian continued to ruminate that perhaps the slaves "could be hung publickly and not allowed to talk any."[7]

More usually, though, the white ideal of the plantation soundscape was one not of silence, but of quietude. Describing his sojourn in the region near Natchez, Mississippi, in the early 1830s, Joseph Ingraham paused briefly to reflect on the nature of plantation life. "No scene," the New England–born traveler intoned, "can be livelier or more interesting to a Northerner, than that which the negro quarters of a well regulated plantation present, on a Sabbath morning, just before church hour." In the free time available to them, slaves were dressing up, combing and styling their hair, and "quietly conversing" outside the doors of their cabins.[8] There is little doubt, however, that the quiet conversations had a different meaning for the Mississippian slaves than for the New England traveler watching from a distance on a fleeting visit to the plantation.

Hardly surprisingly, the recovery of such conversations is difficult, but some of the interviews recorded with former slaves by employees of the Works Progress Administration (WPA) in the 1930s suggest something of what they meant to African Americans. Clara Young, enslaved in Alabama, told how, after supper in the quarters following a long day's work, "we'd set 'round and sin' an talk."9 Green Cumby explained that "at night the slaves would gather roun' the cabins in little bunches and talk 'til bed time."10 Slaves chatted about the weather, the fishing, and the way their vegetables were doing. They gossiped about slaves on neighboring properties and on their own plantation, and about what the whites were doing, and on occasion they fulfilled their owners' nightmares and talked of running away, burning down haystacks, and of wreaking a horrible vengeance on the overseer and other hated whites. Mostly, though, what we know about are the Brer Rabbit and other animal trickster stories, tall tales, and, a subject of particular concern to many of the WPA interviewers, the stories about "haunts." In response to his interviewer's questions, James Southall remembered slaves gathering at someone's cabin to tell ghost stories.11 Arrie Binns, born on a Georgia plantation about 1850, easily recalled how, more than eight decades previously, he had been terrified by some of the stories told to him. "Nigger chilluns was allus skeered to go in the woods arter dark. Folkses done told us Raw-Head-and-Bloody-Bones lived in the woods and git little chilluns and eat 'em up effen they got in the woods atter dark."12 On paper, the dialect that employees of the New Deal's WPA used to transcribe former slaves' words is clumsy, conveying little of the fluent inventiveness of African American speakers, and of the verbal pyrotechnics as gifted raconteurs told their lies, artful performances that would cause Zora Neale Hurston to dub them "lords of sounds."

Some of the clearest examples of the different way in which African Americans and whites used language came from black preachers, archetypes of the black man-of-words. In August 1823, an anonymous Glaswegian attended a Methodist camp meeting in Westchester County. Such gatherings, often of several thousand people, were a commonplace in the immediate vicinity of New York City in the 1820s; some were attended only by blacks, both slave and free, others, as with the one in Westchester County, attracted both black and white believers or seekers after religious truth. After recounting at considerable length details of what the whites were doing, the Scotsman related how he had heard a "prodigious noise" coming "from the bottom of the camp, where the blacks were assembled." Caught up in the throng of whites moving in the direction of the commotion, he eventually "got within sight of a black orator who was standing on the stump of an old tree, and expounding with great vehemence and invective." The preacher railed at his audience, telling them that "they need not expect to get to heaven with their upright backs and starched strict necks for they must bow, and carry the cross on their backs." Here, to render his image palpable, the black man picked up "a huge chair" and "placed it over his shoulder." As the bemused, but fascinated, onlooker noted, the "chair became the topic of illustration, its weight was discussed, then with outstretched arms it was flourished in the heavens, to show how it would be glorified and draw up those who carried it to heaven." The drama of this performance, not just the language the preacher used but the way his entire body was caught up in the delivery of the sermon, was eliciting starkly different reactions from his racially mixed audience. Whites were laughing openly at the preacher's "shouting and mechanical sermonizing," which "was the sport of all around." By contrast, his "negro auditors," tears of joy streaming down their faces, were shouting out "God be praised!" and "Glory! Glory!"[13]

The distinctiveness of the sounds of African American culture may have been most obvious in the hours in which slaves were not toiling for their owners, but it was also clear enough as they went about their daily work. In any consideration of slave life it is important to look at the culture from the inside out, from the place where the slaves were most in control of their destinies to the place where they were under the direct thrall of their overseer or owner. Most of the waking hours of slaves were spent working—that, after all, was the reason for their enslavement—and there is a considerable amount of evidence to suggest that slaves did not view work as a quiet and solitary endeavor. In their working hours, perhaps, the slaves were no longer quite the lords of sounds, circumscribed as they were by whites, whose presence made the slaves somewhat more sly in the way they expressed themselves. But it was still the case that, for example, slaves accompanied seemingly every type of possible work with song, and did so in such a distinctive and unusual fashion that it continually evoked comments from whites who heard it.[14]

One afternoon, while resident on Butler Island in the Altamaha River, Georgia, in the 1830s, Fanny Kemble, best known as one of the leading actresses of the nineteenth century, ventured down to the river to see her plantation-owning husband off on a brief trip to nearby Saint Simons Island. As the boat was pushed off, the eight slave oarsmen began pulling and "set up a chorus, which they continued to chant in unison with each other, and in time with their stroke, till the voices and oars were heard no more from the distance." Kemble was somewhat condescending toward the singing of her husband's slaves—their tunes were invariably plagiarized from those of their owners, she believed, and the new lyrics were "astonishingly primitive"—but even she was forced to concede that the "tune and time" kept by the oarsmen and other slaves singing in unison was "something quite wonderful." And that precision of course was the point— the slaves Kemble watched and heard relied on the beat of their work songs to pace their work.[15] Other travelers made similar comments. A decade and a half before Kemble set foot in Georgia, William Faux, an English farmer, noticed, in Charleston Harbor, the "galley-slaves all singing songs in chorus, regulated by the motion of their oars." Faux also noted that the men made up their own lyrics "either in praise or satire" of "kind or unkind masters," before concluding that "the music was barbarously harmonious."[16]

Throughout British mainland North America and later the United States, whenever slaves were compelled to labor at repetitive, invariably boring, jobs, they preferred to do so to the beat of their songs, in much the same fashion as their African parents and grandparents had done. Not only did slaves row boats as they sang their songs, they also planted tobacco, chopped cotton, swung axes, scrubbed clothes on the washboard, and performed innumerable other tasks. One former slave remembered that "I used to pick 150 pounds of cotton every day," a figure that conjures up images of torn and bleeding hands and hours and hours of backbreaking monotony. She then quickly added that "We would pick cotton and sing, pick and sing all day," which suggests, perhaps, one of the ways slaves made the labor endurable.[17]

Work songs were hardly restricted to the plantation South. Every year in American ports, north and south, tens of thousands of ships' cargoes were loaded and unloaded by African Americans to a deep-voiced musical accompaniment. According to one visitor, not even Liverpool could match the bustle and hustle of the levee in New Orleans from November to July. The only thing that could "drown the noise of singing negroes" was the "fearful roaring and screeching" of one of the steamboats docking, or setting off back up the Mississippi River.[18] Unlikely as it may seem to us today, at least some black factory hands also sang as they worked. In a Richmond tobacco factory, eighty black boys "from the age of twelve years up to manhood" rolled and pressed tobacco plugs and sang psalms at the same time. The owner encouraged the practice as much as possible because "the boys work better while singing."[19]

Some of the most distinctive sounds made by slaves were not easily categorized, being neither speech nor music but more howl or shout. On October 18, 1821, before a crowd of some seven hundred whites and fifteen hundred blacks, the sheriff of Princess Anne, in Somerset County, Maryland, executed Jenny, a seventy-year-old African American woman. Seconds before Jenny was hung, "several hundreds of the colored people" turned their backs to the gallows, squatted on the ground, "covered their faces with their hands, and uttered a simultaneous groan, which while it expressed their feelings, added not a little to the horror of the scene."[20] In June 1820 William Faux, sojourning among the plantations along the South Carolina coast, reported in his diary that close to sunset there "suddenly burst upon my ear an earth-rending shout. It proceeded from negroes shouting three times three, on finishing their task."[21] To many whites, the fact that slaves sang while they worked seemed unusual enough, but these strange, guttural cries were even more unsettling. As far as the onlookers were concerned, these were disconcertingly primitive sounds far removed from their own culture.

The singing of slaves in their brush arbors on plantations, or while chopping weeds in the cotton fields or at a corn shucking or some other type of frolic; the sound of a slave preacher delivering a sermon, or of a pair of blacks exchanging greetings on a New York City street, or of an elderly slave telling Brer Rabbit stories to children; the hollers and cries that punctuated the southern countryside, and even the screams of a slave as the lash bit into her or his skin—all these and many more made up the sounds of slavery, sounds whose deeper cultural meanings this study shall endeavor to explore. Beyond that, our book is an attempt to show how sounds and understandings, whose roots lay deep in the slaves' African homelands, collided with Euro-American musical and speech forms, to create something new.

There are a couple of major problems involved in attempting to recover these sounds of slavery. One is the extent to which African and African American culture have shaped the sounds of American culture. Perhaps this is best illustrated by the example of the blues. One night in the early years of last century, probably in 1904, a train delay forced the black musician W. C. Handy to idle away several hours in Tutwiler railway station, deep in the Mississippi Delta. Handy, then the director of the Knights of Pythias band in Clarksdale, was dozing when, as he later put it, "Life suddenly took me by the shoulder and wakened me with a start." A lanky black man, dressed in rags, toes poking out of his shoes, had sat down and started "plunking a guitar." As he played, he pressed a knife against the strings, creating a sound that was "unforgettable." Three times he sang "Goin' where the Southern cross' the Dog," all the while "accompanying himself on the guitar with the weirdest music I had ever heard." When asked for an explanation, the bemused black man explained to Handy that the line meant he was going to Moorhead, where the north-south and east-west rail lines crossed each other. The reason the tune stayed in Handy's mind, though, lay not in the meaning of the line but in its distinctive and repetitive sound. This incident, which conceivably never happened, is one of the myths of the origins of the blues, a story that sets up an encounter between the sophisticated and technically trained Handy and the vernacular music of ordinary African Mississippians that soon resulted in the commercial form of the blues. Within a few years, the sound that had struck Handy as weird would be known across black America, and nowadays, for example, very few readers of this book would not be familiar with the sound of either a slide guitar or the blues. Indeed, today the guitarist is more likely to be an Eric Clapton, born in Surrey, England, than a black from the Delta. The very success and consequent familiarity of black culture continually threatens to distort our understanding of the sounds of slavery. Part of what we are endeavoring to do in this book, then, is to restore the "pastness" of past sounds, to recover some of the shock value that those sounds would have had for eighteenth- and nineteenth-century whites who heard them, the kind of shock that W. C. Handy experienced as he listened to the black Mississippian's "weird" and "unforgettable" music.[22]

The other major problem involved in writing about the history of sound is that of sources. Seemingly left with only printed and manuscript pages, how effectively can we recover anything of slavery's sounds? Frederick Douglass, easily the most famous survivor of the horrors of the "peculiar institution," was well aware of the strangeness, to whites, of "apparently incoherent" slave musical sounds, even as he urged whites to attempt to understand their "deep meanings." Douglass was alluding here not to the lyrics of the songs but to the "wild notes" of the singers, the "tones, loud, long and deep," every one of which constituted "a testimony against slavery, and a prayer to God for deliverance from chains." Those who wished "to be impressed with a sense of the soul-killing power of slavery," Douglass suggested, should "go to Col. Lloyd's [Douglass's Maryland owner's] plantation, and, on allowance day," as the slaves, singing all the while, passed by on their journey to collect their rations, "place [themselves] in the deep, pine woods, and there . . . in silence, thoughtfully analyze the sounds that shall pass through the chambers of [their] soul."[23]

Unfortunately, of course, we cannot take Douglass's advice. But every now and again, we have come across the writings of someone who has, metaphorically at least, stood in those woods and listened, an observer particularly attuned to the sonic world. Perhaps the best example is Thomas Wentworth Higginson, an idealistic New England abolitionist, who took command of the First Regiment, South Carolina Volunteers, the Union's first black military unit, and who possessed an unusual sensitivity to sound. Higginson's memoir, *Army Life in a Black Regiment,* and the diary and the letters to his wife and mother on which it is based, is saturated with detailed and sharply observed depictions of the strange and intriguing soundscape of black camp life. On one of his "evening strolls among my own camp fires," Higginson came upon black soldiers "telling stories & shouting with laughter over the broadest mimicry," mimicry in which the unit's white officers were "not always spared." Somewhere in the distance "the everlasting 'shout'" was under way, "with its mixture of piety & polka." And here and there "quieter prayer meetings" were in progress, "with ardent & often touching invocations; & slower psalms deaconed out . . . by the leader . . . , in a wailing chant." At one fire, men danced to the accompaniment of "a quite artistic fiddle." At another, a "stump orator perched on his barrel, pour[ed] out his mingling of liberty & Methodism in quaint eloquence."[24] Details such as these eluded the ears of virtually every other observer of black military life.

Higginson listened keenly not merely to this aural world of shouts and song, but to the ways his men spoke. Although disconcerted by certain peculiarities of syntax, he admired his troops' ready eloquence, their striking use of imagery, their pithily expressed abstract thought, their sheer verbal facility and power. One night he heard one of his soldiers deliver a "perfectly thrilling" impromptu speech, which contained "the most impressive sentence about the American flag I ever heard," a sentence he went on to render in dialect:

> Our mas'rs dey hab lib under de flag, dey got dere wealth under it, & ebery ting beautiful for dere chil'en & under it dey hab grind us into money & put us in dere pocket; & dat minute dey tink dat ole flag mean freedom for us dey pull it down & run up de rag ob dere own; but we'll nebber desert it boys, nebber; we hab lib under it for 1862 years (!!!) & we'll die for it now.

Higginson doubted that any of his officers "could have spoken on the spur of the moment with such easy eloquence and such telling effect."[25] Again and again, the New Englander would be struck by his men's verbal inventiveness, their ability to invest images drawn from everyday life with deep and pertinent meaning. In August 1863, as he left the regiment for a twenty-day furlough to recover from war wounds, Higginson was especially touched when a soldier told him: "You's a mighty big rail out ob de fence, sa."[26]

Yet for every Higginson or William Francis Allen and the other compilers of *Slave Songs of the United States* (1867), there were scores if not hundreds of observers journeying through the South who were seemingly oblivious to, or laconically dismissive of, all that they heard.[27] And even had these travelers been as aurally sensitive as we might wish, there is the obvious problem that sound does not reduce well to the printed page. There is, however, another possible source. As part of the documentary impulse of the 1930s, a number of collectors, most notably John and Alan Lomax, traveled through the South, recording all manner of African American sounds for the Library of Congress's Archive of American Folk Song. The fruits of these collecting trips are still deposited in the Library of Congress. In an attempt to illustrate more clearly the nature and meaning of African American sounds, we have included examples of field calls, work songs, spirituals, prayers, and sermons, on the compact disc that is packaged with this book. In most cases, items selected for the CD were recorded in the 1930s and are held by the library's Archive of Folk Culture.

The African Americans whom the Lomaxes auditioned and then recorded on what John Lomax called their "portable-machine for electrical sound-recording"[28]—on the 1933 trip the machine weighed 350 pounds—were the children and grandchildren of slaves. Unlike earlier collectors, whose transcriptions of performances depended on the transcriber's skill and judgment, the Lomaxes relied on technology to secure what they believed was the unmediated original. After one field trip, John Lomax described the 150 tunes with which he had returned as "sound photographs of Negro songs, rendered in their own element, unrestrained, uninfluenced and undirected by anyone who has had his own notions of how the songs should be rendered."

But like the photographs to which Lomax compared his recordings, they contain ambivalences. Recordings, too, can strike a pose. For even though the Lomaxes used machines, they saw themselves as being in pursuit of subjects whom modernity had passed by. And this vision, in turn, shaped both their journeys and the sounds they enshrined. In search of an older, more "authentic" African American culture—in our terms, one closer to the time of slavery—the Lomaxes rummaged through the "eddies of human society" in remote cotton plantations, lumber camps, and, most famously, segregated southern prisons. Part of the reason they were so excited by their "discovery" of the talent of Leadbelly was that they felt that the great blues singer's "eleven years of confinement had cut him off both from the phonograph and from the radio"—the fact that Leadbelly felt otherwise was beside the point.[29] What is exciting about listening to the material from the field trips into the South of the 1930s is that the folk artists whose voices one hears reveal ways of singing and talking that had been heard from the lips of former slaves. It most definitely is not as though a tape recorder had been left on in the woods near the plantation on which Frederick Douglass toiled as a slave, but these recordings bring us about as close as we are ever going to get to hearing some of the famil- iar—and to white ears often "weird" and "unforgettable"—sounds of slavery.

CHAPTER 1

"All we knowed was go and come by de bells and horns"

"When de day begin to crack," the former Louisiana slave Charley Williams told his interviewer, "de whole plantation break out wid all kinds of noises.... You hear de guinea fowls start potracking down at de edge of de woods lot, and den de roosters all start up 'round de barn and de ducks finally wake up and jine in." Then "de wind rise a little, and you can hear a old bell donging way on some plantation a mile or two off, and den more bells at other places and maybe a horn, and purty soon younder go old Master's old ram horn wid a long toot and den some short toots, and here come de overseer down de row of cabins, hollering right and left." As Williams and some seventy-five other slaves on his plantation began work in the fields each day, they could hear too "de anvil start dangling in de blacksmith shop: Tank! Deling-ding! Tank! Deling-ding!, and dat ole bull tongue [of a damaged plow] gitting straightened out," and "de old loom going 'frump, frump,' and you know it all right iffen your clothes do be wearing out, 'cause you gwine git new britches purty soon!"[1]

Williams's interviewer was an employee of the Federal Writers' Project of the WPA, which made an ambitious attempt, in the late 1930s, to gather firsthand testimonies about slavery from those who had survived it.[2] In effect, the WPA project invited large numbers of ordinary African Americans to break a long historical silence, to tell their own stories, often in their own way and to someone other than family and friends, for the first time. As the reminiscences of the former slaves readily show, the sounds of the plantation and its surrounds were an important part of the remembered fabric of slavery, giving both shape and texture to their recollections of the worlds they had once been forced to inhabit. Of course, not all of those worlds were the same as Charley Williams's, and few ex-slaves gave so detailed an account of the soundscapes with which they had once been so familiar. Yet by paying attention to the ex-slaves' memories of sounds that they themselves had created, or that had originated in the natural environment or with whites, and to hints former slaves gave as to what those sounds meant to them, we can at least begin, in Jane Kamensky's words, "to *hear* their history: to restore the voices, the silences, and the clamor amid which people in that distant world made sense of their lives, day by day."3

Former North Carolina slave Tempie Durham, for instance, easily recalled the sounds of domestic industry on the large plantation on which she once worked. "De cardin' an' spinnin' room was full of niggers," she remembered, and all those years later she could still "hear dem spinnin' wheels now turnin' roun' an' sayin' hum-m-m-m, hum-m-m-m, an' hear de slaves singin' while dey spin."4 Jasper Battle, who was interviewed in Georgia, remembered the sounds of washday: the noise made by slave children as they beat the clothes with batten sticks, and the voices of slave women "a-singin' dem old songs," which could be heard " 'most a mile away."5 Heard Griffin, a young boy in slavery times, spoke not of prominent sound-marks—the tolling of the plantation bell, for instance—but of the shifting cadences of ambient sound. Once the slaves on his plantation had reached the field each morning, he remembered, "It wouldn't be long before you would hear the 'geeing and hawing' . . . the squealing of pigs and the barking of dogs—all sounds mingling together."6 The field work to which former Mississippi slave George Weathersby was assigned was burdensome, he told his interviewer, but not without its compensations: "Us laked all being together. Big bunches would be wukin' in de corn or cotton fields, a hollerin' an' a singing an' a telling ghos' tales."7 John Davenport even reproduced, as best he could, the hollers that he and other slaves used to call domesticated animals from the fields: "We used to call de cows on de plantation like dis: 'co-winch, co-winch.' We called de mules like dis: 'co, co,' and de hogs and pigs, 'pig-oo,' 'pig-oo.' "8

A very young Uncle Stepney, eluding the dreaded patrollers by hiding out in the woods near his Alabama plantation, had listened anxiously to "de panthers a screamin' a way off in de fores' an' de wildcats a howlin.' " More ominous, however, had been the cry of a screech owl, a sure sign of impending death. Quickly, the boy had turned the pockets of his overalls inside out, whereupon the bird's raucous cry had ceased.9 In a more nostalgic mood, Aunt Clussey, aged about seventeen when the Civil War began, recalled how, in the days before the conflict, she and the other slaves would gather behind the Big House, where "young massa played his fiddle an' us'd sing, 'Swing Low Sweet Chariot.'" She remembered too "de call of de whip-poor-will ober de ridge at night an' de song of de thrush early in de mornin'," and claimed still to "hear de voices of de tired folks a comin' home singing atter de sun done sunk behin' de mountain."10 For ex-Alabama slave Clara Davis, too, the memory of plantation sounds was richly evocative. "I wants to hear de sound of de hounds in de woods atter de 'possum... an' listen to de wheels [of the old wagon] groanin' as dey rolls along." She longed, also, she said, to hear once more the slaves on boats passing up and down the Alabama River "a singin' at dere work," and to "walk the paths th'ew de woods an... listen to frogs at night."11 Recollections such as these, fragments of African Americans' remembered lives offered in response to interviewers' questions, permit us to eavesdrop on the past, to attempt, in some measure, to "reconstitute the auditory environment" of slavery's hitherto largely soundless world.12

Other recollected sounds carried more traumatic associations. The anguished cries of families whose members were sold away; the repetitive crack of the master's or overseer's whip: these were emblematic sounds for captive African Americans, stark "aural reminders," in Robin Kelley's phrase, of the slaveholder's presence and power.13 "All time, night an' day, you could hear men an' women screamin' to de tip of dere voices as either ma, pa, sister, or brother wus tak without any warnin' an' sell," Augustus Ladson declared. "People wus always dyin' frum a broken heart."14 After lamenting that "babies wuz snatched from dere mother's breas' an' sold to speculators," and "chilluns wuz separated from sisters an' brothers an' never saw each other ag'in," Delia Garlic scornfully rebuked her interviewer's subsequent query: "Course dey cry; you think dey not cry when dey was sold lak cattle?"15 The sounds associated with whippings, too, had stayed with those who had been forced to listen to them. "I's heard old Jack heep o' mornins 'fo day when Marsa would be whippin him he'd say: 'Oh! pray Marsa,'" Alex McCinney testified. "Oh how he did beg an' plead fo' mercy. My! I can hear dat voice now."16 Lou Williams's owners had treated her well, but as she explained, other slaves had not been so fortunate. "We lives close to de meanest owner in de country.... He keeps overseers to beat de niggers and he has de big leather bullwhip with lead in de end, and he beats some slaves to death. We heared dem holler and holler till dey couldn't holler no mo! Den dey jes' sorta grunt every lick till dey die."[17] Martha Jackson called to mind the terrible cries of a runaway slave, subjected to a particularly brutal beating, which she and others had silently to watch. "De holes in de strop dey sucks flesh up th'oo 'em, and de nigger's a hollerin' en ev'ybody so skeered dey right ashy, and dey can't nobody say a mumblin' word 'case dey so skeered."[18]

It was not uncommon, either, for interviewees to recall the doleful baying of hounds on the trail of runaway slaves. Pappy Holloway, born free in Fort Valley, Georgia, in 1848, stated that "you could hear the hounds all hours of the night. Some nigger was gone."[19] "The woods was full of runaways," ex-Texas slave Gill Ruffin declared, "and I heered them houn's a runnin' 'em like deer many a time, and heered dat whip when they's caught."[20] As slaves well knew, a successful capture was often followed by a particularly barbaric punishment. If a slave on Henry Waldon's plantation escaped, the owner of a pack of bloodhounds would be summoned, whose dogs would chase the runaway until they had him or her at bay. When the owner arrived, the dogs would be let loose. "They would tell you to stand still and put your hands over your privates," Henry Waldon declared. "Five or six hounds bitin' you on every side and a man settin' on a horse holding a double shotgun on you."[21]

The baying of the "nigger hound," an animal trained specifically to catch and oftentimes to punish escaped slaves, evoked for slaves not merely their own degraded status (as mere beasts to be hunted down), but also what must often have seemed the master's virtually untrammeled power. When Gabe Emmanuel's master's dog died, its grief-stricken owner announced that the animal was to be given a proper burial, adding ominously that "us Niggers might better be's pow'ful sad when us come to dat fun'al." And, Emmanuel assured his interviewer, "dem Niggers was sad over de death o' dat poor old dog what had chased 'em all over de country. Dey all stan' 'roun a-weepin' an' a-mournin'. Ever' now an' den dey'd put water on dey eyes an' play lak dey was a-weepin' bitter, bitter tears. 'Poor old dog. Amen!...De Lawd have mercy!' "22

Throughout the rural South, the sounds of tolling bells and blown horns, too, must often have been difficult to escape. William S. Walsh remembered that the bugles his father owned, which were similar to those used by other slaveholders in the area, were huge, commonly measuring five or six feet in length. They were made of poplar wood, which was coated with tar and then submerged for several days, a process that gave the instrument "a resonant sound" that "could be heard for miles on a clear night."23 One former Georgia slave estimated that the morning bugle that woke slaves on his plantation could be heard "as far as High Shoals, and us lived dis side of Watkinsville." "Heaps of folkses all over dat part of de country," he declared, "got up by dat old bugle."24

Generally, ex-slaves' memories of plantation bells and horns evoked painful associations. Those sounds had marked for many of them the span of long and arduous working days. Typically, the first bell had sounded at 4:00 AM, but it was not unusual for slaves to have been required to rise earlier. William Byrd explained that his master "had a great iron piece hanging just out side his door and he hit that every morning at 3.30."25 On every plantation in his Mississippi district other than his own, Anderson Williams testified, the first bell of the day rang at three o'clock and by four o'clock every slave had to be ready to go to the fields. In sharp contrast, "Dr's [that is, Anderson Williams's master's] niggers went to de fiel' one hour after sun-up an' quit in time to git de night work done befo' dark," but so unusually lenient were these arrangements thought to be that "de folks around called Dr's niggers 'De Free Slaves.' "26 Not only were field slaves usually forced to rise well before daylight, but they had sometimes to remain in the fields long after dark. "Slaves on our place...had to work night and day," Estella Jones remembered. "Marster had stobs (staves) all over de field to put lights on so dey could see how to work after dark. De men, more so dan de womens, had to work every night 'til twelve o'clock."27 Women hardly escaped, however. After laboring long hours in the field, Callie Bracey's mother would cook for the following day, preparing lunch buckets for the field hands. When the horn sounded at 4:00 AM she went back to work in the field.[28]

Former slaves' recollections of plantation bells also called to mind daily rituals of humiliation that degraded slave women's lives. On Laura Smalley's Texas plantation, the blast of a horn summoned nursing mothers from the fields to feed their babies, a demeaning experience, as her description of the spectacle makes clear. "A cow out there will go to the calf.... Well they [the nursing mothers] come at ten o'clock every day, ... to all them babies.... When that horn blowed... for the mothers, ... they'd jus' come jus' like cows, jus' a-running, you know, coming to the children."[29]

Former Alabama slave Amy Domino learned to identify bells of a different kind. "I 'member w'en I's jes' a li'l gal a-hearin' bells in d' night," she recounted, "d' ol' folks say dat some 'r' d' run-a-way niggers from uder plantation. Dey put bells on d' slaves, wel' [weld] dem on so dey kaint gittum off 'n' dey kin hear dem iffen dey git 'way in d' woods."[30] In an autobiography written after he had escaped from slavery, Moses Roper provided a more detailed description of one variant of this apparatus. Roper's master, a Mr. Gooch, created a U-shaped iron structure, fitted with bells, which was attached to the back of a slave's neck (and presumably, since the apparatus Roper described was seven feet in height, also secured around the wearer's waist). Three crossbars spanned the U-shaped iron frame, the highest having four bells attached to it, the second-highest six bells, the lowest eight bells. The weight of this "very ponderous machine," as well as the minor cacophony of sound that must have accompanied its wearer, effectively discouraged further attempts at flight. Roper noted that devices of this kind were "generally adopted among the slave-holders in South Carolina, and in some other slave states."[31]

Even apparently routine sounds, mainly associated with workaday activities on plantations and farms, could be loaded with deeper-than-expected meanings. After recounting, without apparent animus, how the blast of his master's horn signaled the start of another day's work, Charley Williams suddenly burst out: "Bells and horns! Bells for dis and horns for dat! All we knowed was go and come by de bells and horns."[32] Williams's sudden flare of resentment signaled the restive presence of more fundamental concerns. Mark Smith has argued that, from the 1830s, southern slaveholders' adoption of a mechanical "clock-dependent time consciousness," communicated to slaves through the use of bells and horns, challenged slaves' conception of time. Coming, as they or their forbears had done, from societies in which clocks were virtually unknown, where their sense of time was "task-oriented" and "natural" (time marked by the position of the sun, for example), slaves were increasingly required to accommodate themselves to the demands of a clock-regulated world, to a "mechanical regulation of life and thought."[33] As a resentful former slave, Dave Walker, remembering these transitional years, explained: "We wuz trained to live by signals of a ole cow horn. Us knowed whut each blow meant. All through de day de ole horn wuz blowed, to git up in de mo'nings, to go to de big kitchen out in Mars' back yard ter eat, to go to fields, an' to come in an' on lak dat all day."[34] The tension between clock-dependent time and "natural" or task-oriented time, with all that the former portended for the way in which slaves were able to live their lives, helps to explain Charley Williams's impassioned outburst. It also adds poignancy to an incident that stuck in the memory of former slave Jennie Bowen. In the last years of slavery, a male slave on her plantation had been responsible for ringing the bell that woke slaves in the morning and called them back to the quarters at night. After freedom came, this man remained on the same plantation, but when the owner's son rang the plantation bell to summon black workers from the fields, the former bell ringer ignored it. When asked why, the man answered: " 'Tain't no mo' bell ringin' for dis nigger, 'caze I is free."[35]

It is revealing to attempt to recover the meanings slaves attached to the sounds of the plantation, especially if those sounds signified differently for the whites who had heard them. But slaves also actively and collectively shaped their acoustic environment. Partly they did so by sheer dint of numbers. At most times on most southern plantations slaves far and away outnumbered any whites who may have been present; this was also the case, for example, at events such as the execution of the slave Jenny in Somerset County, Maryland, in October 1821, where there were two slaves for every white, or on market days in Charleston or Richmond. But the impact of African Americans on slavery's soundscape was due also to the different nature, often the apparent strangeness, of the sounds blacks made. This sense of cultural dissonance was perhaps most acutely felt by white observers of slave festivals.

The festival of Pinkster came to America with the seventeenth-century Dutch, but at some time, probably in the second third of the eighteenth century, it became almost entirely an African American event.[36] In 1736 the *New-York Weekly Journal* published an account of a slave festival that may have been Pinkster. On this slave holiday, black people gathered on a plain outside town, divided up into groups "according to their different Nations," and danced "to the hollow Sound of a Drum, made of the Trunk of a hollow Tree, ... the grating rattling Noise of Pebles or Shells in a small Basket," and the sounds of many "Bangers" (banjos), while other blacks accompanied the dancers in song. The seeming cacophony of musical sound, as well as the raucous curses of those "who had been unlucky enough to get a Dram too much," was, declared "The Spy," "enough to raise one's Hair on end."[37] Pinkster occurred intermittently in parts of New York and New Jersey originally settled by the Dutch, but reached its apogee in Albany in the 1790s and 1800s. Here, on "Pinkster Hill" on the outskirts of the state capital, for almost a week and usually in May, King Charles, an African-born slave described as one "whose authority is absolute, and whose will is law during the Pinkster holidays,"[38] presided over a motley crew of slaves, free blacks, and whites. The numbers of those involved were impressive enough—hundreds, indeed quite possibly thousands, of African Americans congregated on these occasions—but what struck spectators even more was the visual and sonic strangeness of this black gathering.

The sense of white alienation is conveyed in the remarks of a contemporary witness. In the "Guinea dance," which climaxed the Pinkster festival, the "chief musician[,] dressed in a horrid manner—rolling his eyes and tossing his head with an air of savage wildness; grunting and mumbling out certain inarticulate but hideous sounds," beat upon a Guinea drum. On either side of this character, two imps "decorated with feathers and cow tails" performed similar "uncouth and terrifying grimaces," while playing on smaller drums and imitating the chief musician's "sounds of frightful dissonance." At the same time, males and females danced to music that, to this observer, possessed "no regular air."[39] Several decades later, a Dr. James Eights recalled Pinkster at its height, sometime in the late eighteenth century. His memories centered on the rhythms of the drumming, and particularly on Jackey Quackenboss's beating on "an *eel-pot,* with a cleanly dressed sheep skin drawn tightly over its wide and open extremity." As Quackenboss wailed away, this African New Yorker slave chanted over and over "the ever wild, though euphonic cry of *Hi-a-bomba, bomba, bomba,* in full harmony with the thumping sounds." Quackenboss's vocals were "readily taken up and as oft repeated" by a chorus of African American females, who accompanied their singing by the "beating of time with their ungloved hands, in strict accordance with the eel-pot melody." Such a performance must have sounded fantastic—little wonder that Dr. Eights claimed that the music was "singular in the extreme"—and about as far removed from anything produced by the respectable and dour burghers of Albany as it is possible to imagine.[40]

Much the same was true of the profusion of sounds created by slaves during Jonkonnu, a festival seemingly restricted on the mainland to antebellum North Carolina. The best account of this slave festival comes from a Dr. Edward Warren, who observed the slaves going "John Koonering" on the Christmas Day he spent at Somerset Plantation in 1829. Warren, too, was struck not only by the fantastic attire of the participants, but also by the weirdness of the sounds they made. The "leading character" in the Jonkonnu procession wore a costume of rags, a pair of ox horns attached to the skin of a raccoon, pulled over his face, sandals made of "some wild varmint," and several cow or sheep bells draped across his shoulders. Behind him came a group of slaves "arrayed fantastically in ribbons, rags, and fethers" and carrying "gumba boxes" or "wooden frames covered over with tanned sheepskins," and bringing up the rear was a "motley crowd of all ages." Once the procession had reached the front door of the "great house," "the musicians commenced to beat their gumba boxes violently," and wild dancing began. Simultaneously, the leader of the bizarre procession "led off with a song of strange, monotonous cadence" that was "extemporized for the occasion," and "the whole crowd joined in the chorus, shouting and clapping their hands in the wildest glee."[41]

In the last three or four decades of slavery's existence in the South, however, by far the most widespread and important slave festival was corn shucking, a ritual event suffused, according to many whites, with unfamiliar, though by no means always unwelcome, sound. After the corn was harvested, slaves from the surrounding plantations would be invited to come on the appointed evening. Competing teams would be organized, and slaves, responding to their captain's, or song leader's, calls, shucked enormous piles of corn. Later, after the work was done, there would be more music, dancing, eating, and drinking, and on some plantations, at evening's end, the slaves would seize their master, carry him around the Big House, occasionally toss him in the air, and take him inside, where, as the former slave George Woods remembered, they would "place him in the chair; comb his head; cross his knees for him and leave him alone."[42] Unusual as such behavior seemed, it was more often than not the sounds that stayed with whites as their strongest memory of the corn-shucking ritual. In a piece published in *Putnam's Magazine* in 1855, an anonymous author wrote of the "wild grandeur and stirring music" of one particular corn-shucking song, and of his difficulty in conveying that haunting power on the printed page. Indeed, he wrote, if one slipped back into the dark and watched "the sable forms of the gang" lit by the flickering flames of the torches as they worked, and listened "to the wild notes of their harvest songs," it was "easy to imagine ourselves unseen spectators of some...savage festival."[43]

The mass slave singing at the core of corn shucking sent shivers down the spine of those lucky enough to witness it. After all, where else in antebellum America could one hear choirs of several score, often hundreds, of voices? One white man, recalling the festival on a North Carolina plantation in the 1850s, wrote that the scene, as "three hundred voices would swell out in the chorus" answering the call of the leader, "simply beggars description."[44] Of course, corn shucking signified rather differently for the slaves and former slaves, few of whom were prone to freighting their accounts of the event with nostalgic references to the peculiar institution. But there was agreement between black and white about the memorable nature of the singing. Decades after he had managed to escape from slavery, William Wells Brown still recalled the exhilaration he felt when listening to the various groups of slaves approaching his plantation in the dark: "To hear three or four of these gangs coming from different directions, their leaders giving out the words, and the whole company joining in the chorus," Brown wrote, surpassed anything that even the best of the blackface minstrels could manage.[45] The irony was, of course, that by the time he wrote this in 1880, Brown's point of comparison was the minstrel show, a genre that in at least some ways was an imitation of the culture that Brown had heard and seen decades earlier in the plantation South.

Seldom did slave behavior seem and sound so different to whites as it did at slave festivals. As slaves created these syncretic events, they drew on their own African past and also what they found around them in America—these events are properly labeled "African American"— but it was also the case that much of the African influence belonged to the sonic realm. Certainly, festivals sounded like nothing most white onlookers had ever heard, and yet, for all their evidentiary value, it is important to bear their limitations in mind. Festivals lasted only for a day or two each year and most slaves were unable even to participate in them. Not only were these events geographically circumscribed, but even when they did occur in a given locale, they seldom seem to have continued for very many years. On the other hand, wherever slavery existed, rituals such as black funerals punctuated the rhythms of the calendar with depressing regularity. The differences between the practices of slaves and their owners are not so spectacularly obvious here as they were in the festivals but, in the end, a close examination of slave funeral rituals may tell us more about the distinctiveness or otherwise of African American slave culture.

Those differences often became apparent even at the moment of death. A little after nine o'clock on a stormy spring evening at Port Royal on South Carolina's coast, a group of whites heard "a strange wild, screaming wail" above the din of the thunder and wind. Initially, Harriet Ware, a young northern woman drawn like so many others to the South to teach the newly freed slaves, had thought the sound was that of the mules stirring, but the manner in which the sound "rose and fell again and again in such agony" soon convinced her otherwise. Next morning she was proved right. Betty, Harriet Ware's maid, came into her bedroom, asked about breakfast, and quietly remarked, "And Bu' Sam dead too." "I dunner if you yeardy de whoop when he gone."[46] Not only did that mournful wail distantly echo the sound made by the fifteen hundred blacks compelled to witness Jenny's execution in Princess Anne some four decades earlier, but it also reverberated with black memories of a now distant African past. According to the French botanist Michel Adanson, in Senegal, the initial "shriek" was made by one of the deceased's relatives, following which "all the women in the village came out, and setting up a most terrible howl, they flocked about the place from whence the first noise had issued."[47] The gender specificity of the ritual may have been lost in the New World—the sources are not clear on that point—but many generations later, even in the last moments of the hated institution of slavery, African Americans were marking death in ways similar to those of their African ancestors.

Of course, the passing of every slave was not memorialized in this fashion. Millions of Africans and African Americans lived and died as slaves in the American North and the South over more than two centuries and, inevitably, the conditions under which they did so varied immensely. Generalizing about something as broad as slave funerary rituals is always fraught with difficulty, not least because it is usually easy enough to come up with counterexamples. Indeed, several former slaves interviewed by the WPA scanted the subject, asserting that the plantation routine was barely interrupted by the demise of one of their number. John Bates, a slave from Limestone County, Texas, remembered that slaves just dug "a hole and rolls em in it and kivers em over wid dirt."[48] Similarly, Mary Gaffney answered her interviewer's question about funerals by detailing that the dead slave was "piled" into the grave and that "no singing, no preaching or praying ever took place during slavery time." She also added that slaves would "not even shed a tear because he was gone where they would not be any more slaves."[49] Kate Darling was another who depicted a heartlessly efficient plantation regime. When slaves died, the owner simply assigned a couple of their compatriots to bury the body, with the admonition "Don't be long." There was no singing or praying, she recalled bitterly, "just put them in the ground, cover 'em up and hurry on back to that fiel'."[50] And yet for all that, the evidence from both slave participants and white onlookers makes it overwhelmingly clear that most owners acknowledged their human property's need to farewell kith and kin after their own fashion. How much they did so varied. One former slave remembered that "whenever there was a corpse on de place Marster didn't make nobody do no wuk, 'cept jus' look atter de stock, 'til atter de buryin'."[51] Other owners were less generous. What slave and white testimony also makes abundantly clear, however, is how the general pattern of ritual associated with most slave deaths and burials differed from that followed by whites, and how those differences were embedded in the slaves' acoustic world.

On the night that "Bu' Sam" died at Port Royal, when the air had been filled with "a strange wild, screaming wail," a couple of white gentlemen keeping company with Harriet Ware had wandered off down the street to investigate. They soon returned to report that there were "a good many people in Uncle Sam's house having a merry time." What these men had stumbled across was the beginning of the "settin' up," or wake, for Sam. Later that night, as Ware was going to bed, "there began, at first quite low, then swelling louder with many voices, the strains of one of their wild, sad songs." The "solemn, wildly sad strains," sounds that Ware categorized as "strange," carried on until sunrise, at which point the participants "ceased and separated."[52] In her telling, she was rather more perceptive than her uncomprehending friends, but the reactions of all three serve to underline the cultural differences between black and white. Most emphatically, death among the slaves was not a subject for muffled tread and black crepe. The fact that Ware's friends mistook the wake for revelry says nothing about the depth of the slaves' feelings for Sam. It merely indicates the different ways in which slaves and their owners chose to mourn their dead.

Hamp Kennedy, a particularly eloquent ex-slave from Mississippi, gave a simple explanation of the wake: "Dey neber lef ' a dead nigger 'lone in de house."[53] That such ideas originated in Africa was certainly suggested by the fact that the "settin' up" was evidently particularly important in the case of the African-born. According to Robert Pinckney, "Wen one uh doze Africans die, it wus bery sad. Wen a man's countryman die, he sit right wid um all night."[54] As soon as news of a death spread, people flocked to the deceased's dwelling, often overflowing onto the street outside. Inside, mirrors were turned to the walls and pictures covered up, and if there were any clocks in the room where the body rested, they were stopped. On being asked why this was so, Rena Clark explained that its purpose was to allow people to hear noises throughout the house, since "they didn't want no haints slipping up on them."[55] And yet, as Harriet Ware and her friends had discovered, wakes could be noisy affairs, more than loud enough, one would have thought, to allow "haints" to move around at will. Elsie Payne remembered the setting-up parties where slaves would "sing and pray and shout, lak at a meeting."[56] When night ended, there was often a leave-taking of the body. Robert Pinckney, detailing in particular the deaths of Africans, remembered that "attuh dey pray, dey come in and put deah han on duh frien an say goodbye."[57]

Something of how a setting up may have sounded is conveyed by Hamp Kennedy's description. "At de wake we clapped our han's an' kep' time wid our feet—*Walking Egypt*, dey calls hit—an' we chant an' hum all night 'til de nigger was *funeralized*."[58] Here the sonic texture of black speech, indicated partly by the clumsy way in which the interviewer has rendered his words, but mostly by the speech's distinctive expressiveness—"*Walking Egypt*" conjuring up both the Old Testament account of the captive children of Israel escaping from bondage and, intentionally or not, the Africa from which the practice derived, and the verb "to funeralize," a neologism that has survived down to our own time—serves to underscore how different slave rituals sounded from those of their owners.[59]

As there were "no 'balmers on de plantations," little time was wasted in burying a deceased slave, particularly in summer.[60] Only specified slaves, often women, could prepare the body, and "dey washed de corpse good wid plenty of hot water and soap" before placing it on the "coolin' board."[61] One former slave was totally bemused by his interviewer's ignorance of this essential item. "Lordy, Missy, ain't you never seed no coolin' board?" He then explained that these items were a "good deal lak ironin' boards, only dey had laigs to stand on."[62] Corpses were prepared on these boards—women were usually wrapped in "windin' sheets," men were dressed in homespun suits.[63] Coffins were spare and wooden, although at least one slave remembered one as being "blackened 'til it looked right nice," an effect achieved by painting coffins "wid smut off of de wash pot mixed wid grease and water."[64]

The burial occurred on the day following the death, and it too was hardly a quiet affair. Isaah Morgan from Alabama recalled that the coffin "was taken in a ox cart to de grave, wid all de slaves a-walkin' 'long behine de cart singin' de spirituals."[65] Initially, the loudest sounds were the creaks and groans of the wagon bouncing over what passed for a road on most southern plantations: Annie Davies remembered with a smile that "if you hadn't been dead, it sure would have woke you up, going up and down hill and bumping over the road."[66] And then, starting low but swelling into a full-throated rendition of favorite hymns, the mourners, sometimes a mere handful but at other times numbering in the hundreds, found their collective voice, filled the air with those oft-commented on "wild" and "plaintive" sounds, and for a short time at least, claimed some portion of the plantation South as an African American place. Decades later, Arrie could still remember the sound of the funeral processions slowly making their way to the burial ground. "I've heard 'em 'nough times clear 'cross the fields, singin' and moanin' as they went," she said, adding wistfully that "dem days of real feelin' an' keerin' is gone." [67]

Proceedings at the graveside did not last long, indeed seem almost perfunctory. The coffin was lowered into the grave, some planks were placed over it, someone, occasionally a white but more usually a fellow slave, said a few words, and the hole was filled in. And all the while the mourners kept up a continual accompaniment of song. Ex-slave after ex-slave noted that the song most closely associated with funerals was "Hark from de Tomb a Doleful Sound," not infrequently remembered as "Harps from de Tombs." That variation significantly reminds us that this was, to all intents and purposes, an oral society: this particular hymn was important to many slaves, but consistency in the words or music to which it was sung could hardly have been expected. WPA interviewee Bert Strong clearly recalled one of the hymns sung at his grandpa Gloster's funeral:

> Hark from the tomb my ears a tender cry,
> A living man can view the ground where
> I may shortly lie,
> And must this body die and this frame decay,
> And these active limbs of mine lay molten
> in the clay.[68]

Here, the first two lines are derived from the original hymn (the phonetic resemblance is clear, even if the meaning has been lost), but the last two lines have been taken from somewhere else entirely. Yet for all that, the new words have an expressive force and appropriateness of their own. Doubtless, similar variations also occurred in the tune to which "Harp [or Hark] from de Tombs" was sung. For all the variety, though, what was impressively consistent was the memory of how the hymn was a vital part of the observance of a slave death. Carrie Hudson, for example, told her interviewer that "I 'members how us used to holler and cry when dey come to de part of de fun'ral whar dey sung: 'Hark F'um De Tomb, A Doleful Sound.'"[69]

Slave interments were often almost unseemly in their haste, a response both to the climate and to the participants' circumstances as slaves. In South Carolina and Georgia in particular, slave funerals were often held at night, which allowed rather more friends and relatives from nearby plantations to attend, but even this hardly permitted a satisfactory farewell to the deceased.[70] What generally happened throughout the South was that many of the rituals of the funeral were separated from the burial, sometimes by a few weeks, but often by months or even years. As the Reverend John Dixon Long wrote in the 1850s, "a negro funeral is different from the 'burying.'"[71] James Bolton, a former slave from Oglethorpe County, Georgia, told his interviewer that "sometimes it were two or thee mont's atter the burying fo' the funerl sermon was preached."[72] Another former slave from Georgia declared that "de reason dey had slave fun'rals so long atter de burial wuz to have 'em on Sunday or some other time when de crops had been laid by so de other slaves could be on hand."73 According to Long, these funerals were frequently held out in the woods, and "sometimes as many as three funerals are preached at once." He also noted that such an arrangement was "a unique affair," being unaware of course that this practice of delayed funerals was common in West Africa.74 Indeed, what is likely is that both African ideas and the restrictions of slavery easily combined to establish the custom of double funerals in the New World. The practice of two rituals occurred in the eighteenth century, but in the middle decades of the nineteenth century, by which time the majority of slaves were Christian, such a procedure appears to have been ubiquitous.75 It was important to slaves that they heard the right words, delivered by one of their countrymen, spoken about their dead, a fact acknowledged by Long when he wrote that "unless a colored person is preached...there is no peace of mind to his friends."76 Given that these men and women were slaves, the practice of double funerals allowed a surprising amount of solace on this count.

For many whites, the rituals of slave death and burial were deeply disconcerting. The singing of hymns by slaves, or, though less commonly, the preaching of sermons, was familiar enough to Euro-American observers, but this very familiarity made the transformations wrought by the slaves all the more unsettling. Liberal embellishment of hymn tunes; the commingling of lyrics from several sources; the preaching of the funeral sermon some months after the slave's interment, and its content, delivered in Black English and either almost incomprehensible or completely nonsensical to most white listeners; all this and much more contributed to the feeling that things were somehow awry. Embedded in what whites saw and heard were echoes of their own practices, but when they came to describe slave funerals their accounts were suffused with a sense of strangeness. After witnessing a nighttime slave funeral that attracted scores of slaves from nearby plantations, the clergyman Hamilton W. Pierson wrote that "the appearance of such a procession, winding through the fields and woods, as revealed by their flaming torches, marching slowly to the sound of their wild music, was *weird and imposing* in the highest degree."77

In much the same way that viewers of the first cubist paintings were confronted by a new way of seeing, by what seemed like a distorted image disturbingly at odds with their usual experience, and yet for all that still recognizable, so too white witnesses to slave funeral rites were forced to contemplate cultural difference. In this case, however, the shock of the new was mostly in the sonic rather than the visual realm and, importantly, after decades of living together, a small minority of whites began to appreciate and then gradually to love this new sound. "White folkses would come lissen to slave fun'rals," one ex-slave casually remarked, but we would suggest that the word "lissen" here can bear some weight.[78] More and more whites acknowledged their liking for many of the sounds of slavery, sounds that had by then saturated the fabric of southern life.

Much as would later happen with the paintings of Picasso and Braque, antebellum whites continued to use words such as "wild" or "strange" to describe the sounds that they had heard, but they also acknowledged the haunting power of what had been revealed to them. "Viator" was present at the nighttime burial of an important and much-liked slave on a large Georgia plantation in the 1850s. The wagon carrying the coffin was followed by in excess of one hundred and fifty slaves, in the middle of whom "was stationed the black preacher, a man of gigantic frame and stentorian lungs, who gave out from memory the words of a hymn suitable for the occasion." Rooted to the spot, this northern white watched as darkness swallowed up the cortege and then listened for some time to the singing "mellowed by distance." It was, he wrote later that night, "the most solemn and yet the sweetest music" that he had ever heard. Indeed, he concluded, "no incident of my life has impressed me with more powerful emotions than the night funeral of the poor negro."[79]

During the institution's final years, it was quite common for whites to go out of their way to watch and listen to slaves. They attended funerals, corn shuckings, church services, or other black performances, and they did so not so much for the purposes of surveillance, although no one was likely to forget their color or position, but out of an aesthetic appreciation of and inquisitiveness about slave culture. On Sundays in Richmond in the 1850s, curious whites frequently attended services at the First African Baptist Church. Mary Virginia Hawes Ter-hune, better known in some circles as the novelist Marion Harland, re-membered that "what were known as the 'Amen benches,' at the left of the pulpit, were reserved for white auditors." The attraction was not the performance of Robert Ryland, the white minister, but the singing of the congregation and the impassioned eloquence of the black ex-horters. In Mary Terhune's memory the amen benches of this black Baptist church "were always full."[80] These whites who sought out African American singing in black churches and elsewhere were the forebears of later generations who would be entranced by the sounds of blues and jazz.

CHAPTER 2

"To translate everyday experiences into living sound"

In the course of his journey through South Carolina in the years before the Civil War, Frederick Law Olmsted encountered a group of African American slaves, members of a railroad work gang, gathered around a fire. Suddenly, one of the men "raised such a sound as I never heard before, a long, loud, musical shout, rising, and falling, and breaking into falsetto, his voice ringing through the woods in the clear, frosty night air, like a bugle call." Olmsted guessed that the cry was a form of "Negro jodling";[1] in fact the sounds that had intrigued him were those of a richly embellished field call, a free musical form common among the slave population of the South.

It is not surprising to find that the West African practice of using a variety of calls to announce important events, greet friends, summon meetings, and so on, carried over to the New World.[2] As deployed by North American slaves, these seemingly elemental kinds of musical expression took various forms, ranging from the relatively simple to the complex, and served a range of purposes, not all of them readily appreciated by outsiders. Particularly when African influences were strong—in the early years of slavery, for example, or wherever groups of newly arrived slaves were kept together—calls functioned as an alternative communication system, conveying information through the medium of sounds that whites could neither confidently understand nor easily jam. Calls constructed from the languages of the slaves' homeland were, of course, unintelligible to whites, and to many slaves. But, just as West African drums could "talk" by imitating the rhythmic and tonal characteristics of speech, so too, in all probability, could some of the wordless calls of North American slaves. As Harold Courlander, who interviewed a number of elderly African Americans in the rural South in the early part of last century, has pointed out, this process could become extremely complex.

It is now well understood that African signal drumming is based largely on simulation, through rising and falling inflection, of speech tones. Voice signalling in Africa is sometimes based on this same principle, and signal horns are used in the same manner. In some instances, voice signals are not modeled directly on speech tones, but on the sound of instruments imitating speech. Many of the early day slave calls and cries in the United States may have utilized these communicative devices. In such disguise, seemingly wordless messages could have been quite unintelligible to outsiders.[3]

As slaves became acculturated, their calls incorporated English-language words, a development that would have made them intelligible to whites, at least in some degree. Such calls were often simple expressions of loneliness, pain, or despair. Harold Courlander was told that a slave "working under the hot sun might give voice to such a cry on impulse, directing it to the world, or to the fields around him, or perhaps to himself." The call "might be a phrase like 'I'm hot and hungry,'" or it could, as in the case of the following Alabama cry, contain a more detailed message:

> Ay-oh-hoh!
> I'm goin' up the river!
> Oh, couldn't stay here!
> For I'm goin' home![4]

Readers may listen to the "Arwhoolie" holler sung by Thomas J. Marshall, at Edwards, Mississippi, in 1939 (track 1) to hear something similar.[5]

Other calls had a more obvious practical purpose. Yach Stringfellow, formerly a slave in Texas, told his WPA interviewer how, "ef de oberseer wuz comin'," a slave named Ole man Jim, the possessor of "a big boom voice," would "wail out loud like an say: 'Look-a long black man, look-a long; dere's trouble comin shore.'"[6] An ex-slave who was interviewed in Alabama revealed that hollers could even be used to measure distance: wagons leaving his plantation "got outer hearing" once they had traveled "about a holler and a half," he explained.[7] Much more commonly, calls were employed to aid work routines.

Soon after the "strange cry" of the black railroad worker whom Olmsted encountered had died away, Olmsted heard another member of the work gang "urging the rest to come to work again, and soon he stepped towards the cotton bales, saying, 'Come, brederen, come; let's go at it; come now, eoho! roll away! eeoho-eeoho-weeioho-i!'—and all the rest taking it up as before, in a few moments they all had their shoulders to a bale of cotton and were rolling it up the embankment."[8]

But even after slaves had become relatively well acculturated, they continued to employ calls that contained either no or very few English words; if a few such words were included, they tended to function as do syllables in scat singing—as pure sound rather than as vehicles for the conveying of information. The former slave Julia Frances Daniels revealed that her brother, a skilled hunter, used a celebratory but wordless call to broadcast his success. "We would know when we heard him callin', 'OoooooOOOooo-da-dah-dah-ske-e-e-e-t-t-ttt,' that he had sumpin. That was just a make-up of his own, but we knowed they was rabbits for the pot."[9] A boastful Hector Godbold incorporated some English words into the call he reproduced for his WPA interviewer, but those words were obviously valued for sound rather than sense. "I was one of de grandest hollerers you ever hear tell bout. . . . Here how one go: O—OU—OU—O—OU, Do—MI—NICI—O, BLACK—GA—LE—LO, O—OU—OU—O—OU, WHO—O—OU—OU. Great King, dat ain' nothin'."[10]

Of course, contemporary white observers of the peculiar institution, as well as those who managed later to interview former slaves, were able to give only a very imperfect representation of the calls they heard. On many occasions, interviewers appear to have recorded only or mainly the words of a particular cry. African American voices could, however, transform such words into richly detailed patterns of sound. As visually represented by Yach Stringfellow's interviewer, Ole man Jim's warning call: "Look-a long black man, look-a long; dere's trouble comin shore" seems simple in form and straightforward in meaning, but sweeping tonal glides and intricate melismas (melismas occur when one syllable of a word is carried over several tones), which the interviewer may have lacked the time or ability to represent, could easily have translated this call into a complex vocal utterance. Again, the wordless "plantation holler" that ex-Texas slave Jeff Calhoun performed for his interviewer, was merely written down as "Uh, Uh, Uh, Uh, Uh, Uh."[11] However, as Harold Courlander points out, apparently simple wordless calls of this type—he instances a call consisting merely of a long "Hoo-Hoo"—could be "filled with exuberance or melancholy," and "stretched out and embellished with intricate ornamentation of a kind virtually impossible to notate."[12]

Whether with or without lyrics, slave calls were often elaborate vocal creations that drew heavily, as Ashenafi Kebede points out, on "many African vocal devices, such as yodels, echolike falsetto, tonal glides, embellished melismas, and microtonal inflections that are frequently impossible to indicate in European staff notation."[13] Some of these characteristics may be heard in the "Arwhoolie" call (track 1) performed by Thomas J. Marshall at Edwards in Mississippi, in 1939, which features half-yodels, portamenti (a continuous gliding from one pitch to another), and richly ornamented melismas.[14] They also occur in the anguished and liberally filigreed levee holler of Enoch Brown, which John and Ruby Lomax heard while sitting on the front porch of folklorist Ruby Pickens Tartt's home near Livingston, Alabama, in the same year. Every evening, Mrs. Tartt explained, this elderly black man walked out onto a bridge leading to Livingston and "crie[d] out his woes to heaven." Although the caller was some distance away, his plaintive cry seemed to the Lomaxes "to fill completely the void of dark silence about us." Two days later they managed to capture the call on their primitive recording equipment. Brown's levee holler, which makes use of impassioned falsetto and descending tonal cadences, may be heard on track 2.[15] Tracks 3 and 4 contain two further calls. The call of Roosevelt "Giant" Hudson (track 3), recorded at Cummins State Farm, Varner, Arkansas, features a series of high to low note figures, interspersed with tonal glides. As the spoken words with which he begins his holler—"Hey, Joe Green, I'm waitin' on you"—indicate, Hudson simulates a work situation in which he is driving a mule.[16] Willie Henry Washington's levee camp holler, also recorded at Cummins State Farm (track 4), is ornamented with vibrato effects, descending tonal glides, and note-bending melismas. Like Hudson, Washington simulates a work situation, every so often calling out instructions to an imaginary mule.[17]

In the African American folklorist and teacher Willis Laurence

James's estimation, the more complex, or "coloratura," calls rank "among the most amazing and remarkable vocal feats in folk music."[18] It was a coloratura call that had attracted Olmsted's attention as he came upon the group of African American railroad workers; the yodel- ing sounds that so intrigued him originated with the rainforest Pyg- mies of Central Africa, whose musical styles influenced, in turn, the Kongo peoples of West Africa, and, ultimately, broad segments of the North American slave population.[19] As we have seen, Olmsted had been puzzled by the lone railroad worker's richly filigreed cry; the more in- teresting issue, however, is what meanings that cry had communicated to those African Americans who heard it.

At the deepest cultural level, coloratura slave calls were emblematic African (and African American) sounds, and deeply evocative on that account. Robert Farris Thompson's comment that "the textlessness of [Pygmy] yodeling, unshackling sound from words, unlock[ed] extraor- dinary freedom of voice" is applicable to many of the more complex New World calls as well.[20] These, too, were free musical forms, allow- ing virtually limitless scope for improvisation, for the admixture of the vocal leaps, glides, moans, yells, and elisions that gave to African American musical expression its characteristic rhythmic and tonal complexity, its perennial inventiveness and love of surprise. Slave calls exemplified, that is to say, what Olly Wilson has termed "the heteroge- neous sound ideal," defined by Wilson as an "approach to music mak- ing" that deploys "a kaleidoscopic range of dramatically contrasting qualities of sound," qualities that characterized the West African tonal languages from which that music was derived.[21]

In West African societies, dramatic variations in timbre, or tone "color," had been in evidence, of course, not merely in calls, but when- ever music was made, and most saliently in the African dancing ring, the symbol, as Samuel A. Floyd Jr. points out, of "community, solidar- ity, affirmation, and catharsis."[22] In the New World, the African circle or ring was initially shattered, as members of cultural groups were de- liberately dispersed or indiscriminately distributed among competing buyers. The ring would take periodic shape again in the ring shout (a quasi-religious slave dance) and, most publicly and dramatically, in the dancing formations of slaves at New Orleans' Congo Square, but to those who remained outside the ring—who lived relatively isolated lives or belonged to owners determined to suppress "primitive" ritual —the calls, cries, and hollers that drifted across an often hostile southern soundscape constituted a musical idiom with which slaves must have felt a high degree of affinity. In emotional terms, slave calls fleetingly reconstituted the West African ring, the center of communal life and locus of culture-affirming movement and sound. They evoked, that is to say, not merely a time-honored African and African American means of communication but deep-seated cultural memory.[23]

There is little reason to expect that former African American slaves, interviewed by employees of the federal government, would have attempted to put such feelings into words, but an anecdote from the writings of Willis Laurence James conveys in some imperfect degree the evocative power of wordless but culturally compelling sound. The incident that James relates occurred during a conference on African American folk music.

> One morning at a lecture I presented on Negro cries...I sang a florid Negro cry. [Ragtime pianist and composer] Mr. [Eubie] Blake leaped halfway from his seat and yelled, "Oh, professor, professor, you hit me, you hit me." He placed both hands over his heart and continued with great emotion: "You make me think of my dear mother. She always sang like that. I can hear her now. That's the stuff I was raised on."[24]

For African American slaves, however, the more complex sonic textures of communal, interactive singing had an even stronger cultural resonance.

During the eighteenth century, there is a relative silence about slave music, an as-yet-unexplained lack of historical evidence regarding a subject that one might expect would have been, in those years, integral to the slave experience.[25] Increasingly in the nineteenth century, however, southern whites and numerous travelers to slaveholding states recorded their varying impressions of the music slaves made. One well-documented musical encounter between a group of whites and some newly freed blacks took place in the South Carolina low country in 1865. In May of that year an official party, dispatched by President

Andrew Johnson, reached Saint Helena Island, off the South Carolina coast. Saint Helena was one of the Sea Islands, which had been captured by Northern forces early in the Civil War, with a view to enforcing the blockade against the Confederacy. Cut off from the mainland and outnumbering whites by a ratio of something like nine to one, Sea Island blacks had developed a culture in which African influences were strong. The government group's immediate purpose was to assess the condition of Saint Helena's former slaves, who, under the guidance of Major General Rufus Saxton, the Union general in command of the Port Royal area, had worked the land since the hurried flight of their former owners some years before. Included in the party were General Saxton, Secretary of the Treasury Salmon P. Chase, the Reverend Doctor Richard Fuller, former owner of some hundreds of the island's slaves, and the northern journalist Whitelaw Reid. It is on Reid's sound-rich account of the day's events that the following discussion largely relies.

Arriving, without notice, on a Sunday, the official party found the roads thronged with African Americans, "gay with holiday attire," heading for the island's main church. When Reid and the others reached the church they discovered large numbers of blacks massed in front of it, the building being too small to contain them. Presently, a "white-wooled deacon" arrived and informed General Saxton that "de people is gathered, sah, and was ready for de suvvices to begin," whereupon Saxton led the official group to a small platform under some live oaks. Once members of the party had taken their seats, "a quaint old African" moved to the front of the stage as if to welcome them.

Instead of delivering an address, the man began to sing. "Leaning, like a patriarch, on his cane," Reid recorded, "and gently swaying his body to and fro over it, as if to keep time, he struck up, in a shrill, cracked voice, a curiously monotonous melody, in which, in a moment, the whole congregation were energetically joining." Reid quickly found himself agreeing with those who held "that the language of these sea islanders (and I am told that, to some extent, the same is true of the majority of plantation hands in South Carolina), is an almost unintelligible patois"; the journalist found it "impossible, for a time, to make out [the song leader's] meaning." Not only this, but "the vocal contortions to which the simplest words seemed to subject" the aged singer were "a study that would have amazed a phonetic lecturer."[26]

The first person whose presence the former slaves acknowledged in their song was Rev. Dr. Fuller, who had earlier won their affection by giving up his law practice in order to preach to them. The singing followed the usual call-and-response pattern, which Reid, in his later account, represented as best he could.

> Ma-a-a-assa Fullah a sittin' on de tree ob life,
> Ma-a-a-assa Fullah a sittin' on de tree ob life,
> Roll, Jordan, roll.
> Ma-a-a-ssa Fullah a sittin' on de tree ob life,
> Roll, Jordan, roll.
> Ma-a-a-assa Fullah a sittin' on de tree ob life,
> Ro-o-oll, Jordan, roll,
> Ro-o-oll, Jordan, roll,
> Ro-o-oll, Jordan roll.

Eventually, after "repetitions that promised to be endless," the lyrics changed, and the name of General Saxton, who had assisted the former slaves as they struggled to adjust to a dramatically changed postslavery world, was substituted for that of Master Fuller.

> Gen-e-ul Sa-a-axby a sittin' on de tree ob life;
> Gen-e-ul Sa-a-axby a sittin' on de tree ob life;
> Roll, Jordan, roll.
> Gen-e-ul Sa-a-axby a sittin' on de tree ob life;
> Ro-o-oll, Jordan, roll,
> Gen-e-ul Sa-a-axby a sittin' on de tree ob life;
> Ro-o-oll, Jordan, roll,
> Ro-o-oll, Jordan, roll,
> Ro-o-oll, Jordan, ro-o-oll!

When it came the turn of the treasury secretary to be honored, the song leader "struck out in harsher tones, and more indescribably bewildering difficulties of punctuation than ever," and the answering chorus was sung, Reid wrote, "with a vehemence that pierced the ears."

> Me-is-ta-ah Che-a-ase a sittin' on de tree ob life,
> Me-is-ta-ah Che-a-ase a sittin' on de tree ob life,
> Roll, Jordan, roll;
> Me-is-ta-ah Che-a-ase a sittin' on de tree ob life,
> Roll, Jordan, roll.
> Me-is-ta-ah Che-a-ase a sittin' on de tree ob life,
> Roll, Jordan, roll,
> Roll, Jordan, roll,
> Ro-o-oll, Jordan, ro-o-oll.[27]

Following this impromptu musical performance, a decided shift in musical styles occurred. A white teacher from one of the island's schools led the black congregation in the singing of some of "the ordinary hymns of the church," and soon, Reid observed, "great volumes of sound rang like organ peals through the arches of the oaks." If Reid now found the tones of the singers "harsh," or their diction difficult to follow, or the repetitions in the song tedious, he did not say so.

After questioning members of the audience as to their well-being, Dr. Fuller pronounced the blessing to end the day's formal proceedings. No sooner had he done so than he was surrounded by about one hundred of his former slaves, who "pushed up against him, kissed his hands, passed their fingers over his hair, and crowded about, eager to get a word of recognition." Whitelaw Reid attempted to capture the ex-slaves' speech in dialecticized English. "Sure, you 'member me, Massa Rich'd; I'm Tom." "'Laws, Massa Rich'd, I mind ye when ye's a little 'un." "Don't ye mind, Massa Rich'd, when I used to gwine out gunnin' wid ye?" "How's ye been dis long time?" "'Pears like we's never gwine to see 'ou any more; but, bress de Lord, you'm cum." "Oh, we's gittin' on cumf'able like; but ain't 'ou gwine to cum back and preach to us sometimes?"[28]

Like the WPA interviews, Whitelaw Reid's narrative of these events returns us, in some senses, to what Ronald Radano has termed the "sound-filled, preliterate past."[29] It does so, of course, in only a partial and unsatisfactory way. As Winthrop Jordan has pointed out, we cannot really recover the sounds of "the long past." The music of slaves (or, as in this case, of people not long out of slavery) could be described by whites but not recorded, except through conventional transcriptions, which, in the despairing words of William Francis Allen, a compiler of the volume entitled *Slave Songs of the United States* (1867), were "but a faint shadow of the original." The slaves' voices, Allen declared despairingly, "have a peculiar quality that nothing can imitate; and the intonations and delicate variations of even one singer cannot be reproduced on paper."[30] Slave speech has, to a degree, been preserved in written, and often, as in Reid's narrative, in dialecticized form, but, as Winthrop Jordan has warned, such visual records tell us nothing of its nuances and cadences, of "the nearly infinite variety of human inflections and accents as they resonated in different places, situations, and time." Even if "something of [the] timbre and rhythm" of slave speech can be approximated "by listening to twentieth-century audio electromagnetic recordings," Jordan cautions, "there is always danger in listening backward in time by a process of extrapolation from the sounds of later years."[31]

Although we are attempting, in some measure, to "listen" once more to the sounds of the past, our main objective is to reach an understanding of what those sounds meant to enslaved African Americans, and to whites who were within earshot. Limitations in the historical record often require historians to "look" at slavery through the eyes of whites; the same limitations mean that we shall often have to "hear" it through their ears. In the present instance, fortunately, we listen through the ears of a shrewdly observant and more than usually perceptive journalist who, however, knew very little about a people whom he was encountering for the first time.

In the main, Reid reacted negatively to the manner in which Saint Helena Island's former slaves sang. In that respect, of course, he was hardly unique. If Reid disliked the harsh tones and vehement delivery of the African American singers, so also had the Scottish traveler Laurence Oliphant, who, after touring the South in 1856, objected that slaves' religious songs were performed "with great vehemence and unction," and that, where they were mentioned, sacred names "were generally screamed rather than sung, with an almost ecstatic fervour."[32] Such comments become something of a testy refrain in white contemporaries' accounts of slave life. Occasionally a more sympathetic observer detected deeper messages in these apparently dissonant

tones; for instance, the musician Lucy McKim, who, with her abolitionist father, Rev. James Miller McKim, first came to the South Carolina Sea Islands in 1862, concluded that "the wild, sad strains" of
slave song "tell, as the sufferers themselves never could, of crushed
hopes, keen sorrow, and a dull daily misery which covered them as
hopelessly as the fog from the rice swamps."[33] Even in such cases,
however, the more fundamental importance of tone color and tonal
variation in African American music was not understood.

Underlying whites' objections to the "harsh" and "aberrant" tones
of slave vocal music lay a different conception of the role of sound in
musical performance. In the slaves' African homelands, Francis Bebey
has argued, musicians sought "not . . . to combine sounds in a manner pleasing to the ear," but "simply to express life in all its aspects
through the medium of sound,"[34] to "translate everyday experiences
into living sound," "to render emotions and desires as naturally as
possible."[35] Reflecting the tonal nature of African languages, on which
much African music is based, the tones employed by an African singer,
Bebey writes, "may be soft or harsh as circumstances demand." Thus, a
"mellow tone" may be used "to welcome a new bride; a husky voice to
recount an indiscrete adventure."[36] In the same way, impassioned
falsetto might effectively express grief, a grainy rasp anguish, a
sonorous wail despair. If, as we might anticipate, southern slaves too
made freer use than did whites of different tones (strictly timbres, or
tone "colors") to express the pain and emotional trauma that must
have been part and parcel of their lives, it is not surprising to find
whites describing such sounds as "wild and barbarous,"[37] "uncouth,"[38]
"a dismal howl,"[39] or "hideous noise."[40] The African and African
American practice of weaving a variety of wordless intensifiers—
shouts, cries, yells, groans—into a melody, translating, thereby, their
strongly felt emotions into sound, can only have increased whites'
sense of alienation.

African American vocal music sounded dissonant to many whites
not only because of its harsh, impassioned, or gravelly tonalities, but
also because slave singers inflected the pitches of notes "in ways quite
foreign to regular melodic practice in Western art music."[41] As the
historian William Francis Allen, one of the compilers of *Slave Songs*

of the United States, pointed out, "like birds," slaves often seemed "to strike sounds that cannot be precisely represented by the gamut," and abound in "slides from one note to another, and turns and cadences not in articulated notes."[42] Mrs. Roger Pryor made a similar observation. After accompanying a slave funeral procession through the woods on her Virginia plantation in 1861, she declared the mourners' song to be "a strange, weird tune no white person's voice could ever follow."[43] This tendency of black singers (and instrumentalists) to "play" with pitch, to worry, for example, the third and seventh degrees of the scale by "slurring or wavering between flat and natural," was disconcerting to those whites who first encountered it in black musical performance.[44] To Mrs. C. J. B., who transcribed the spiritual "The Day of Judgment" for the publication *Slave Songs of the United States*, for instance, a "tone" that would later have been described as a worried third merely sounded like "a sort of prolonged wail."[45]

Similarly disconcerting to whites were what Lucy McKim termed the "odd turns made in the throat" of black singers, another of the characteristics which, like the presence of "worried" notes, made it "difficult to express the entire character of...negro ballads by mere musical notes and signs."[46] Lucy McKim may have been referring here to various forms of vocal embellishment practiced by slaves, the use of yodels, bends, or slides, for instance, or most probably to melisma. When Whitelaw Reid called attention to the "vocal contortions to which the simplest words seemed to subject" the former slave who led the Saint Helena Island blacks in song, he may have been describing certain difficulties of pronunciation, or alluding to the leader's Gullah or Gullah-inflected speech (Gullah was a Creole language spoken by blacks who inhabited the Sea Islands off the South Carolina and Georgia coast and adjacent low country).[47] But it is more likely that Reid, too, was referring to the African American practice of extending the number of syllables in a sung word in order to give greater scope for melismatic play. By representing the song leader's enunciation of the word "Massa" as "Ma-a-a-assa," Reid reveals that the man had turned a two-syllable word into a five-syllable one. And when, instead of singing "Mr. Chase" the caller sang "Me-is-ta-ah Che-a-ase," he had effectively transformed three syllables into seven. The carrying of

African American voices over the additional tones these extra syllables allowed for may have produced the "odd turns in the throat," those puzzling, and to whites "unnatural" sounds to which McKim had alluded.

Like Reid, many whites regarded the words of slaves' songs as almost meaningless, a mélange of mispronunciation, trivial content, and pointless repetition. In 1842 the Presbyterian minister Rev. Charles Colcock Jones, anxious to replace the slaves' religious songs with "approved hymns," described the former as "extravagant and nonsensical chants."[48] In a similar vein, Colonel Thomas Wentworth Higginson, commander of the First Regiment, South Carolina Volunteers, the Union's first black military unit, whose troops were encamped on the Sea Island of Port Royal, characterized the nightly singing of his troops as "incomprehensible negro methodist, meaningless, monotonous, endless chants, with obscure syllables recurring constantly."[49] So generally "absurd and unmeaning" were the lyrics of the "so-called hymns" in the recently published volume *Slave Songs of the United States*, a reviewer complained in March 1868, "that it would be as well for the teachers in the schools and meeting-houses where they are sung to commence, as speedily as possible, the destruction of the entire lot."[50] Even slaves, it sometimes seemed, did not comprehend the meaning of the words they sang. Puzzled by the term "cater nappen," included in the song line "Wid a white a cater nappen tied 'roun' he [Jesus's] wais'," schoolteacher Elizabeth Kilham and her companions inquired of several of the slave singers as to its meaning, but "received no further explanation than, 'Why dat's jes' in de hymn.'" Kilham was similarly bemused by the way in which slaves appended a hymn chorus—"Shall we know each other there?"—of which they were particularly fond—to "almost everything, sometimes in rather startling association." She cited the following examples:

> Hark from the tombs a doleful sound,
> Chorus—Shall we know each other there?

And

> Hell is a dark an' a drefful affair,
> An' ef I war a sinner I wouldn't go dar,
> Chorus—Shall we know each other there?[51]

Such seemingly odd alignments of song lines would not have appeared incongruous to Saint Helena Island's blacks. On being asked by a white woman what an African American preacher had preached about at a camp meeting, Jenny, a recently freed slave, had replied that, while she could not "tell de perticulars" (though "I's got dem all in my heart"), she could "sing some of de hymns I larned dar." Encouraged to do so, Jenny began:

> I hears a rumblin' in de skies,
> Jews, screws, de fi dum!
> I hears a rumblin' in de skies,
> Jews, screws, de fi dum!

When asked the meaning of the second and fourth lines (which were the same in each of several additional verses), Jenny replied, with some impatience: "La, dear soul, don't you know what dem is? Dem is de chorus!" Further efforts to secure a satisfactory reply provoked the following rejoinder: "Mean?" cried Jenny, with a deprecating glance at the inquisitive mistress, "dey don't mean nothin', as I knows on, dey's de chorus, I tell you!" Later, the white woman learned that the "correct" words of the chorus were "Jews crucified him."[52]

In all probability, the song Jenny described had originally been a white hymn that had been recast by an African American gathering into the familiar call-and-response format. In this context, the main function of the chorus (response) was not to "make sense," when placed after every call line that preceded it, but to base the song, to provide a stable foundation against which the lyrical, melodic, and rhythmic improvisations of the caller would be set. The chorus that Jenny used could adequately perform this task even if the "words" of which it was composed had been scrambled in translation.

But something deeper was involved here. To Elizabeth Kilham, the surprising juxtaposition of different elements within African American songs seemed almost deliberate; the slaves made nearly "all their hymns into this kind of patchwork," she wrote, "without apparently, the slightest perception of any incongruity in the sentiments thus joined together." She speculated that the future publication of a collection of African American religious songs would prompt the question as to whether they were "composed as a whole, with deliberate arrangement and definite meaning, or [were] fragments, caught here and there, and pieced into mosaic, haphazard as they come?"[53] To the Texas schoolteacher William P. Stanton, too, his black students' hymns "seem[ed] to be a sort of miscellaneous patchwork, made up from the most striking parts of popular Methodist hymns."[54] And, endeavoring to describe the singing of companies of black soldiers as they marched along, Colonel Thomas Wentworth Higginson wrote that "for all the songs, but especially for their own wild hymns, they constantly improvised simple verses, with the same odd mingling,—the little facts of to-day's march being interwoven with the depths of theological gloom, and the same jubilant chorus annexed to all."[55]

Once again, the puzzled, or fascinated, or hostile reactions to slaves' religious songs measure the cultural gap between black and white. Whites expected song lyrics to follow an orderly course, whereas the kind of spontaneous "sampling" in which the creators of spirituals engaged reflected the imperatives of a culture that prized improvisation and was not bound by the processes of linear thought. In the manner of slave quilt-makers, slave musicians pieced their compositions from different, often provocatively juxtaposed elements.[56]

Whitelaw Reid was scarcely alone in finding the Saint Helena Island blacks' singing "curiously monotonous," in expressing puzzlement over "repetitions that promised to be endless."[57] In similar vein, as we have seen, Thomas Wentworth Higginson referred to the nightly singing of his troops as "monotonous, endless chants."[58] Yet, in some senses, repetition, through the time-honored practice of call-and-response, facilitates improvisation rather than hindering it. As John Miller Chernoff has written, "a repeated rhythmic response provides a stable basis to clarify the rhythms which change."[59] That is to say, it is against the regularly recurring rhythmic response that the varying rhythms of the caller are set, creating a more complex rhythmic pattern. For instance, overlapping antiphony, a feature of slave choral music that occurs, for example, where the basers (chorus) overlap the end of the lead singer's lines and the lead singer cuts in again before the basers have finished, introduces an element of polyrhythmic, as well as polyphonic, complexity, musical characteristics that African Americans prize. William Francis Allen observed that slaves "overlap in singing...in such degree that at no time is there any complete pause." Overlapping created thicker sonic textures and a more complex interweaving of rhythms, characteristics that, as Lucy McKim and others quickly discovered, rendered slave singing virtually impossible to notate.[60] Criticisms of the repetitive nature of slave singing miss, also, imaginative forms of vocal embellishment—melisma, yodels, glides, falsetto swoops, and other vocal techniques—that invariably characterized the lead singer's performance.

Listening, in quizzical fashion, to the performance of Saint Helena Island's former slaves, Whitelaw Reid almost certainly missed not only the complex rhythmic colloquy between lead singer and basers, but the various forms of vocal embellishment. He failed too to appreciate that cyclical rather than linear in form, the ex-slaves' singing continued not, as in Western practice, until the song had finished, but until the singers had finished. In the case of the Saint Helena blacks, the reiteration in song of the names of each of the white men who had either helped them in the past or intended now to do so was exuberantly prolonged until the former slaves' celebration of those individuals was complete. This was not something to hurry over.

There is a degree of uniformity in whites' reactions to African and African American vocal music not only in the United States across time, but also in the diaspora. Whitelaw Reid's complaints had been anticipated, decades earlier, by George Pinckard, who, in 1796, described the singing of a group of Africans on the deck of a slave ship at anchor in Carlisle Bay, Jamaica, on its way to Georgia. "Their song," Pinckard declared, "was a wild yell, devoid of all softness and harmony, and loudly chanted in harsh monotony."[61] Here again are the objections to harsh tones, to timbres that clash rather than blend, to dissonance, and to repetition. There is more than a rough similarity, too, between the recollections of Jeanette Robinson Murphy and those of George Pinckard, Whitelaw Reid, and numerous other white observers. As a child during the early postbellum years, Murphy had listened to the singing of aged former slaves who had either come directly from Africa or whose parents had been born there. A more sympathetic observer than Pinckard or Reid, Murphy had been enchanted by the sounds of the former slaves' voices, by "all the intonations and tortuous quavers of [their] beautiful music" (use of contrasting timbres and tremolo). To her, "some of the strange, weird, untamable, barbaric melodies" possessed "a rude beauty and... charm." It would, however, be futile for whites to attempt to reproduce these sounds, since, to be effective, a singer's voice needed to be made "exceedingly nasal and undulating" (harsh tones and yodeling) and "around every prominent note" there needed to be placed "a variety of small notes" (use of melisma). It would also be necessary for such a white singer to "sing tones not found in our scale" (pitch inflection), to "drop from a high note to a very low one" (possibly yodeling, but more likely octave leaping or swooping to inject an element of surprise), to "intersperse his singing with peculiar humming sounds" (use of wordless intensifiers), and to "carry over his breath from line to line and from verse to verse, even at the risk of bursting a blood-vessel" (overlapping call-and-response, producing polyphony and cross-rhythmic complexity).[62]

What whites who decried, or were puzzled or intrigued by, slave music often failed to realize was that blacks were listening to different things. Where whites wanted intelligible lyrics, accurate pitch, and purity of tone, blacks needed to hear the complex rhythmic patterns, inflected pitches, and timbral diversity that delighted them, the sort of characteristics that could create what Olly Wilson has termed "a kaleidoscopic range of dramatically contrasting qualities of sound."[63] Whites' attempts to discover a clear melody were oftentimes defeated not only by odd tonal shadings, but by melismatic embellishment and a seemingly inexhaustible repertory of vocal interjections—moans, shouts, grunts, hollers, and screams—used to intensify musical expression. Listening for harmony, whites heard only heterophony, as voices were pitched in relation to, and conversation with, other voices, weaving melodic and tonal improvisations into the fabric of sound. Listening for song lyrics that "made sense," they heard, instead, a "kind of patchwork, without, apparently, the slightest perception of any incongruity in the sentiments thus joined."[64]

The abrupt encounter between various northern whites—the somewhat disdainful Whitelaw Reid and such basically sympathetic reformers as James Miller McKim, William Francis Allen, and Lucy

McKim—and South Carolina's Sea Island blacks was something of an extreme case, a particularly vivid illustration of the mistranslations and mutual incomprehension that can occur whenever dramatically differing cultures collide. Across large areas of the South and long periods of time, however, African American and Euro-American cultures were not so far apart. Forced into a degree of intimacy on southern plantations, both slaves and their owners borrowed from each other; functioning as *bricoleurs,* they built their cultural products from what they or their forebears brought with them and from what they found about them in the New World. But there is a sense in which, because slaves recognized more things *as* bricks, their pile of bricks was larger, and was composed of bricks of sharply contrasting colors and odd-seeming designs. What we see in slave cultural creations, for the most part musical ones in this instance, is a playful sampling and rearrangement of what to whites seemed unexpected elements. At times this process is strikingly obvious: the creators of a slave work song draw apparently indiscriminately on biblical texts, lines from secular songs, and contemporary references from everyday life; a slave musical creation incorporates yells, moans, complex rhythmic patterns, and sharply differing tone colors; a slave clothing ensemble mixes items in ways that whites see as bizarre. At other times, the mixing of disparate elements seems more muted. But despite the inevitable advance of acculturation, slave *bricoleurs,* exhibiting a sensibility that seems close to what might now be called postmodern, continued to create cultural products that drew components from unexpected sources and arranged them in surprising ways.

CHAPTER 3

"De music [of the slaves] make dese Cab Calloways of today git to de woods an' hide"

"As the teams of slaves approached" the Kentucky plantation at which the evening's corn shucking was to occur, Jonathan Dorris, a guest of the owner, began to hear the sounds of mass slave singing. The sounds came first from one direction, then from another, and the effect was "simply fascinating," the "melodies echoing and re-echoing from the hills beyond the [Kentucky] river and from the hills across Muddy Creek [sounding] like the intermingling of voices singing in unison near and far away." On their arrival at the home plantation, the slave volunteers were greeted by its owner, who thanked them for coming and offered each a glass of whiskey. Then, as the slaves set about their task, heaping the ears of corn ready for shucking, a famed singer named Pike, from the Oldham plantation, struck up a song, each line of which was thunderously answered by the great slave chorus. "Old marster shot a wild goose," came Pike's "call," upon which a hundred voices gave the response: "Juranzi hoi ho." The song continued:

> It wuz seben years fallin'
> Ju-ran-zie, hoi ho.
> It was seben years cookin'.
> Ju-ran-zie, hoi ho.
> A knife couldn't cut it.
> Ju-ran-zie hoi ho.
> A fork couldn't stick it.
> Ju-ran-zie hoi ho.

All during that evening, Dorris would later write, the slaves continued to sing with "great harmony and perfect concord," and as the home plantation was on higher ground than the surrounding land, "the great volume of sound rolled off across the river and echoed and re-echoed in the Estill County hills beyond."[1]

38

The corn-shucking festival was but one of a number of occasions on which the sounds of mass slave singing must virtually have filled the air. Gangs of slaves laboring together in the fields could produce similarly spectacular effects. As they worked side by side among the cotton, one traveler remembered, large groups of slaves "often sing some wild, simple melody, ... which usually ends in a chorus, in which all join with a right hearty good will," and with voices so powerful that they could be "heard from one plantation to another, and the welkin is made to ring for miles with musical echoes."[2] Crowds of slaves gathered for a camp meeting could also make the woods resound with their jubilant songs. Writing in 1856, a correspondent of *Dwight's Journal of Music* declared that, when hundreds of blacks "join[ed] in the chorus of such a hymn as 'When I can read my title clear, / To mansions in the skies,' the unimpassioned hearer is almost lifted from his feet by the volume and majesty of the sound."[3] Former slaves, too, recalled similar sound-filled occasions. Fannie Berry remembered the rousing songs of a large gang of slaves from her own and surrounding plantations, hired out to cut timber for a railroad:

An' chile, you order hear dem niggers singin' when dey go to wuk in de mornin'. Dey all start acomin' from all d'rections wid dey ax on dey shoulder, an' de mist an' fog be hangin' over de pines, an' de sun jes' breakin' cross de fields. Den de niggers start to sing:

> A col' frosty mo'nin',
> De niggers mighty good,
> Take yo' ax upon yo' shoulder,
> Nigger, TALK to de wood.

As they sang the word "talk," their axes cut deeply into the timber, and the woods rang "wid dis song. Hundreds of dem jes' asingin' to beat de ban'."[4]

Spectacular choral performances such as these involved large numbers of slaves, but, as contemporary observers frequently noted, in whatever circumstances slaves found themselves, and whether alone or in groups, they exhibited a seemingly inextinguishable desire to sing. "The negro is a great singer," the Reverend C. F. Sturgis, a resident of Greensboro, Alabama, declared in 1851. "They sing at their work, at their homes, on the highway, and in the streets. . . . How common to see an old woman at her work, 'lining out' a hymn to herself, and then singing it in a spirit of rapt abstraction from earth and all earthly things."[5] Daniel Robinson Hundley, whose treatise on social relationships in southern states would be published a few years later, agreed. "No matter where they may be or what they may be doing, indeed, whether alone or in crowds, at work or at play, ploughing through the steaming maize in the sultry heat of June, or bared to the waist and with deft hand mowing down the yellow grain, or trudging homeward in the dusky twilight after the day's work is done—always and everywhere they [the Negroes] are singing."[6] Interviewed in the 1930s, the former slave Vinnie Brunson put the matter this way: "De nigger used to sing to nearly everything he did. . . . De timber nigger he sings as he cuts de logs and keeps de time wid his axe. De wimmen sing as dey bend over de washtub, de cotton choppers sing as he chops de cotton. De mother sing as she rock her baby to sleep. De cotton picker sing as he picks de cotton, and dey all sing in de [religious] meetin's an at de baptizin' an' at de funerals." Singing, Vinnie Brunson emphasized, "wuz des de way [the slave] 'spressed his feelin's an hit made him relieved." If slaves were happy, this former bondsman declared, their happiness could be broadcast through song; if sad, singing could lighten their mood. Singing, Vinnie Brunson elaborated, was "de niggers mos' joy, an his mos comfort w'en he needs all dese things."[7]

Underlying North American slaves' unquenchable desire to sing was a West African tradition that saw music as functional, as part and parcel of the ordinary course of daily life, rather than as something abstracted from it. Music in the slaves' African homeland was integral to most activities; it was used to time the rhythms of work, to mourn a death, to celebrate a wedding, to placate a spirit, to express, through song, criticism that could not otherwise be voiced.[8] And if strong functional imperatives underlay Africans' and enslaved African Americans' determination to sing, powerful aesthetic ones mandated the total artistic context within which singing should ideally take place. "In the homelands of West Africa," Glenn Hinson has pointed out, "artistic expression defined the very texture of daily life." Art, however, was the province not of the few, but of the entire community,

"with every individual considered as both creator and contributor."
Thus, "music making . . . invariably invited song, dance, rhythmic accompaniment and spoken calls of encouragement," musical, or indeed
any other type of performance, achieving beauty "only when it became *co*-performance—only when the different areas of artistry came
together to forge a balanced, collectively created whole."9 Although
modified to some extent by conditions in the land to which they or
their forbears had been brought, these traditions continued to influence the nature of African American musical expression.

Whites often enthusiastically described this phenomenon of collective artistic performance, even if they failed to understand its full
significance. While traveling down the Mississippi River on the
steamer *Belle Kay* in the 1850s, the Swedish traveler Fredrika Bremer
recognized artistry (of rhythmic movement, improvised lyrics, musical sounds) in the performance of the black firemen who kept the ship's
furnaces supplied with wood; indeed, as we shall see, she stated specifically that the men's display would have made excellent theater. A
friend had asked whether Bremer would like to hear the black crew
sing, and on being told that she would, had taken her to the bottom
deck. There she "beheld a strange scene. The immense engine-fires are
all on this deck, eight or nine apertures all in a row; they are like
yawning fiery throats, and beside each throat stood a negro naked to
his middle, who flung in fire-wood. Pieces of wood were passed onward
to these feeders by other negroes, who stood up aloft on a large place
between them and a negro, who, standing on a lofty stack of firewood,
threw down with vigorous arms food for the monsters on deck." The
man standing on the pile of firewood sang an improvised song in stanzas, and "at the close of each the negroes down below joined in vigorous chorus." To the Swedish traveler, "it was a fantastic and grand sight
to see these energetic black athletes lit up by the wildly flashing flames
from the fiery throats, while they, amid their equally fantastic song,
keeping time most exquisitely, hurled one piece of fire-wood after another into the yawning fiery gulf. Everything went on with so much
life and so methodically, and the whole scene was so accordant and well
arranged, that it would have produced a fine effect upon any theater
whatever."10 To abstract singing from labor would not only have been

to decrease blacks' efficiency as workers, but also to render their performance of their appointed tasks arid, artistically incomplete.

Time and again, whites watched almost uncomprehendingly as slaves used sound and coordinated bodily movements to turn work into performance.[11] In 1824 the traveler Arthur Singleton was struck by the collaborative efforts of a group of slaves who had been directed to make a quantity of cider. "Instead of having a cheap apple-mill," Singleton observed, the slaves "scoop out a long trough, and into this empty the apples; and then you may see long rows of slaves, of both sexes, arranged up and down the sides, with ponderous pounders, and their shining black arms lifted up and down in order, as they quash the pomace; and, as they drink what juice they please, they get merry, and sing lustily to the strokes of their tall weighty wood pestles."[12] There were practical imperatives that drove the slaves to accomplish this task, but there was artistry, too, in the way they went about it—in the antiphonal singing, the coordinated bodily movement, and the thudding rhythms of the pestles as they simultaneously struck the floor of the trough.

The desire to turn work into performance is evidenced in black work songs recorded in the 1930s. In the work song "Roxie" (track 5 of the compact disc), sung by a group of black convicts at the penitentiary in Parchman, Mississippi, in 1939, we again envisage blacks' bodies moving in unison as the thud of ax chops maintains the rhythms of the toilers' song.[13] "New Buryin' Ground" (track 6), illustrates not only the fluidity of black cultural forms, but also the playfulness of John Brown and a group of convicts at the State Penitentiary in Raiford, Florida, as they partially recast what was originally a funeral song as a work song. The ejaculation "huh" at the end of each line simulates the point at which axes or hoes simultaneously strike their targets, and occasional calls for the water boy also mimic a work song situation. The singing is antiphonal—in effect, the first line of each stanza is the lead singer's call, the remainder of the stanza becoming the imaginary workers' response. The singing is also heterophonic, with individual voices being pitched in relation to, and in conversation with, other voices in the group, and improvisation by individual singers being encouraged.[14] "Long Hot Summer Days" (track 7), sung by Clyde Hill and a group of convicts at Clemens State Farm, Brazoria County, Texas, in 1939, is a type of work song designed not to pace unison activity, but to ease the burden of labor for groups of blacks working in close proximity with one another. In this group's rendition of the song, Clyde Hill's initial call, in the first line of each stanza, is answered by a prolonged burst of moaned heterophony, but in the succeeding lines of each verse the singers move toward unison. The artistry here would lie in the deep expressiveness of the singers, their song's slow, mournful cadences simulating the workers' longings and pain.[15]

In the slave South, the bringing together of various areas of artistry to form "a balanced, collectively created whole"[16] was perhaps most closely and spectacularly approximated in the great slave dancing rings of New Orleans' Congo Square, which the traveler Benjamin Latrobe had happened upon while out walking in the city in 1819. As he recounted, circular groups had formed on this open space, and in the center of each was a ring in which African Americans were dancing and singing, while others played strange-looking musical instruments. It was these musical instruments, and the odd sounds they produced, that seem particularly to have caught Benjamin Latrobe's attention.

In one of the dancing rings, Latrobe saw "an old man [sitting] astride of a Cylindrical drum about a foot in diameter and beat[ing] it with incredible quickness with the edge of his hand and fingers." A second man beat an "open staved" drum in a similar manner, while holding it between his knees. The resulting noise, Latrobe declared, was "incredible." Latrobe also observed a "curious" stringed instrument, which he felt must have come from Africa, and which was being played by an old man. On top of the fingerboard of this instrument was "the rude [carved] figure of a Man in a sitting posture, and two pegs behind him to which the strings were fastened. The body [of the instrument] was a Calabash." While these instruments were being played, several women "squalled out a burthen [refrain] to the playing, at intervals, consisting of two notes."

Most rings contained ensembles of this general type, but at one, the largest, Latrobe discovered instruments of markedly different design.

One resembled "a block cut into something of the form of a cricket bat with a long and deep mortice down the Center." Another was "a square drum looking like a stool." The noise of the cricket bat drum, which was being "beaten lustily on the side by a short stick," was "considerable"; that of the stool-like drum "abominably loud." The instruments in this, the largest of the dancing rings, also included "a Calabash with a round hole in it, the hole studded with brass nails," on which a woman was beating with two sticks. Meanwhile, as a vocal complement to the sound these instruments made, a man "sung an uncouth song to the dancing which I suppose was in some African language, for it was not french," and some women "screamed a detestable burthen [refrain] on one single note."[17]

Since the cylindrical and open-staved drums in the first of Latrobe's dancing rings were constructed differently and from different materials, they would necessarily have yielded sounds of strikingly different pitch and timbre. And by using a variety of hand and finger movements, for instance, or beating the drum membrane in different places, each drummer would have been able to vary, even more dramatically, his instrument's sonic range. As the African scholar J. H. Kwabena Nketia explains, on many drums a broad range of tone quality and pitch may be obtained through a drummer's use of "the cupped hand, the palm, palm and fingers, or the base of the palm in different positions on the drum."[18] The player of the open-staved drum, the sides of which appear, from a sketch that Latrobe made of this and other instruments, to have been composed of strips of wood, could have achieved additional tonal differentiation by applying pressure with his knees, between which the drum was held, squeezing the sides of the drum to increase tension on the membrane and relaxing such pressure when lower tones were desired. Just such a method is used by players of the Yoruba two-headed hourglass drum, which is held under one arm and beaten with a curved stick. "Variations in tension of the skins are obtained," Francis Bebey writes, "by exerting pressure with the forearm on the longitudinal thongs that connect the skins," a procedure so effective that it "gives different sonorities which can produce all the tones of speech."[19] The open staves that formed the sides of the drum that Latrobe described would seem to correspond very closely to the "longitudinal thongs" mentioned by Bebey, and were almost certainly worked on in the same way.

The "cricket bat" drum in the largest of the Congo Square dancing rings bears at least some resemblance to the African slit drum, which, Nketia tells us, is "made out of a hollowed log of wood, a section of which is slit open to provide it with a pair of 'lips' that can be struck with beaters." Lips of different thickness produce different sounds when struck.[20] But whatever sounds this Congo Square drum was capable of producing, they were certain to have differed markedly from those made by the drum which "resembled a stool," and even more so from those of the "calabash with a round hole in it, the hole studded with brass nails which was beaten by a woman with two short sticks." The responsive singing and clapping by the blacks who formed the various dancing rings would have created even more complex sonic textures. As we have seen, several decades after Latrobe's visit to Congo Square, Colonel James Creecy, too, described a diverse collection of musical instruments (including African-style jingling idiophones) capable of producing sounds of strikingly different pitch and timbre.[21]

West African musicians strove for just such an effect. In the playing of idiophones, for instance, sharp variations in sound were sought. As Nketia explains, "the tones produced by shaking a rattle may be varied by hitting the instrument against the body or the palm, or by slapping it with the fingers. Similarly, a stamping tube may be played in such a way as to produce sonority contrasts which can be exploited in the formation of rhythmic patterns."[22] Differences in the pitch and timbre of idiophones would allow the individual rhythms created by the players of the idiophones to be heard. In the same way, differences in pitch and timbre as between the drums and the other instruments to which Benjamin Latrobe and James Creecy listened would have made the rhythms of those musical instruments audible, allowing both dancers and other participants to hear and respond to the exciting musical conversations that were taking place—drummers engaging with drummers, drummers with dancers, dancers with singers, and so on. The striking of the calabash with sticks and the scraping of its ring of brass nails could have initiated further rhythmic exchanges. Variations in

vocal timbre and the singers' slides, yells, yodels, and melismatic embellishments would have created even more complex sonic textures,
"kaleidoscopic" in their "range of dramatically contrasting qualities of
sound."[23]

Here, then, in the largest of Congo Square's dancing rings was the
exhilarating mix of vocal and instrumental sounds in which slaves delighted, the complex play of rhythms they loved to hear. Here too in all
probability was what Robert Farris Thompson has called that fusion
of "energy and decorum...that confounds the either/or categories
of Western thinking." Individual performers might have drummed,
or sung, or danced "apart"—might have improvised—but they would
need to have done so without becoming unruly, without losing touch
with the whole. In a dynamic context of this type, Thompson points
out, call-and-response becomes "a means of putting innovation and
tradition, invention and imitation, into amicable relationships with
one another," and in this sense, "it...is cool." Musical conversations of
the type we have been considering at Congo Square—voice with voice,
voice with instrument, instrument with instrument, instrument with
body, and so on—were additive, rather than disruptive, and "cool in
[their] expressions of community."[24]

None of these things could Benjamin Latrobe have appreciated. As
we have seen, he had declared that he had never seen anything "more
brutally savage, and at the same time dull and stupid than this whole
exhibition"[25] (an exhibition to which, however, he had listened carefully and described meticulously, suggesting at least a degree of ambivalence on his part). But the African Americans who came by the
hundreds each Sunday to Congo Square heard not a frenzied cacophony of earsplitting noise, but an exciting, yet at the same time cool mix
of culturally evocative sound.

The degree of license enjoyed by Congo Square's black dancers and
musicians was all but unique; New Orleans' unusual demographic
and religious character had bred a relative tolerance of African American cultural display. From the earliest days of slavery in the British
colonies of North America, however, owners had been wary of slave
musical instruments. They knew enough about African societies to
understand that such instruments could be made to "talk," possibly

subversively. They had tried, periodically, to keep these potential speech surrogates out of the hands of their human property, though with only partial success. A 1740 act, passed by the South Carolina legislature shortly after the Stono slave rebellion of the previous year, banned the "using and keeping [of] drums, horns or other loud instruments which may call together or give sign or notice to one another." A half-century later, North Carolina passed a similar law, and in 1839 Louisiana, too, placed restrictions on the use of drums, though prohibition was never complete.[26] As WPA testimony makes clear, however, in the decades before the Civil War, slaves often managed to assemble an impressively large array of instruments, some of which they had been able to buy, others of which they received as gifts, but most of which they crafted themselves, using whatever materials were to hand.

The former slave Wash Wilson described for his WPA interviewer the makeshift musical instruments that slaves of his plantation used for their frolics and how these instruments were played. Slave musicians beat "pieces of a sheep's rib or cow's jaw or a piece of iron," or "an old kettle" with a stick or other implement. They played drums made from "a hollow gourd and some horsehairs," or from a section of a tree trunk with goatskin or sheepskin stretched over one end, or from a barrel with an ox's hide stretched across its top. Two slaves beat on the gourd drum with fingers or sticks, while another man "sot 'stride de barrel and beat on dat hide with he hands, and he feet, and iffen he git to feelin' de music in he bones, he'd beat on dat barrel with he head." Wash Wilson also remembered how the slaves fashioned flutes from scraped-out buffalo horns, and how, for added percussive effect, they would "tak a mule's jawbone and rattle de stick 'cross its teeth."[27]

Other slaves showed similar ingenuity. During Saturday night frolics on ex-slave Marshal Butler's Georgia plantation, one slave played a fiddle, while a second beat with straws on the fiddle's strings, and a third beat with his hands on a tin can. The sounds the straws made on the strings were similar to those made by a banjo.[28] Slaves on Litt Young's Texas plantation danced on Saturday nights to the music of fiddles made out of gourds, banjos constructed partly from sheep hides, and bones knocked together.[29] When they gathered around the cabin doors after supper during the week, slaves on Bob Maynard's Oklahoma plantation sang to the accompaniment of sounds and rhythms made by striking the cupped hand or palm or fingers over the mouth of "a jug or big bottle," hitting "a skillet lid or frying pan...with a stick or a bone," and playing "a flute...made out of reed cane."[30] There is an unmistakable sense of pride in the descriptions that WPA interviewees gave of slave-created musical instruments and of the ability of slaves to play them. Quill player George Fleming, for instance, explained that "[de] quills was made frum cane, same as de spindles was but dey was cut longer and was different sizes. All de quills was put in a rack and you could blow any note you wanted off of dem. Boy, I sho could blow you out of dar wid a rack of quills. I was de best quill blower dat ever put one in a man's mouth. I could make a man put his fiddle up; hit you so hard wid Dixieland dat I knock you off de seat. Gals wouldn't look at nobody else when I start blowing de quills."[31] In the estimation of former slave Willie Blackwell, the music slaves produced by such means was so good as to "make dese Cab Calloways of today git to de woods an' hide."[32] Like the instruments Benjamin Latrobe and James Creecy saw at Congo Square, those described as being played in the quarters could be used to create tones of strikingly different pitch and timbre as well as the complex rhythmic conversations that slaves greatly prized.

Where instruments were hard to come by, or even when they were not, slaves could beat out rhythms on parts of their bodies, clapping or patting to accompany vocal music and dance. "Patting," the ex-slave Solomon Northup explained, was performed "by striking the hands on the knees, then striking the hands together, then striking the right shoulder with one hand, the left with the other—all the while keeping time with the feet."[33] Former slave Frederick Douglass noted that "almost every farm has its 'Juba' beater," or patter, who, in the absence of musical instruments, could provide vocal and rhythmic accompaniment for dancing. "The performer improvises as he beats, and sings his merry songs," Douglass explained, "so ordering the words as to have them fall pat with the movement of his hands." And, Douglass added, into the "mass of nonsense and wild frolic, once in a while a sharp hit [was] given to the meanness of slaveholders," as in the following example:

We raise de wheat,
Dey gib us de corn;
We bake de bread,
Dey gib us de cruss;
We sif de meal,
Dey gib us de huss;
We peal de meat,
Dey gib us de skin,
And dat's de way
Dey takes us in.
We skim de pot,
Dey gib us the liquor,
And say dat's good enough for nigger.[34]

Even whites found the complex rhythms that Juba patters could achieve impressive. The southern poet Sidney Lanier wrote of hearing a southern plantation hand, who was patting for a companion to dance by, "venture upon quite complex successions of rhythm, not hesitating to syncopate, to change the rhythmic accent for a moment, or to indulge in other highly specialized variations of the current rhythmus."[35]

The sounds of Congo Square dancing rings found their distant musical echo in some of the dances that slaves performed at the frolics, which were a common feature of plantation life. Many masters allowed their slaves to frolic on Saturday nights, but as ex-slave Paul Smith explained, frolics could be held on other occasions as well. "At harvest season dere was cornshuckin's, wheat-thrashin's, syrup-cookin's, and logrollin's," Smith recalled. "All dem frolics come in deir own good time."[36] Frolics might also be held after chimney daubings (coating wood chimneys with thick mud),[37] or evening quilting bees,[38] and on Christmas Day and the Fourth of July. Tourist Charles Lanman described a frolic that came at the conclusion of a corn shucking that he had attended on a large plantation. "The scraping of fiddles and the thumping of banjos having been heard above the clatter of *spoons, soup-plates,* and *gourds,* at the various supper tables," Lanman wrote, "a new *stampede* takes place, and the musicians are hurried off to the dancing ground, as if to trip the light fantastic toe were deemed the climax of earthly happiness." A hundred blacks now formed up for the

Virginia reel, and when the music started, "the head couples dash[ed] into the arena, now slowly and disdainfully, now swiftly and ferociously, and now performing the *double shuffle* or the *pigeon-wing*." As these dancers tired, others went through "the same fantastic performances, with the addition perhaps of an occasional leap or whirl." With the music wailing louder and louder, "order [was] followed by confusion—and in the madness of the dance there [was] no method." The frolic was ended only by the coming of day.[39] Former slave Sally Paul was another who eagerly recalled one of the obviously less elaborate frolics that took place on her plantation. "Oh, my Lord," she declared, "dey would dance en carry on all kind of fuss. Yes, mam, blow quills en knock bones together dat would make good a music as anybody would want to dance by."[40] Elisha Doc Garey, too, cherished the memory of these exuberant events. "Sadday nights us had a stomp down good times pickin' de banjo, blowin' on quills, drinkin' liquor, and dancin'. I sho' was one fast Nigger den."[41]

Not surprisingly, many of the dances performed at slave frolics took place within a circle, on the perimeter of which other slaves sang, patted, played musical instruments, and called out encouragement to the participants. In the widely popular slave dance-form known as buck dancing, for example, attention was initially fixed on the fast-stepping dancer, a solo performer, who beat out exciting rhythms with his feet. But, typically, buck dancing took place within a communal context, with those who had formed the ring—instrumentalists, patters, clappers, and so forth—engaging with the dancer in exciting rhythmic exchanges, urging the performer on to greater feats of artistry. As the dance progressed, the spirited participation of onlookers invited others to jump into the central space, challenging the current performer's dancing skills. In these ways, individual and community combined "in a celebration of collectively created artistry."[42] At such times, slave frolics became, in effect, the dancing rings of Congo Square writ small.

When he visited New Orleans in 1819, Benjamin Latrobe had been repelled (though subliminally fascinated) by the sounds of Congo Square, sounds that seem to have evoked in him images of the "primitivism" of "deepest, darkest, Africa." But on many slave plantations, whites' attitudes to black musical noise were more ambivalent. The sounds of slave frolics, for instance, must often have intruded into, and indeed occupied, whites' aural space.43 This was so not only because frolics were commonly held in the yard behind the Big House, but also because slaves sometimes danced on wooden platforms assembled for the occasion, with the result that, as Roger Abrahams has pointed out, "the sound of feet dancing flat against the boards was amplified by the enclosed space beneath the platform that operated like a sound baffle."44 On occasions, slaves also danced on the split logs that formed their cabin floors, a practice that once again greatly magnified sound. Yet, as whites' not infrequent presence at frolics suggests, they seem to have found the sounds of the frolics nonthreatening, even intriguing. Appreciating that slave cultural preferences were different from their own, slaveowners "encouraged a display of those differences,"45 sometimes even providing musical instruments for the slaves' added enjoyment, and, of course, their own. Slave frolics became, for owners, a form of "home entertainments,"46 offering not merely some relief from the tedium of plantation routine, but also a glimpse of the exotic. Over time, more and more plantation owners came to enjoy the sounds of slave music and dance, and increasingly managed to do so without the sense of repugnance or foreboding that Latrobe had experienced.

But although the sounds of frolics, or corn shuckings, or similar celebratory events made noisy intrusions into whites' acoustic space, the more decisive impact on the processes of acculturation came from the everyday sounds of slave life and work and worship. On plantations throughout the South, these sounds set up an insistent cultural antiphony, subtly interrogating whites' ways not only of making music, but also of using language, or treating their human property, or worshipping their God.

In ways not immediately apparent, the sounds of slave music located themselves within a much broader African American cultural context. When she explained to Jeanette Robinson Murphy how spirituals were created, one of the former slave women, to whose singing Murphy had listened appreciatively, pointed to a significant difference between the religious music of African Americans and that of whites. "Notes is good enough for you people," the woman declared, "but us likes a mixtery."47 It may have been that, in using the word "mixtery," the woman was referring to the process by which the lyrics of slave songs were created, a process that often seemed to whites to entail an almost haphazard piecing together of texts drawn from the Bible, or expressions used in everyday speech—"fragments, caught here and there, and pieced into mosaic," as Elizabeth Kilham had characterized it.[48] It seems likely, however, that in juxtaposing the words "notes" and "mixtery," the woman had more than lyric content in mind, that the "notes" she deemed "good enough" for whites referred to the sounds of a relatively simple tune sung in a straightforward manner, whereas the "mixtery" preferred by blacks was the more complex sonic texture of the slave spiritual, with its overlapping rhythms, sharp timbral contrasts, and liberal tonal embellishment. Whether this was so or not, there are clear indications that North American slaves did like a "mixtery," and that in so doing they were reflecting West African cultural preferences.

In the realm of music, for instance, West Africans mixed tones of great range and diversity. African instrumentalists, Francis Bebey reminds us, "experiment with unusual sonorities," seeking "to produce all manner of weird and complex sounds that often strike Western ears as being impure." In an effort to create new sounds, "metal jingles may be attached to instruments or dried seeds placed in the sound-box to add their dancing rhythms to the music; drums sometimes have snares. All manner of contrivances are used to produce a variety of sounds—muted, nasal, or strident—that are intended to bring the music as close as possible to the actual sound of nature."[49] In their efforts to replicate the world of sound, African singers also used "explosive sounds or special interjections, vocal grunts, and even the whisper."[50] To the extent that circumstances permitted, Afro-American slaves attempted to replicate these practices.

But the principle of mixing has a wider application in West African and African American culture, extending to cultural spheres as diverse as textile design, speech, and dance. In textile production, for instance, West Africans mixed colors and designs in ways that whites found surprising. As Robert Farris Thompson has pointed out, "African cloth has for centuries, as it is today, been distinguishable by deliberate clashing of 'high affect colors,'...in willful, percussively contrastive, bold arrangements." In the widely influential Mande culture, Thompson asserts, "visual aliveness" and vibrancy in textile production are achieved not only by the aggressive mixing of colors, but by the apparently haphazard placement of the variously designed narrow strips of which the material is made. In the so-called "rhythmized" cloth of West Africa, rhythms are irregular and complex, mixing elements of color and design in ways that disturb white sensibilities.[51]

In the early nineteenth century, when North American slaves became involved in the manufacture of cloth and clothing, they, too, mixed colors and patterns in ways that seemed strange to whites. Former South Carolinian bondsman Charlie Meadow explained to his WPA interviewer that, whereas the slaves' winter clothing had been "drab and plain," "for our summer clothes we plaited de hanks to make a *mixtry* of colors."[52] Lizzie Norfleet, interviewed in Mississippi, remembered that the dresses slave women made for themselves out of such cloth were "beautiful," with "one dark stripe and one bright stripe." "Folks them days," she averred, "knowed how to mix pretty colors."[53] Whites, however, were less impressed. Fanny Kemble, resident on her husband's Sea Island plantation in the late 1830s, called the Sunday clothing of the slaves "the most ludicrous combination of incongruities that you can conceive . . . every color of the rainbow, and the deepest possible shades blended in fierce companionship; head handkerchiefs, that put one's very eyes out from a mile off; chintzes with sprawling patterns, that might be seen if the clouds were printed with them; beads, . . . flaring sashes, and, above all, little fanciful aprons, which finish these incongruous toilets with a sort of airy grace, which I assure you is perfectly indescribable."[54] Kemble alluded here not just to the propensity of slaves to create seemingly bizarre mixtures of color and design, but also to their tendency to combine various items of clothing within the one ensemble in ways that whites considered wildly inappropriate.

The slaves' creation of such mixed and odd-seeming clothing ensembles reflected not simply privation, a sort of catch-as-catch-can mentality, but a tendency, also observable in West Africa and particularly among the elite, to add to their clothing ensembles any garment that caught the wearer's fancy or that he or she happened to acquire, without any westernized sense that such an item should coordinate in style, color, or anything else with the rest of their garb. Writing shortly after the end of the Civil War, an anonymous correspondent of

Harper's New Monthly Magazine, who had spent several years in Guinea, mocked this very practice. "What a union of civilized and barbarous costume was here!" he declared, referring to the garb of one "Hamitic Dandy," who had offset more usual African forms of dress with a European-style hat and cane and a prominently displayed collection of keys. In this writer, the juxtaposition of items of European clothing or accessories, or items of European manufacture, with more recognizably African garments, excited feelings of puzzlement and disdain.55 The *Harper's* correspondent's reaction recalls Elizabeth Kilham's observation that Sea Island blacks made "nearly all their hymns into [a] kind of patchwork, without apparently, the slightest perception of any incongruity in the statements thus joined together."56 It also echoes Thomas Wentworth Higginson's remark that "for all their songs, but especially for their own wild hymns, [his black soldiers] constantly improvised simple verses, with the same odd mingling,— the little facts of today's march being interwoven with the depths of theological gloom."57 The abrupt dismissal by some whites of slaves' color and clothing preferences is the analogue, in the sartorial realm, of the often disdainful white reaction to slave music, to its unseemly loudness, bewildering mixture of rhythms, and often sharp timbral dissonance.

Of course, not all whites viewed slave music in such a negative light. Some, while acknowledging its strangeness, found such music intriguing (sufficiently so, in the case of James Miller McKim, William Francis Allen, Charles Pickard Ware, Lucy McKim Garrison, and others, to collect it, write about it, and have it published). As for the slaves themselves who danced to makeshift musical ensembles in the slave quarters or at Congo Square, or joined in the antiphonal singing, or clapped or patted to intensify the basic pulse, they heard in their music not the chaos and disorder that Benjamin Latrobe had described, but a complex and culturally resonant chorus of black American sound. Not only this, but the mixture of sounds and rhythms in the music slaves made fit easily into a cultural aesthetic that gave a reassuring sense of unity to their lives and offered a brief respite from the rigors of a hard and often capricious existence.

CHAPTER 4

"Sing no hymns of your
own composing"

"They didn't allow us to sing on our plantation," declared former Alabama slave Alice Sewell, who was just fourteen when the war ended, "'cause if we did we['d] just sing ourselves happy and get to shouting and that would settle the work."[1] Anderson and Minerva Grubbs, who labored on a plantation near Marshall, Texas, faced similar constraints. If they or their fellow slaves wished to sing their favorite religious songs around the fireplace at night, "it would be just whispering like so the white fo'ks not hear us." And when at work in the fields, instead of singing their songs, they quietly hummed them, against the threat of punishment by the overseer or owner.[2] The former bondsman Louis Meadows's situation had been equally dire. "Honey," he informed his WPA interviewer, "de only music us knew was de hoe ringin' 'round de cotton plants."[3]

But such restrictive attitudes were rare. Most owners understood that slaves worked better if they were permitted to sing, to move their bodies rhythmically to the beat of their songs. They appreciated too that allowing slaves some respite from their labor by permitting them to sing at night in the quarters, or at Saturday evening frolics, was also likely to be to the slaveholders' economic advantage, as well as a source of enjoyment for those in the Big House. Moreover, the real or imagined "happy" singing of supposedly contented slaves confirmed in slaveholders their belief in the inherent rightness of the system, their sense that, contrary to the fervid cries of abolitionists, this was the way the world was meant to be.

The most concerted opposition to slave singing came not from slave owners, who understood its practical value, but from religious leaders, whose sense of spiritual decorum it violated. In a book entitled *Methodist Error*, published in 1819, the Reverend John Watson cautioned against "the practice of singing in our places of public and society worship, *merry* airs, adapted from old *songs*, to hymns of our composing." Watson made it clear by whom this practice had been begun. The hymns that resulted, "often miserable as poetry, and senseless as matter," had been "most frequently composed and first sung by the illiterate *blacks* of the society." Had not John Wesley himself, Watson asked, declared his own book of hymns "amply sufficient for all our purposes of rational devotion?" Had he not expelled three ministers for singing *"poor, wild, flat, disjointed hymns,"* that pointlessly repeated the same verse again and again "to the utter discredit of all sober christianity?" Yet at camp meetings, Watson complained, black people were doing these very things, making up lyrics as they went along; singing, for hours at a time, "short scraps of disjointed affirmations, pledges, or prayers, lengthened out with long repetition *choruses"*; singing, moreover, "in the merry chorus-manner of the Southern harvest field, or husking frolic method of slave blacks."⁴ To Watson, such music, with its "merry airs," jaunty rhythms, and "long repetition choruses," was inimical to true religious observance.

Nor was it simply white ministers of religion who found slave musical practices unsettling. Two years before Watson's book was published, in a work entitled *The Doctrines and Discipline of the African Methodist Episcopal Church,* a member of that black denomination had issued the following curtly expressed instructions: "Do not suffer the people to sing too slow." "Let the women constantly sing their parts alone. Let no man sing with them unless he understands the notes, and sings the base as it is composed in the tune book." "Introduce no new tune till they [members of the congregation] are perfect in the old." And, the churchman added, leaving the most egregious of faults till last, "Sing no hymns of your own composing."⁵

Despite efforts to stamp them out, the practices complained of evidently died hard. Some five decades after these warnings were issued, the seventh annual session of the Virginia Conference of the African Methodist Episcopal Church resolved that the "common practice for members of our churches to sing songs which are without meaning and sense" must cease, such singing being "detrimental to true, intelligent worship." "K. C.," the correspondent of *Zion's Herald* who covered this conference, offered an example of the type of song to which objection was being made. "Imagine," he wrote, affecting a sense of outrage he seems not entirely to have shared, "the dear pastor greeted on a bright Sunday morning with—

> Good morning to you, stranger,
> The sheep all going astray;
> You promised the Lord to take care of the lambs,
> And pay him at the coming day."

Obviously, members of black church congregations were continuing to make up verses and rhymes as they went along. "Our people in Lexington," the *Zion's Herald* correspondent reported, with poorly disguised admiration, "sang a piece about Pharaoh and the children of Israel at the Red Sea, which would beat Shakespeare before any Boston audience." In another of the Lexington members' songs, which began with the familiar words "swing low," the congregation had

> seem[ed] to realize the actual coming of the chariot, and their elevation to the golden seats. The shouts are indescribable.... They all sing, ... and what voices! full of the sweetest melody. Just fancy six or eight hundred blacks wrought up to the highest pitch of excitement, in one vast chorus chanting,

> > Swing low, chariot in the East,
> > And let God's people pass in peace;
> > Swing low, chariot in the North,
> > And let God's people all come 'crost;
> > Swing low, chariot in the West,
> > And let God's people come to rest;
> > Swing low, chariot in the South,
> > And let God's people rise and shout.

Efforts to stamp out such practices, the *Zion Herald's* correspondent seemed to be suggesting, would merely split the church. A "brother" at the Washington conference of the African Methodist Episcopal Church had told him that "if they don't sing these songs, the masses will not sing at all." Another brother reported that a congregation in Norfolk had been "literally broken up by the pastor's telling his people that he would have 'no such foolishness.' " "If we are not allowed to enjoy ourselves here," the dissidents informed their minister, "we will go elsewhere," and they had since done just that, frequently holding their meetings until one or two o'clock in the morning.[6]

The dissidents' demand for freedom of musical expression had deep roots. Drawing on the cultural traditions of West Africa, slaves often spontaneously created songs that expressed their deeply felt emotions or the immediate circumstances of their lives. An ex-slave woman explained how spirituals could be created in this fashion. "We'd all be at the 'prayer house' de Lord's day," the woman stated, "and de white preacher he'd splain de word and read whar Ezekial done say—Dry bones gwine ter lib ergin. And, honey, de Lord would come a'shinin' thoo dem pages and revive dis ole nigger's heart, and I'd jump up dar and den and holler and shout and sing and pat, and dey would all cotch de words and I'd sing it to some ole shout song I'd heard 'em sing from Africa, and dey'd all take it up and keep at it, and keep a'addin' to it, and den it would be a spiritual."[7] Work songs were improvised by slaves in much the same way. Former Mississippi bondsman John Crawford explained that "when they pick cotton a bunch a-going one side lift up they head and roll out 'uhm-m-m-m-m, yo-o-o-o,' and then those on tuther side pick it up and go the same way and jest put some make-up words to it." Crawford had even heard slaves in a coffle singing to ease their pain. "I seen some niggers chained in a line that they was a-driftin' to the west," Crawford recalled. "They swing they ankle chains and it clinks to most a music and the[y] champs a song, Yo-o-o—o—o, Yo-ho-ho-ho-ho—, Swing long my bullies, swing, swin-n-ng long my bullies."[8] (In this case, there was an immediate practical imperative for the slaves' song: had those in the coffle not marched to the music, the chains would have torn their ankles to pieces.) And when freedom came, slaves on Charlotte Brown's Virginia plantation celebrated in communally created song. They "was all sittin' roun' restin' an' tryin' to think what freedom meant," Charlotte Brown stated, when suddenly

ole Sister Carrie who was near 'bout a hundred started in to talkin':

> Tain't no mo' sellin' today,
> Tain't no mo' hirin' today,

> Tain't no pullin' off shirts today,
> Its stomp down freedom today.
> Stomp it down!

An when she says, "Stomp it down," all de slaves commence to shoutin' wid her:

> Stomp down Freedom today—
> Stomp it down!
> Stomp down Freedom today.

As a result, Charlotte Brown declared, there "wasn't no mo' peace dat Sunday. Ev'ybody started in to sing an' shout once mo'. Fust thing you know dey done made up music to Sister Carrie's stomp song an' sang an' shouted dat song all de res' de day. Chile, dat was one glorious time!"[9] Again, slaves often began a song with lyrics that were familiar, but improvised additional lines as they went along. The traveler J. Kinnard recalled that, as he and some other members of a group were being rowed by a crew of black oarsmen down a Florida river in 1845, "the negroes struck up a song to which they kept time with their oars." "There seemed to be a certain number of lines ready-manufactured," Kinnard noted, "but after this stock was exhausted, lines relating to surrounding objects were extemporized. Some of these were full of rude wit, and a lucky hit always drew a thundering chorus from the rowers, and an encouraging laugh from the occupants of the stern seats."[10] The church leaders' requirement that blacks should sing no "hymns of [their] own composing" collided head-on with this African and African American tradition of lyric improvisation.

But there was a further dimension to slave musical creativity. For large numbers of slaves, a song was never a stable text and an unvarying tune; it was a frame to be filled as the moment dictated. The frame was to be filled by a loosely defined melody, and perhaps a chorus grounding the song, but there was never a set text. Song lyrics were made up either from words improvised on the spot (as was the case with the song Charlotte Brown described), or, more usually, from words drawn by the lead singer from the vast storehouse of traditional African American lines, couplets, and entire stanzas that the black tra-

dition of textual innovation had created and that awaited artful use.
Lines, couplets, and stanzas in this lyric pool did not belong to one particular song, but floated freely, able potentially to be inserted in many.
Decisions as to precisely which lines, couplets, and so on were "sampled" were left to the creative choice of the individual singer.[11] In the
process of this artful selection, the often-commented-on ability of
slaves to fit sampled lyrics to the existing rhythms of a song was
clearly displayed. "The negroes keep exquisite time in singing," William Francis Allen had realized, "and do not suffer themselves to be
daunted by any obstacle in the words. The most obstinate Scripture
phrases or snatches from hymns they will force to do duty with any
tune they please."[12] Whites were often puzzled by these cultural practices, being unaware of the creative processes involved. For example,
having completed a tour of the South in the mid-1840s, J. Kinnard observed that, in their songs "the blacks . . . leave out old stanzas, and introduce new ones at pleasure. . . . You may, in passing from Virginia to
Louisiana, hear the same tune a hundred times, but seldom the same
words accompanying it."[13]

An examination of the spirituals that former slaves recalled for
their WPA interviewers shows how lyrics were able to float between
any number of slave songs. For instance, the line "swing low, sweet
chariot" appeared not merely in the now familiar slave song of that
title, but in many others. Slaves on Lorenza Ezell's South Carolina
plantation, for instance, employed it thus:

> Swing low, sweet chariot,
> Freely let me into rest,
> I don't want to stay here no longer;
> Swing low, sweet chariot
> When Gabriel make his las' alarm
> I wants to be rollin' in Jesus arm,
> 'Cause I don't want to stay here no longer.

"Sampled" from the lead singer's lyric store, the line "swing low,
sweet chariot" was easily incorporated into a new song. In the same
way, the couplet "When Gabriel make his las' alarm, / I wants to be
rollin' in Jesus arm," probably coined long in the past, had once more
found an appropriate home.[14] In a spiritual called to mind by ex-

Alabama bondsman Hilliard Johnson, the words "swing low, chariot" were once again used differently.

> Trouble here and dey's trouble dere,
> I really do believe dere's trouble ev'ywhere.
> Swing low, chariot, I'm gwine home.
> Swing low, chariot, I'm gwine home.

Successive verses of Hilliard Johnson's spiritual read:

> Oh, dey's a moaner here, dey's a moaner dere,
> I really do b'lieve dey's a moaner ev'ywhere.
> Swing low, chariot, I'm gwine home.
> Swing low, chariot, I'm gwine home.
>
> Oh dey's a sinner here, dey's a sinner dere,
> I really do b'lieve dey's a sinner ev'ywhere.
> Swing low, chariot, I'm gwine home.
> Swing low, chariot, I'm gwine home.
>
> Oh, dey's a Christun here, dey's a Christun dere
> I really do b'lieve dey's a Christun ev'ywhere
> Swing low, chariot, I'm gwine home.
> Swing low, chariot, I'm gwine home.

This last song illustrates not merely the process of lyric borrowing, but the African American tradition of parallel statement, which allowed singers to expand the lyrics of a song by altering merely a word or a phrase ("moaner," "sinner," etc.)[15] As Hilliard Johnson explained: "Den dey's a heap of 'em [verses] to dat song lac a 'deacon' and a 'member' and a 'prayer' and a 'singer,' jes' a whole passel dem verses, but I reckon dem will do today."[16] Again, "Little Annie" remembered her father, a Texas slave, singing:

> Gwine try on my starry crown, Down by the riverside,
> Down by the riverside, Down by the riverside,
> Gwine try on my starry crown, Down by the riverside,
> Down by the riverside.
> I aint gwine study war no more, I aint gwine study war no more.[17]

But Ellen King, formerly a slave in Mississippi, recalled the phrase "down by the riverside" being associated with different words:

Down by the river side,
Jesus will talk and walk,
Ain't going to study the world no more,
Ain't going to study the world no more,
For down by the river side,
Jesus will talk and walk.[18]

As with song texts, so too with tunes: African American slaves treated these "not as unchangeable traits of song, but rather as freely variable vehicles for conveying one's innermost feelings."[19] To express the emotions of singers, tunes were freely embellished, tempos slowed or quickened, vocal textures constantly shifted.[20] When Henry Russell, an English singer who toured the United States in the late 1830s and early 1840s, visited a black church in Vicksburg, Virginia, he was surprised by the choir's rendition of a psalm that the minister had introduced. Before long, choir members "commenced singing so rapidly that the original tune absolutely ceased to exist—in fact, the fine old psalm tune became thoroughly transformed into a kind of negro melody; and so sudden was the transformation, by accelerating the time, that, for a moment, I fancied that not only the choir but the little congregation intended to get up a dance as part of the service."[21] In March 1863, Charles Coffin, correspondent of the *Boston Herald*, described an equally dramatic musical transformation effected by a black congregation at Hilton Head. A hymn was "lined off" by the new plantation owner, a Mr. Norton from Massachusetts, after which "William, a stout, middle-aged man, struck into St. Martin's, and the congregation joined, not reading the music exactly as good old [William] Tansur composed it, for there were crooks, turns, slurs, and appoggiaturas, not to be found in any printed copy. It was sung harshly, nasally, and dragged out in long, slow notes."[22] During their journey through the South in 1939, John and Ruby Lomax were able to record Deacon Harvey Williams's lining out of the slow-meter hymn "Go Preach My Gospel" for the congregation of the New Zion Baptist Church in Clemson, South Carolina to sing. Against the slow tempo of the hymn, Deacon Williams and his congregation liberally adorned the melody with vocal glides and slurs of their own (track 8).[23] Another lined hymn, "Jesus, My God, I Know His Name," which the Lomaxes recorded at Cummins State Farm, near Varner, Arkansas, in May 1939, featured an all-but-incessant use of melisma, vibrato effects created by the lead singer, and the changing timbres of the singers' voices, all of these thickening the texture of sound (track 9).[24] Lining out, which is to say, having someone read one or two lines of a hymn so that those who could not read or who had no hymn books could sing it, had been introduced by whites, but later adopted by blacks, whose call-and-response style of singing it resembled. In black hands, however, lining out often changed its character, becoming not so much a device for helping those who lacked the ability or opportunity to read, as part of the hymn itself, the lined-out "calls" having melodic and structural characteristics of their own. The typically slow tempo of lined-out hymns threw the improvisational and richly ornamental styles of black singers into sharp relief.

Black cultural preference was expressed in other ways as well. Slave singing was not harmonic, in the Western sense, with soprano, alto, tenor, and bass parts, but rather, in many cases, heterophonic. Heterophonic singing did not mean that members of the group sang whatever notes they chose, but that they sang in response to, and in "conversation" with, one or more of the other singers. Voices were pitched purposefully, but in a way that left generous scope for improvisation and personal expression, and indeed invited them. (Readers can find examples of heterophonic singing in "New Buryin' Ground" [track 6], sung in 1939 by John Brown and a group of convicts at the State Penitentiary, Raiford, Florida,[25] and "Long Hot Summer Days" [track 7], sung by Clyde Hill and a group of convicts at Clemens State Farm, Brazoria County, Texas.[26]) The effect that could be created by such means has been called by Glenn Hinson "a symphony of improvisation and personal statement,"[27] a complex sonic effect that whites found great difficulty in describing. William Francis Allen, one of the compilers of the volume *Slave Songs of the United States* (1867), made by far the best attempt:

> I despair of conveying any notion of the effect of a number [of black people] singing together.... There is no singing in parts, as we understand it, and yet no two appear to be singing the same thing—the

leading singer starts the words of each verse, often improvising, and the others, who "base" him, as it is called, strike in with the refrain, or even join in the solo, when the words are familiar. When the "base" begins, the leader often stops, leaving the rest of his words to be guessed at, or it may be they are taken up by one of the other singers. And the "basers" themselves seem to follow their own whims, beginning when they please and leaving off when they please, striking an octave above or below... or hitting some other note that chords, so as to produce the effect of a marvellous complication and variety, and yet with the most perfect time, and rarely with any discord. And what makes it harder to unravel a thread of melody out of this strange network is that, like birds, they seem not infrequently to strike sounds that cannot be precisely represented by the gamut, and abound in "slides from one note to another, and turns and cadences not in articulated notes."[28]

Allen's reference to the lead singer's making way for another member of the group, a common occurrence at ring shouts, corn shuckings, and on any number of impromptu occasions, reminds us that, in this as in other ways, a slave song was a frame that invited co-construction. Among others who attempted to capture in words the heterophonic nature of slave singing were the English traveler William Faux, who declared the singing of black oarsmen in Charleston Harbor in 1823 to be "barbarously harmonious,"[29] and the white southern woman Victoria Clay, who, having listened to the songs of slaves on a South Carolina plantation in 1864, wrote of "dozens of voices blended in weird and melodious harmonies."[30] Decades later, Zora Neale Hurston would refer to the "jagged harmony" of old-time spirituals.[31]

The Reverend John Watson's protest against a growing tendency of Methodist congregations to sing "in the merry chorus-manner of the Southern harvest field, or husking frolic method of slave blacks," probably reflected also his concern over what he saw as an entirely inappropriate mixing of the sacred and secular realms. In this matter, too, a sizable cultural gap remained between blacks and whites. Whatever the degrees of acculturation that had occurred by the time Watson wrote, many slaves retained a worldview that spoke to the unity of work, worship, leisure, and play, that saw them all as belonging to a single realm. And if, as we attempt to enter the slaves' world, these white-created genres seem to collapse, that is because they were never there. There were some marked situations, where blacks attended white church services, for example, in which white-stipulated boundaries were more likely to be observed by blacks, but with work songs, and in a host of other situations, there was often a free interspersing of sacred and secular expression.[32] Examples abound. As a group of blacks rowed Charles Lyell down the Altamaha River in Georgia in 1845, they improvised songs praising their master's family and likening the beauty of a black woman of their acquaintance to that of a red bird. Every so often, however, the rowers "struck up a hymn, taught them by the Methodists, in which the most sacred subjects were handled with strange familiarity, and which, though nothing irreverent was meant, sounded oddly to our ears, and, when following a love ditty, almost profane."[33] In the late 1850s, Mary Dickson Arrowood heard slave boatmen singing songs that exhibited the same indifference to the supposed sacred/secular divide:

> De ship is in de harbor, harbor, harbor,
> De ship is in de harbor,
> To wait upon de Lord. . . .
>
> 'E got 'e ca'go raidy, raidy, raidy,
> 'E got 'e ca'go raidy,
> Fo' to wait upon de Lord.[34]

A song that slaves in a Virginia factory sang began as a spiritual, but made references to the task in which the workers were engaged:

> Shine alon', shine alon'
> My home is over Jordan.
> One o' dese mornin's bright an' fair,
> We goin' shine mos' much in de air.
>
> Shine alon', shine alon',
> My 'bacca, my bacca,
> I goin' stem alon',
> One o' dese mornin's bright an' fair,
> We goin' shine mos' much in de air.[35]

The same kind of indiscriminate mixing appears in the slave lullaby "Go to Sleep" (track 10), which Florida Hampton sang for the Lomaxes in Livingston, Alabama, in 1939. Several times the singer warns the baby not to cry or "de bugger-bear get you," but shortly afterwards reassures the child that "there's nobody but the Saviour."[36] In the ring shouts, too, lead singers often set sacred and secular lines side by side.

Whites also heard cultural dissonance in the seemingly directionless nature of work song lyrics. Stanzas in these songs seemed to follow no linear sequence; two or three verses relating to one subject might be succeeded by another group of verses that bore no connection to the first, or indeed to any others in the song. The same kind of mixing, without regard to consonance or continuity, occurred not only between verses but also within them. In part, these disjunctions reflected the exacting demands of improvisatory music, the need to come up with new lines or verses that would keep the song going while the laborers continued to work. In a sense, anything that dropped into the song leader's mind would serve as long as the beat was maintained, as long as the workers could time their ax cuts or oar strokes or hoe chops to the rhythm of the song. Sometimes, as we have seen, work songs were created not to pace unison activity, but to ease the burden of labor for groups working in close proximity with one another. Even with such songs, however, the same imperative for rapid improvisation applied.

Yet the very fluidity and adaptability of work song lyrics, their untroubled incorporation of immediate contemporary references or selected lines or couplets from a song leader's lyric store, allowed more easily for the elliptical criticism of a master, or the expression of a deeper range of feelings than would have been possible through the medium (and tedium?) of linear, "logical" thought. The disjunctive character of the lyrics, the narrative "cut" to an unrelated topic, imparted a freshness and spontaneity to a slave work song, a welcome element of surprise. Roger Abrahams has written that "[The literary critic] Houston Baker's analysis of the way in which blues lyrics are constructed effectively describes the continuum from the great African bardic traditions of disjunctive improvisation through the corn shucking and other work songs...to the present." He quotes Baker:

"Like a streamlined athlete's awesomely dazzling explosions of prowess, the blues...erupts, creating a...playful festival of meanings. Rather than a rigidly personalized form,...[these songs] offer...a nonlinear, freely associative, non-sequential meditation."37 Linking the apparently chaotic character of slave work-song lyrics to ancient bardic traditions might seem fanciful until we recall that in African American quilting and textile design, what is surprising, what is prized and enjoyed, is precisely this element of "disjunctive improvisation," the arresting juxtaposition of apparently incongruous elements. In African American music, too, improvisation, creative intervention and change, occur on the break, the point at which an individual performer does her or his thing.38 In part, then, what we may be looking at in the random lyric arrangements of slave songs is not simply a hastily selected and uncoordinated sequence of ideas or observations, but a different set of cultural preferences. Far from being obvious, meaning in work song lyrics is left open, dissonance is unresolved, creative tension survives.

Karin Barber's discussion of "oriki," the praise poetry of the Yoruba people in Africa, is valuable here and not simply because it reminds us that there are other ways of presenting ideas and creating dramatic effects than through the processes of linear, sequential thought. She writes: "Oriki are essentially and not accidentally fragmentary and non-narrative. There is no attempt to link, causally or temporally, the events they allude to. In fact their tendency is the opposite." And again, "a performance of oriki appears to lack unity—to be a centreless agglomeration of only tenuously related items....It appears to lack closure and boundaries."39 Barber's description recalls the observations of a "gentleman," who, after attending a corn shucking in 1836, reported that the song leader, a man noted for his skill at improvising lyrics, "seemed to have no object in view but to sing," and that he "passed from one subject to another without regard to connexion." The gentleman offered the following as an example:

> Oh, Jenny, gone to New-town
> CHORUS Oh, Jenny gone away!
> She went because she wouldn't stay,
> CHORUS Oh, Jenny gone away!

> She run'd away, an' I know why,
>   CHORUS Oh, Jenny gone away!
> For she went a'ter Jones's Bob,
>   CHORUS Oh, Jenny gone away!
>
> Mr. Norton, good ole man,
>   CHORUS Oh, Jenny gone away!
> Treats his niggers mighty well,
>   CHORUS Oh Jenny gone away!
> Young Tim Barnet no great thing,
>   CHORUS Oh Jenny gone away!
> Never say, come take a dram.
>   CHORUS Oh Jenny gone away!
> Master gi's us plenty meat,
>   CHORUS Oh Jenny gone away!
> Might apt to fo'git de drink.
>   CHORUS Oh Jenny gone away![40]

The gentleman's example is not especially well chosen. On one reading, the series of lines lamenting the fact that the singer's woman had left him for a slave named Bob, owned by a Mr. Jones, seems to bear no relation to the evaluative comments about slaveholders, with which it is awkwardly juxtaposed. An alternate reading, however, could be that Jenny had "gone away" in order to follow "Jones's Bob," whose master, the unsympathetic and miserly "Tim Barnet," had sold him to a person in New-town. An outsider such as the gentleman, unaware of the contextual references contained in the song's lyrics, would not have seen that possible connection between the two verses. To those slaves who supplied the song's chorus, however, the connection might well have been obvious enough.

The gentleman's observation does, however, accurately reflect a general expectation among whites that song lyrics, and indeed narratives of any kind, should take a linear form; that they should have a beginning, a main part, and an end; that overall they should "make sense." But in this expectation whites, when they listened to slave music, were often disappointed. Traveling to Savannah in 1808, in a canoe rowed by four slaves, John Lambert admired the men's antiphonal singing and the way in which they used the song to time the strokes of their oars, but concluded that the words of their improvised song "were mere nonsense; anything, in fact, which came into their heads."[41] (We could recall also the gentleman's comment that the song leader to whom he had listened at the corn shucking "seemed to have no object in view but to sing," and that he "passed from one subject to another without regard to connection.") As would later be true of blues lyrics, stanzas in slave songs often tended to be randomly placed, or grouped in almost haphazard fashion, perhaps around some central theme or themes. Moreover, not merely the lyrics, but also the tunes of slave music tended to take a nonlinear form, with their horizontal progression or flow constantly being "interrupted" by more complex melodic phrasings, surprising changes in tempo and pitch, and, in the case of hymns, by the practice of lining out.[42] Again addressing the issue of nonlinearity, Roger Abrahams observed that "with black song, there is not only not such a profound sense of squaring off with a beginning and ending, but the tunes tend toward the circular, as do the dances that accompany them."[43] Beginnings and endings are ragged or indeterminate; songs continue until the performers have finished, not at some predetermined point; rather than being silenced, the music ebbs untidily away. Nonlinearity is characteristic also of certain types of black speech. In a series of interviews conducted in the 1930s, the African American linguist Lorenzo Dow Turner recorded, on phonograph disc, the recollections of some of the survivors of the terrible earthquake that struck the Sea Island of Edisto in 1886. Subsequently, Turner transcribed the memories of some of these informants—Gullah speakers all—who witnessed these events, using conventional systems of phonetic notation. He thus allowed those of his readers who were familiar with phonetic symbols to "hear" something of the Gullah speakers' vowel and consonant sounds and patterns of intonation. Turner's rendition of Diana Brown's narrative, without phonetic symbols and as abridged by the present authors, is reproduced below:

> When that first storm been here, when that first storm been here, you—I don't think you been born. And that first storm—you know about earthquake? You know about dark night? I ain't afraid about a dark night now in August. Well, when that—when that first storm

been here, I had seven head of children in my house. And Miss Barton—and she give you ration. And she give me [some] for every head.
That was a woman.... And that storm—all the people what been with
me on the island, every God one gone.... [The tide] carry the people
right down in the creek.... You go there and meet some man broken.
The man and he wife hang to the tree. Them lick to pieces. Man, some
shocking time been here.... And after them storm, them what get
away from the tide sleep in wood.... The people come home naked;
come home naked!... [T]hey catch birds. Lord! Lord! Catch birds to
eat them raw to get home. The tide carry them out.... [T]oday when I
look, when the storm is coming, I say I don't care for freedom.... I say,
"I ain't care for freedom, because I done been through it." ... When
the earthquake been here, we gone to meeting ... I couldn't get home.
I had to walk on my hand and knee, because the world going upside
down.... When God create that midnight.... See this here God? this
here God what people don't pray to? Huh! I been through all them
thing.44

Writing of the narrative style of Diana Brown, Alex Bontemps is
able to see past its apparent structural formlessness and experience
something of its elusive power. To Bontemps, this former slave's description of the traumatic event of 1886 is both "strangely compelling,
even riveting" and at the same time "exasperatingly disjointed, juxtaposing remembered fragments of experience without any indication of
their relationship," and this is certainly how it at first appears.45 Yet
there is more structure in this Gullah speaker's account than we might
think. In her telling, Brown creates a refrain—"When that first storm
been here" (she uses the terms "earthquake" and "storm" inter-
changeably)—from which she journeys away but to which she keeps
returning, each journey providing a fuller picture that will make her
account of the disaster more powerful. Thus, she tells, for example, in
no particular order, how Clara Barton (founder of the United States
Red Cross) provided food for herself and her family; of the many
islanders who drowned, whose bodies hung in trees; of destitute survivors eating birds raw to say alive; of having to crawl across the
heaving ground to return to her home, and so on. She asserts that deliverance from the earthquake was a greater deliverance than that

from slavery: "I ain't care for freedom [emancipation]," Brown declares, "because I done been through it [the earthquake]." And at the end of her story she makes a moral of it. Having talked about the power of God, who created "that midnight" (that is, the earthquake), she laments the fact that people no longer pray to him, even though he had demonstrated a power greater than that which delivered Brown from slavery.

With its restive chronology and often random mixing of vividly recalled impressions, Diana Brown's story of the earthquake may yet take us closer to the experience itself than any tightly organized narration could do. We feel that we have an understanding of what she went through, because her vividly recalled impressions, taken as a whole, give a *sense* of the experience rather than an *account* of the experience. Like the blues singer, she offers not an orderly arrangement of events and ideas but a field of meaning, an evocative whole. The seeming preference of many African American slaves for what, to the "gentleman" quoted above and to many other whites, seemed disjunctive, nonsequential song lyrics reflected, in part, the exacting demands of lyric improvisation. It also hinted at something as deep-seated as a different way of making sense of the world.

CHAPTER 5

"He can invent a plausible Tale at a Moment's Warning"

Late in the evening, when Colonel Thomas Wentworth Higginson had time to take up his pen and write of the day's events in the black army camp at Port Royal, his account was saturated with the sounds of black voices and the sudden gales of laughter prompted by the wit of some black raconteur. Not only did these sounds constitute that part of his troops' lives that intrigued and puzzled him the most, but they were also, as he himself recognized, the sounds that were most difficult to capture on paper, and whose power was impossible to convey fully to someone who had not witnessed them. One night, soon after his arrival in late August 1862, as he strolled through the unit's camp after dark, the young commander came upon a "circle of thirty or forty soldiers sat around a fire of logs." From inside the ring, "one old Uncle, Cato by name was narrating an interminable tale to the insatiable delight of his auditors." Of Cato's story, Higginson would later write: "It was a narrative, dramatized to the last degree, of his adventures in escaping from his master to the Union vessels; and even I, who have heard stories of Harriet Tubman, and such wonderful slave-comedians, never witnessed such a piece of acting."

As Higginson sidled up to the edge of the group, Cato was relating how, at one stage during his flight to freedom, he had boldly approached a plantation house and asked a white man for food.

> Den I go up to de man, very humble & say would he please gib ole man a mouthful? He say, he must hab the valeration ob half a dollar. Den I go away, Den he say, gib him de hatchet I had! Den I say (with infinite comic seriousness) "I mus hab dat hatchet for defend myself *from de dogs!*" (Immense applause, & a sympathetic auditor says chuckling, "Dat was your *arms,* ole man," which exploded the house again.) Den he say, de Yankee pickets was near by & I must be very careful. Den I say *Good Lord, Mas'r, am dey?*

Referring to the final line of this exchange, Higginson observed that "words cannot express the unutterable dissimulation with which these accents of terror were uttered," since, of course, the location of the Yankee pickets was precisely the information that Cato had been hoping to obtain.

Next, Cato described how he had made his escape from his owner's plantation, "all in a style of which Gough alone among speakers can give any impression, so thoroughly was every word dramatized." He then related how, having eventually reached a certain river, he had had to decide which of the ships moored there were hostile and which belonged to the Union forces:

> "Den I see guns aboard & I feel sure ob it." "Den it pop in my head, *Seceshky hab guns too*—" Then he described sleeping in the bushes till morning. "Den I open my bundle & take my ole white shirt & tie um on ole pole and wave um, & ebry time de wind blow, I tremble all over & drop down in de bushes"—because the Secessionists were on shore & he might be seen from that side first. And so on, with a succession of tricks beyond Molière, of acts of caution, foresight, patient cunning such as seemed incredible to hear, while they were yet listened to with perfect comprehension & infinite gusto by every listener.

Cato's performance illustrated well Zora Neale Hurston's claim that the Negro's "entire self" was permeated by drama. And we can sense Higginson grappling with the language as he tries to convey the expressive power of his black soldier. When he wrote that "every word" of Cato's address was "dramatized," and that he himself had "never witnessed such a piece of acting," he alluded not simply to the words the ex-slave spoke, but to other factors—to the communicative bodily movements and manipulation of such vocal qualities as timbre, tone, volume, and stress—that characterized this storyteller's style. But Higginson, too, had difficulty in depicting the influence of such factors. Indeed, when, in describing Cato's feigned expression of alarm on being told the location of the Yankee pickets, Higginson wrote that "*words cannot express* the complete dissimulation with which these accents of terror were uttered" (italics added), he conceded that language simply was not capable of conveying the essence of the black orator's storytelling skills.[1]

Higginson discerned something of the power of Cato's performance from the noise and laughter of the black audience. He himself felt that power, favorably comparing Cato's dramatic skills with those of the best orators of the day, black as well as white. Yet, as between Higginson and the African American soldiers there is a detectable difference in response. Higginson can neither match nor fully understand the black crowd's enthusiasm. He can record, but not share their "insatiable delight." Nor does his attempt to convey a sense of Cato's verbal force and artistry by quoting the former slave's own words really succeed. The drama dissipates, the humor does not translate. Higginson seems bemused by the fact that Cato's protestation that he must retain his hatchet against the possibility of attack by dogs elicits "immense applause," and so are we. The black troops' hilarious response to the double entendre contained in the soldier's reference to "arms" puzzles him as it does us. Culturally as well as physically, Higginson remains on the edge of things, putting words down on paper that lack the essential qualities that must, for the black audience, have brought them thrillingly to life. It is doubtful whether this New England officer, to whom the sounds and speech rhythms of this former slave orator would have seemed strange, picked up as many of these meanings as did members of Cato's black audience. Intent on creating a written record of the night's proceedings, and unused to the cadences and tonal embellishments of black speech, the highly literate, even bookish, Higginson, may merely have tuned out sounds for which he possessed no written equivalent. In the manner of wordless field calls, the speech rhythms and tonal play of Cato's dramatic narration communicated meanings that eluded language, that were, as Higginson correctly perceived, beyond the power of words to express.

Although not apparent at the time, the situation was replete with irony. Higginson came from a New England Brahmin family and could trace its ancestors back to first-generation Puritans. Born in Cambridge, educated at Harvard, and an ardent abolitionist, for him army life with a black regiment was a complete revelation. Higginson had hardly led a sheltered existence but his troops behaved in ways that were radically different from those of the African Americans he had met in the abolitionist movement. On the other hand, most of Higginson's counterparts on the Confederate side had been hearing black voices from birth and, indeed, many probably were the scions of families that had owned slaves since at least sometime in the eighteenth century. But if many young Confederate officers, who of course commanded white and not black troops, had an at least rudimentary understanding of some of the nuances of black culture, very few, if any, were fascinated, in the way that Higginson was, by its aesthetics. Although it was undoubtedly true that on the eve of the Civil War there was a growing minority of southerners who appreciated, for example, the sounds of black singing, it was still the case, particularly among the young white men who became Confederate officers, that a knowledge of slave culture was little more than another tool of plantation management, something to be used to help extract the maximum amount of labor from their human property.

For all its freshness for Higginson, then, there was nothing particularly new about the way Cato told his story. By the 1860s the sounds of African and later African American voices had been part of the American, especially the southern, landscape for well over two centuries. We should not fall too easily into the assumption that the first languages spoken by blacks in America in the seventeenth century were African, for as Ira Berlin has shown, the first generation of blacks were Atlantic Creoles, who were often multilingual and fluent in an Atlantic patois. But by the eighteenth century, the era of what Berlin has termed the plantation generations, ship after ship was unloading its cargo of Africans along the Chesapeake and in South Carolina, transforming the economy, culture, and very appearance of the southern colonies. Indeed in 1737 one Swiss settler opined that "Carolina looks more like a negro country than like a country settled by white people."[2] Inevitably, these areas of the plantation South also began to sound more like a "negro country" as well.

About the only thing, other than the clothes they happened to be wearing on their backs, that the slaves were able to bring with them from Africa was their voices. And they spoke an almost bewildering variety of languages. In Africa today there are some sixteen hundred languages, some eleven hundred of which come from an area that was the catchment for the slave trade that supplied North America. Even as, or if, they learned English, many of these Africans also continued to speak their native language, often for the rest of their lives. In 1774 Bucharah and Cupid, two Africans who had been in South Carolina for about two years, spoke English "so as to be understood," but according to their owner, John Savage, they both spoke as well "the Bombra [probably Bambara] language and Cupid the Fulla language."3

By far the best source for revealing the sheer variety of the ways in which slaves talked is the thousands of runaway advertisements, such as the one describing Bucharah and Cupid, placed by inconvenienced and often irritated owners in eighteenth-century newspapers. These notices are the standard coin of most studies of slavery in the colonial and early national periods. Concerned to return their wayward property to work as quickly as possible, slave owners penned often quite detailed accounts of their runaways, in the hopes of hastening their recapture. These thumbnail sketches frequently included a reference to an ability or otherwise to speak English as one possible means of identifying the miscreants.

Many runaways could speak at best a few words of English. Charles, who absconded from a Virginia plantation in 1771, could utter his name but, according to his owner, that was "every word of English he can speak."4 Learning English as a slave could not have been easy. Population ratios and densities were clearly factors that influenced how long the process would take. It was, for example, likely that an African enslaved in New York City and coming in constant contact with English would be forced by her or his circumstances to pick up the language rather more hastily than one living on a plantation in the Carolina low country. According to Edward Fenwicke, Sambo, who was originally from the "Guinea country," and who ran away from his plantation on Johns Island, South Carolina, in 1786, spoke "bad English" even though he "has been many years in this State."5 In a place like Johns, where a high proportion of Sambo's fellow slaves were also African-born, a little "bad English" was probably more than enough to get by with. It should also be remembered that, as Michael Gomez has pointed out, English was the language of the slaves' owners and masters, those responsible for stripping them of their freedom and treating them inhumanely, and some slaves, quite possibly including Sambo, may well have deliberately refused to make the effort.[6]

And yet what impresses most as one reads the runaway advertisements is the facility and speed with which many African-born slaves picked up the English language. According to his owner, Colonel Lewis Burwell, a Mandingo runaway from Burwell's plantation near Williamsburg had been in Virginia only about two years, yet he was able to speak "pretty good English." George Washington's detailed account of several runaways who absconded from his Fairfax County plantation in 1761 revealed that Neptune and Cupid, who had been bought from a slave ship two years previously, still spoke "very broken and unintelligible English," but their countryman, Jack, who had been in Virginia only a year or two longer, spoke "pretty good English." Washington described Peres, another African-born slave, as speaking "something slow and broken, but not in so great a Degree as to render him remarkable," a level of fluency that was much better than that achieved by Washington's other escapees. Indeed, Peres had "little of his Country Dialect left, and is esteemed a sensible judicious Negro."[7]

Even when African-born slaves spoke English well, their speech sounded different from that of their owners. Tomboy, a mature slave, may have been ensnared by the slave trade and brought to Virginia when he was very young, but according to Tomboy's owner, he "retains much of his country dialect." Similarly, although Charles, who ran away from John Champneys in South Carolina in 1773, was said by his owner to speak English "remarkably well," he could "easily be distinguished from one born in this Province by his Speech."[8] Occasionally, owners described their slaves' voices in a way that suggests that they were referring to speech characteristics imported from Africa. In 1770 Wood Durman thought that his slave Sirrah, who was "of the Guiney Country," spoke "tolerable good English, not very thick." Durman's other runaway, Glasgow, spoke English "indifferently" and "with a squeaking Voice in common" with others from "the Ebo Country."[9] Conceivably, as Philip Morgan has surmised, this allusion to a "squeaking" voice referred to "the use of falsetto common to African American speech patterns," but while such terse descriptions are suggestive they are hardly conclusive.[10]

Most frequently, it was those blacks who had been born into slav-

ery who were described as speaking very good English. Nine of John
Ainslie's ten slaves, who absconded while en route to his plantation on
the Santee in South Carolina in 1771, were "born in this Country" and
all were "sensible and speak good English." Similarly, Jenny, a twenty-
year-old who departed from her owner's house in Charleston ten years
later, spoke "exceeding good English."[11] Although it was difficult for
them to express the matter succinctly on paper, many of the owners of
American-born slaves appear to have been trying to indicate that the
English spoken by their recalcitrant property sounded different from
that which they themselves spoke. Peter, a Maryland-born twenty-
five-year-old, was said to affect "a lofty stile of speech," and Phebe,
a Georgia slave, to speak "proper and artful."[12] The owner of Jacob, a
Pennsylvania-born slave who absconded in 1776, explained to readers
of his runaway advertisement that "in Conversation," Jacob "frequently uses the Words moreover and likewise," and the "very proud
and stately" George Quacca, who fled his Virginia owner in 1785, was
said to have a "masterly speech."[13] Occasionally, blacks who were enslaved in Africa and had endured the Middle Passage were categorized
in a similar fashion: "although an Affrican," the thirty-five-year-old
Ayre, who ran away from his Virginia plantation in 1778, "affects to
pronounce the English language very fine, or rather to clip it."[14] As
usual, it is very difficult to come to any firm conclusions from such
terse evidence, but there is at least the suggestion, and we would argue
it is rather more than that, that these slaves were embellishing the language in distinctive ways, demonstrating a cultural tendency that
Zora Neale Hurston would later label the "will to adorn."[15]

Other instances of that which Hurston later described as the artfulness of black speech are also readily apparent in runaway advertisements. Christmas, who ran away in 1772, had been James Mercer's
servant since childhood. Now an adult, he could read, was "very fluent
of Speech," and talked "with great Propriety." Indeed, "so artful" was
Christmas's language "that he can invent a plausible Tale at a Moment's Warning," a talent that led Mercer to believe that his slave
would now "pass unmolested, under some Pretence or other, as a Freeman." Similarly, both Quamino and Quacco, who ran away in South
Carolina in 1733, could "speak English very well," and, furthermore,

were "so crafty, that they would almost deceive any Body, and if taken, will frame a very plausible Story that they are not runaways."[16] Often this facility with words was developed at a young age. Levi, a fifteen-year-old runaway from New Jersey, was described by his owner in 1780 as being "very modest in speech" and having "a sober look," but no matter how unprepossessing that made him sound Levi was still more than capable of manufacturing "a smooth story from rough materials." Nor was it only American-born slaves who demonstrated this high level of proficiency with English. Even though Cuff was a "Guinea Negroe," his Dutchess County, New York, owner stated that he was "very flippant" and "a plausible smooth Tongue Fellow."[17]

As David Waldstreicher has reminded us, however, "one man's or woman's lying, of course, was another's resistance to brutal exploitation."[18] Resentful of their situation, and skilled in adapting African storytelling traditions, many slaves demonstrated a fluency and skill with words more than adequate to fool most whites with whom they came in daily contact. When one irate New York slave owner in 1795 described his slave Jude as speaking "very good English" and being "a sly cunning girl," he was in effect issuing a warning to whites to be wary.[19] Indeed, judging by the evidence from the runaway advertisements, the sound of a slave talking at length and fluently was little more than an indication to whites that they were being deceived. When Colonel Higginson had watched the performance of Cato at the campfire reenacting his conversation with the white planter, his breath had been taken away by the "unutterable dissimulation" with which his black soldier delivered his lines, and the way the knowing audience had roared with laughter at the deception, but, of course, the talents of the confidence man and woman, the "puttin' on" of "ole massa," as it was known in the quarters, made the lives of slaves just that little bit easier. White slave owners were caught in a trap. On the one hand they valued skilled, linguistically competent slaves highly; on the other hand they must have realized that their smooth-talking human property was much more likely to effect a successful escape.

The variety of ways in which slaves spoke hardly ended with African languages and varying levels of English. Further complicating the already bewildering situation were slaves who had picked up or developed different accents and/or dialects used by their owners. According to his master, Joe, "a plausible rascal" from South Carolina, "sometimes affects to speak broad Scotch or Northumberland dialect," while Jacob, originally from Pennsylvania, used a "Scotch-Irish Dialect."[20] By the second half of the eighteenth century, in the minds of some whites, at least, there were regional American dialects as well: in 1781 Will was said by his owner to speak "with the Virginia or North-Carolina accent." In 1776 Elijah, who was described as "Virginia born," spoke "with the accent of that country." According to his owner, Grotis, who had been raised on Long Island, was "yankified in his speech, and likewise slow in his motion," while Jasper "was either born or lived in the West-Indies, by which he has acquired their peculiar Way of speaking."[21] At times, too, it was not region that determined one's manner of speaking but trade or occupation: in 1779 a mulatto named Jerry who ran away was described as having been "bred a sailor, and speaks much in that dialect."[22]

In addition, in the eighteenth century there were large numbers of slaves who were bi- and often multilingual in European languages. In the New York City area, for example, many slaves were raised speaking Dutch. In 1792 John De Wint's runaway Maria spoke "very broken English and good Negro Dutch." Cuff, who ran away from nearby Hackensack in 1789, spoke "broken English as he was brought up in a Dutch family," and David Banks of Newark spoke "Low Dutch and middling good English, although he frequently gives his words the Dutch accent."[23] Others, who had come from the West Indies, spoke French. A Guinea-born slave who ran away in New York in 1794 spoke "a little English and a little French," and Lindor, who absconded in 1789, called himself a native of the West Indies and was able to speak "pretty good English, French and Creole."[24] Similarly linguistically adept slaves were also common in the South. Five runaways from Purrysburg, South Carolina, were able to speak "good English, French and German," and Peter, the slave who delivered the *South Carolina Gazette* in Charleston in the 1730s, spoke "good English, French and Dutch."[25]

Overwhelmingly, then, the evidence suggests that in the eighteenth century it was impossible to fix with any degree of certainty how slave speech sounded. In the very last years of the eighteenth and early decades of the nineteenth century, however, this situation began to change. What happened was that, principally through the medium of print but later through the precursors of the minstrel show and then the minstrel show itself, whites insisted on the existence of a uniform Black English, a dialect that they saw as embodying cultural difference and black inferiority. As David Waldstreicher has aptly observed, "White Americans found in culture—in language turned into performance and print—something they could not always depend upon in biology."[26] The northern states, where, not coincidentally, slavery ended in these years (by the 1820s only a very few were still enslaved), took the lead in this development. As African northerners attained their hard-won freedom, unprecedented numbers of whites took to imitating, parodying, and burlesquing blacks. It was as though the now-free blacks were more visible than they had ever been as slaves, and that their activities were attracting the eye of "witty" whites. Yet there was something brittle and rather uneasy about this humor. "Black dialect" and the various "humorous" stories that were told about blacks were designed to separate blacks from whites, to ensure that although all were now free, the two groups could not be confused.

In early January 1813, when *Poulson's American Daily Advertiser*, a Philadelphia newspaper, reprinted from the *Boston Weekly Messenger* a supposedly comic piece in "black dialect" entitled a "Dialogue Between Sambo & Cuffy," the editor thought it necessary to append a brief notice. "It must be recollected," he warned his readers, "that the people of colour in Boston talk in a dialect peculiar to themselves, of which here is an excellent specimen."[27] Perhaps there were some minor peculiarities of African Bostonian English that marked its speakers off from African Philadelphians' or African New Yorkers' English, but those differences would hardly have caused problems of comprehension. More to the point was the fact that there was as yet no accepted way of rendering black speech on the printed page. It is easy enough to find examples of "black dialect" in the newspapers or almanacs of the New York or Philadelphia or Boston of the 1790s, but by the 1810s and 1820s, what had been a trickle of such material rapidly developed into a torrent.[28] With this increased volume came an increased standardization and the development of an orthography of "black dialect." The conventions of this white version of black speech—the inclusion of numerous malapropisms and the use of phonetic spellings, for example—were being worked out in the northern cities in the early decades of the nineteenth century at the same time that large numbers of free blacks were becoming a highly visible and often raucous presence. That was hardly coincidence. "Black dialect" comprised a curious mixture, one ingredient of which was an occasional closely observed representation of the way in which some blacks did actually speak, the other ingredient of which was a complete invention of black speech forms. Overall, this amalgam of fact and fantasy purported to show, often in the most demeaning and unpleasant fashion possible, that blacks were comically inept imitators of their supposed betters, who, even if now free, remained clearly differentiated from whites. Refined, and above all amplified, by white performers in blackface, this manufactured black dialect, with all its pernicious legacy of racial denigration, has lasted down to our own time.

In Boston of the 1810s and 1820s, much of this material was centered around the so-called "Bobalition" parades celebrating the end of the African slave trade. In New York, the material often focused on the African Grove Theater, the site at which a black acting troupe performed, among other things, some of Shakespeare's plays.[29] Black dialect was ubiquitous and its use was almost invariably an ill-concealed, surly, and bad-tempered attempt to lampoon any independent black activity or achievement. Often too this distorted representation of black speech was used in little filler items. In 1828 the *New-York American,* seemingly apropos of nothing, printed a supposed black account of the origin of the white man. After Cane had killed Abel,

> de massa cum and say—"Cane, whar your brodder Abel?"—Cane say—"I don't no, massa." But de niggar no'd all de time. Massa now git mad, cum gin; peak mity sharp dis time. "Cane, whar you brodder Abel, you niggar." Cane now get friten, an he turn *wite;* and dis is de day de fus wite man cum pon dis yerth! an if it hadn't been fur that plaggy nigger Cane, we'd never ben tubled wid dese sassy wites, pon de face ob dis circumblar globe.[30]

For all the verisimilitude of this story (not only is it similar to other documented African American accounts of Genesis, but the dismissive attitude exhibited toward whites fits in so well with the prickly mood of black New York in the 1820s), the language in which it is recounted seems less an attempt to render the sound of Black English than a strained effort to demonstrate difference, clearly equated with inferiority. Who, after all, does not pronounce "know" as "no" or "mighty" as "mity"? Much the same demeaning techniques were used in the reporting of blacks' court appearances, accounts of which provided the press with its most frequent opportunity to render black speech, and became the very foundation on which numerous parodies of blacks were based.

As one plows through the surviving written record of these years, the deluge of material in dialecticized Black English is quite striking. Clearly, many blacks were using Black English, which was different from the English spoken by whites, but whites were exaggerating those differences to create what rapidly developed into an accepted caricature of black speech. The reasons for this deliberate distortion were bound up in the ambivalent attitude of whites to the realities of black freedom. What particularly unnerved many whites were the similarities between black and white, the fact that, too often, as far as they were concerned, black men and women could now be mistaken for whites themselves. Inserting an often ludicrously distorted, dialecticized language into black mouths was a way of reassuring whites not only that blacks sounded different from whites, but that blacks really were as different from whites as whites wished to believe. This desire to segregate blacks went hand in hand with another linguistic innovation, the use of the term "nigger" in the public prints. All such devices were designed to remind everyone that although African northerners might now be free, they were anything but equal.

Occasionally this newly conventional way of rendering black speech puzzled strangers who actually encountered African Americans. A Mrs. Felton, for example, after conversing with many black females in New York City, commented that "they generally express themselves in good language, and with an enunciation, as bold and as clear as any Englishman." "This struck me with surprise," she continued, "as I had formed my judgement of their conversational capabilities, from the dialogues given in broken English, that I had met with in the course of my reading."[31] Mostly, though, people heard what they expected to hear, and the caricatured speech perpetuated through print culture and the minstrel show was insidiously effective in demeaning blacks, as it has been since that time.

By the 1840s and 1850s, then, slaves had to contend with an implicit, albeit often only half-formed, assumption on the part of many whites that not only was there a relatively homogenous way in which African Americans spoke, but also that the language they used was a clear sign of their intellectual inferiority. When Sally Baxter Hampton visited Columbia, South Carolina, in the 1850s she thought that the "darkies" were "irresistibly comic." Indeed, the slave who "attends on us is the fac-simile of George Christy—superb in demeanor, language & deportment—using the most high sounding words in rather a Mrs Malaprop fashion." George Christy, of course, was a white man wearing blackface, probably one of the greatest performers in the history of minstrelsy.[32] To be sure the linguistic variety was not as great as it had been in the eighteenth century, but an abundance of evidence, both from whites who listened carefully to black speech and from African Americans themselves, makes it clear that there was anything but homogeneity in the way slaves spoke.

Even in the last years of slavery and almost half a century after the official cessation of the slave trade, there were still African-born slaves scattered throughout the plantation South. For most slaves Africa was by then at some remove, but clearly the presence of Africans made an often indelible impression on a few of the young slaves who, as it turned out, would later be interviewed by the WPA. The former slave Richard Carruthers remembered "a story about a black feller called Old Pete," who had "come fresh from Africa and he din' know no talk hardly but that African talk." The old man persisted in using the word "'Whitta-ka-plum-pick' for the name we-all call screech owl."[33] Perhaps it was the strangeness of the old African, or perhaps it was the fact that slaves associated the screech owl's penetrating cry with impending death, but whatever the reason, one probably terrified slave boy remembered the word for the rest of his long life, and as a result one small sound of Africa reverberated down at least until the 1930s. Other WPA interviewees also recalled the strange sounds of African languages. Richard Jones from South Carolina spoke of "Uncle Tom" and

"Granny Judith," who, "when dey talk, nobody didn't know what dey was talking about." Granny Judith "never could speak good like I can," the former slave added. "She talk half African, and all African when she git bothered."[34]

No "dialect" sounded stranger to white ears than did Gullah, a creole language that drew most of its vocabulary from English and much of its syntax, pronunciations, and intonational patterns from diverse African languages. Gullah was spoken by blacks who inhabited the Sea Islands off the coast of South Carolina and Georgia and the adjacent lowlands.[35] Whites who encountered Gullah for the first time were deeply puzzled by its strange tones and cadences and peculiar syntax. For instance, the English actress Fanny Kemble, introduced to Gullah when she visited her husband's Saint Simons Island plantation in the late 1830s, wrote that an account given her by "Old House Molly," of incidents that had occurred on the plantation during the War of 1812, had been "full of interest, in spite of the grotesque lingo in which it was delivered, . . . which once or twice nearly sent me into convulsions of laughter."[36] Others were equally dismissive. "The lowland negro of South Carolina has a barbaric dialect," Edward King declared. "The English words seem to tumble all at once from his mouth and to get sadly mixed whenever he endeavors to speak."[37] James Miller McKim complained that the lyrics of songs sung by Port Royal blacks were "couched in a barbarous, African sort of English,"[38] and to Charles Nordhoff, who spent time on the Sea Islands in 1863, their inhabitants' speech seemed a "rude jargon," whose speakers' highly dramatic manner of delivery made it "extremely difficult to follow their rapid and thick utterance."[39] Even African Americans in other parts of the South had difficulty comprehending Gullah. James Lucas, who was interviewed in Mississippi, remembered that, when his grandmother spoke, "folks couldn' un'erstan' a word she say." "It was," he concluded, "some sort o' gibberish dey called gullah-talk, an' it soun' *dat* funny."[40]

Although Thomas Wentworth Higginson also found Sea Island speech strange, he was notably more sympathetic toward it. In late 1862, soon after he arrived, he sought to convey in a letter home to his mother the disorienting effects of the camp's ambient sounds. Seated at the door of his tent, he wrote, he was attempting to settle disputes between members of the regiment whose "lingo is almost inexplicable." "The very listening to these people," he declared, "is like adjusting the ear to some foreign language." As an example, he related for his mother how one of the camp's washerwomen had protested to him that a girl whom she had adopted and for whom she had long cared had suddenly left her. "I took she when she am dat high," the woman declared, "& now if him wants to leave we, let he go."[41]

Intrigued by his troops' mode of speech, Higginson began entering examples of it in his diary. An anxious husband urged the young colonel to dispatch the camp doctor to attend his wife: "Him sick, Sa, in he tent," the man explained. "Him c'ant come to de surgeon, surgeon must go to he."[42] A soldier who had been dissuaded by one of the regiment's white officers from marrying a certain woman complained testily to Higginson that "Cappen Scroby (Trowbridge) he acvise me not for marry dis lady, 'cause she hab sever children,—what for use?— Cappen Scroby can't lub for me, I must lub for myself, and I lub he."[43] Later, when he noticed that his men were beginning to modify some of their cultural practices, introducing a degree of levity, for example, into their "shouts," the commander expressed the hope that "they will never grow so civilized as to lose their piquant use of personal pronouns." The remark had been prompted by his overhearing a black soldier facetiously issuing an imaginary general order: "Heretofore no man must fry he meat, must always boil he."[44]

William Francis Allen, Higginson's contemporary, who conducted a school for contrabands on Port Royal, was also initially disoriented by a form of speech whose "strange . . . pronunciations," "frequent abbreviations," and "rhythmical modulations" gave it "an utterly unEnglish sound." It seemed to Allen that in Gullah, "the process of phonetic decay" had gone as far as it could. Port Royal blacks softened the English sound made by the letters *th*, difficult for Africans to pronounce, to that produced by the letter *d*, so that "this" became "dis." They clipped English words, rendering "little brother" as "lee' bro'," and "plantation" as "plant'shun." The word "sh'um," which had at first puzzled Allen, turned out to be a contraction of "see 'em." "Where's your brother?" a teacher had inquired of one of Allen's pupils. "Sh'um dar. Wid bof he han' in he pocket," came the reply.

Allen noted that Sea Island speech was largely uninflected. Nouns did not indicate number, gender, or case; verbs failed to indicate tense. In the sentence "Him lick we," for instance, the pronoun "him" might equally refer to a male or female, and the verb "lick" could designate past, present, or future tense. Possession was indicated by juxtaposition. The expression "Sandy hat" denoted ownership, but not the number of hats that Sandy possessed. Strange words appeared in the islanders' vocabulary, and English words assumed new meanings. The term "buckra" referred to a white man; "churry" meant "spill"; "oona" signified "you"; "yeardy" meant "hear," as in the exchange "Flora, did you see that cat?" "No ma'am, but I yearde him holler." "Study" referred not to an examination of some object or issue, but to "any continuous or customary action." "He studdy 'buse an' cuss we," was the complaint of a group of Port Royal children who were being bothered by an older girl.[45]

Though Higginson often felt that his troops spoke in an "immature and childlike" way, he was still struck by their eloquence, by the power of their imagery.[46] On one of the unit's route marches, Higginson refused to allow the men to stow their knapsacks on the unit's wagons, believing it important for them to learn to move efficiently, even while carrying their equipment. Later, when he discovered that a number of knapsacks had been placed on the wagons, he promptly ordered their removal. At this, some of the men "looked a little disconcerted, till one, heaving up his big black burden, shouted consolingly 'Every man he own hoss,' which practical witticism created a general guffaw, & the knapsacks were resumed with perfect cheerfulness."[47]

Clearly, then, in the 1850s, as well as a few Africans still speaking African languages there were also many more slaves using a language that owed something to West African speech forms. Of course, the Gullah that Demus Green used in the 1970s in his animal trickster story of the buzzard and the cooter (track 11) is not the Gullah that Lorenzo Dow Turner would have heard from the lips of Diana Brown and Turner's other informants in the 1930s, or the snatches of Gullah that Thomas Wentworth Higginson would have overheard in the conversations of his black troops. As Alice Boyle, who recorded many of Demus Green's stories in the 1970s, points out, the black storyteller's speech reflects his exposure to Standard English. For instance, sometimes in his storytelling he distinguishes tense and number but at other times he does not. The rapid-fire delivery and shifting patterns of "peculiar" intonation are, however, characteristic.[48]

Even in the last decades of slavery it was not that unusual to find slaves who were at least bilingual. This was particularly the case in Louisiana, with its French and Spanish heritage. In the 1850s, as Frederick Law Olmsted strolled through the New Orleans marketplace, he noted that "some of the coloured women spoke French, Spanish, and English as their customers demanded," an observation he supported by including a footnote in his traveler's account reprinting an advertisement from the *New Orleans Picayune* for a mulatto runaway named Mary, who "talks *French, Italian, Dutch, English and Spanish*."[49] When interviewed by the WPA, the former slave Elizabeth Ross Hite reminisced about the preacher on her Louisiana plantation, the Reverend Jacob Nelson. According to Hite, Nelson spoke French, English, Latin, Greek, and Spanish, and "was a slave just 'cause he was too smart." Whites too came to hear his sermons, but he always had more impact on his slave congregation. "Oh, dat man could preach! He went a-growlin', cryin' from de hart, and talkin' in all dose many languages dat de people didn't know anything about. De crowd went wild [and] most of dem fainted."[50]

But by the 1850s most slaves spoke English and did so in ways that ranged from a language that was virtually indistinguishable from that of whites through to a version that has since been labeled Black English. As was typically the case, finding extended examples, for the purposes of analysis, of the language of slaves is difficult. In 1842 Lewis Clarke, a fugitive slave from Kentucky, spoke before a white audience in Brooklyn on the subject of slavery in his home state. Later, Lydia Maria Child, who had heard Clarke speak, reproduced his address as accurately as she was able. "I have taken this imperfect sketch from memory," she explained to readers of the *National Anti-Slavery Vanguard*, in which her version of Clarke's words appeared, "and may, perhaps in some instances, have confounded facts together, which should have been kept separate. I believe, however, that it is very nearly as he uttered it."[51]

Among other things, Clarke had sketched in his family background, decried the moral degradation that slavery inevitably brought, and explained that slaveholders did virtually as they wished with their human property, and that there was no way slaves could effectively protest. "A horse *can't* speak," Clarke told his audience, "and a slave *darn't*." Clarke also spoke of the widespread sexual exploitation of female slaves, of the cruel treatment of slave children, of forced separations of family members, and of the brutal behavior of the patrollers. Child felt that Lewis Clarke had impressed his audience as a truthful person, testifying to events he had actually witnessed. The fugitive had "conveyed much information," in words "valuable for their honest directness and simplicity."[52] Child also remarked, rather oddly in view of the fearful images that Clarke had invoked for his audience, that she had "seldom been more entertained by any speaker."[53]

Child felt, however, that the fugitive slave's speech had been marked by structural frailty and an extremely loose (even random) association of ideas. His address "had no thread, but was as discursive and uncertain as the movement of fallen leaves in the autumn wind." Clarke had been hampered too by the "uncouth awkwardness of his language," although this awkwardness in itself had possessed "a sort of charm, like the circuitous expression, and stammering utterance, of a foreign tongue, striving to speak our most familiar phrases." Although the escaped slave's mind was "full of ideas, which he was eager to express[,] ...the medium was wanting." " 'I've got it in *here*,' said he, laying his hand on his heart; 'but I don't know how to get it out.' " The "great idea," which Clarke obviously espoused, that the main evil of slavery was the "moral and intellectual degradation" it inevitably occasions, "shone through his awkward language, like fragments of rainbow through a fog."[54]

At one point in Clarke's speech, the audience had laughed at the slave's faulty grammar. Child recalled the incident.

> "I an't a going to tell you first about the whippings," said he; "though I'm the boy that's got 'em, times a plenty. But as I was saying, 'tan't the slave's sufferings I care so much to tell about; though they do suffer some, some of them a big, vast quantity." The audience laughed audibly, and he at once understood its meaning. He smiled, as he said, "Now, you oughtn't to expect words out of the grammar from me; for how should I know what's in the grammar?"[55]

There is no sign that Child appreciated the power of Clarke's language, its cumulative emotional force as example after example of slavery's cruelties was set before the audience. Speaking of the sexual depredations of slave patrollers, for example, Clarke had explained:

> [Female slaves] know they must submit to their masters; besides, their masters, maybe, dress 'em up, and make 'em little presents, and given 'em more privileges, while the whim lasts; but that an't like having a parcel of low, dirty, swearing drunk patter-rollers let loose among 'em, like so many hogs. This breaks down their spirits dreadfully, and make 'em wish they was dead.[56]

Such a passage was not atypical, making it difficult to understand why Child spent so much time drawing attention to the supposed "uncouth awkwardness" of Clarke's language. Child sees Clarke's impassioned cry, "I've got it in *here*...but I don't know how to get it out," as a lament prompted by the slave's lack of formal education, by his inability to use language in an effective way. Perhaps, though, what Clarke is saying is not that *his* language was inadequate to express the horror and anguish he feels—over the sexual violation of his sixteen-year-old sister, for instance, and her subsequent sale and death—but that *any* language was.

Similarly puzzling is Child's assertion that Clarke's narrative "had no thread, but was as discursive and uncertain as the movements of fallen leaves in the autumn wind." The thread, the central theme around which specific examples of cruel treatment, drawn from the fugitive slave's own experiences, were clustered, was "the evils of the slave system." And in the elaboration of that theme, neither the sequence in which Clarke's experiences are recollected, nor the smoothness of the transitions between one topic and the next, were important. Clarke's narrative may have been disjointed in the sense that sharp breaks occur between his discussion of some particular facet or other of Kentucky slavery, but the relationship between any of those facets and his central theme was always clear.

As should be evident from the examples of Lewis Clarke and the soldiers overheard by Higginson, the Black English used by many slaves was often extremely eloquent. Many whites, though, when they heard such speech, framed their accounts as humor, echoing often the ludicrous exaggerations and distortions of the minstrel-show stump speech. After listening to the talk of African Americans as they thronged the levee and streets of New Orleans in the early 1840s, Bishop Whipple concluded that, not least of their "oddities" and "strange conceits" was their "love of high flown words."[57] The Scottish traveler David McRae agreed. "The Negroes have a curious weakness for big words," he observed, adding that "a black man clutches at a polysyllable as a hungry man would clutch at a loaf."[58] Similarly, when in 1822 a New York mulatto accused of theft gave his testimony, the court reporter commented that, on the witness stand, he "afforded the most laughable display of *consequential cuffee*—of the ludicrous distortion of language, into which he runs when attempting display, that has been witnessed for a long time."[59]

The roots of black eloquence lay in a deeply embedded West African tradition. Having spent some time with the Ashanti of Ghana, R. A. Freeman observed that "the art of oratory is in West Africa carried to a remarkable pitch of perfection." At "public palavers," Freeman wrote, "each linguist [official spokesman] stands up in turn and pours forth a flood of speech, the readiness and exuberance of which strikes the stranger with amazement." Indeed, it seemed to Freeman that "every African native is a born orator and a connoisseur of oratory."[60] Eloquent speech was also highly valued by, among others, the Ibo of eastern Nigeria, the Limba people of northern Sierra Leone, and the Anang of Nigeria, whose very name signified an "ability to speak wittily yet meaningfully upon any occasion." In the traditional kingdom of Burundi, too, eloquence was "one of the central values of the cultural world-view."[61] Africans carried this tradition of eloquence with them to the New World.

On occasion, at least some whites recognized and were prepared to acknowledge the eloquence of their slaves. "How remarkably eloquent the Negroes are!" Gertrude Clanton Thomas declared as she listened to the prayers of slaves mourning the death of a black child. "They can rise and continue speaking for a great length of time without being at a loss for a single word."[62] A few whites did sense that more was involved in such instances than an inept attempt by blacks to imitate white speech. Far from hesitating or stumbling when they spoke, many of these blacks used language with extreme fluency, and with an artfulness that was widely appreciated by their peers. In a piece entitled "Negro Eloquence," a writer in the *New York Transcript* in July 1834 acknowledged that blacks were "as fond of set speeches as professional orators." Although condemning these black "harangues" for being "verbose and tautological"—missing the importance of the flights of linguistic fancy that blacks valued—the writer was willing to concede that a degree of conscious artistry was involved. Buried within what was perceived as the excesses of these speeches, "we meet, if not good argument, at least that which resembles it, and even supersedes its necessity—that is to say, acute illustration." If a black wished to warn of the folly of taking unnecessary risks, he would do so not "by mode and figure; but will at once say—'Crab what walk too much go 'na pot.' Similarly, to express the idea that after death people are soon forgotten he will say—'When man dead, grass grow at him door.'"[63] As we shall see in a later chapter, cultural differences in the creative use of language were best demonstrated by black preachers, archetypes of the black man-of-words.

What should also be remembered is that so often the voices of slaves—be they talking Gullah, Standard English, or some version of Black English, or even code shifting, which is to say, switching from one mode of speech, Gullah, for instance, to another style perhaps closer to Standard English—were often accompanied by the sound of their laughter. Of course it is not as though laughter was the sole preserve of African Americans, but it was still the case that time after time observers associated it with slaves. Commenting on African Americans promenading along the streets of Charleston, Henri Herz, a concert pianist, remarked on "their almost continual bursts of laughter, quick gestures, and rolling gait, which are the most characteristic traits of their race."[64] Similarly, when he attended a black market linked to an African Baptist church in Washington, D.C., Frederick Jobson was struck by the well-dressed men and women "joking, laughing, and jabbering away."[65]

Here too the stereotype of the happy, laughing slave, perpetuated by the minstrel show, among other cultural vehicles, has had its insidious effects, interfering both with the observations of contemporaries in antebellum America and with our twenty-first-century reading of their accounts. There are, of course, different types of laughter. Undoubtedly some slaves, for whatever reasons, fulfilled every expectation of the stereotype. There were also times, during corn shuckings, for example, at which whites, implicitly, were invited to join in the laughter with their slaves. Sometimes, as when Higginson listened to Uncle Cato, whites did not entirely "get" the humor, but they were still included. At other times whites were excluded, were indeed the butt of the humor, and it was often the resulting type of guffaw that, for whites at least, seemed totally inappropriate to blacks' status as slaves. This laughter was, in Peter Bailey's apt phrase, "sound out of place,"[66] a bodily effusion that unnerved, sometimes even disturbed, white auditors. William Thomson, not the usual gentleman traveler but a self-confessed tradesman touring America in the 1840s, remarked that the slaves he had observed "laugh and sing more than any class of men on earth." He had even seen slaves "laughing at the jokes of the auctioneer who was selling them at a public auction." Thomson was envious, wishing that he "could laugh as hearty and as often as they do," but of course he had no interest at all in "being in their stead" or experiencing one minute of their lives as slaves.[67]

More than a quarter-century ago, in his seminal *Black Culture and Black Consciousness*, Lawrence Levine demonstrated the centrality of black humor to African American culture. For those with the least power in society, jokes and humor, often about the more powerful, are a way of trying to assert some control over circumstances.[68] As he explicated the world of Rabelais, the Russian literary theorist Mikhail Bakhtin took great pains to recover the sheer physicality of sixteenth-century folk culture. For Bakhtin, laughter was both regenerative and subversive, a bodily eruption that belonged to the people even as it mocked authority.[69] The parallels with slavery are compelling. Tales of Brer Rabbit and Brer Fox, of Anansi and John the Trickster, or stories about the slaves' own mistresses and masters, and the gales of laughter they often prompted, revealed, in an aesthetically pleasing fashion, an alternative universe, one that differed considerably from that of the slaves' owners.[70]

There are few contemporary accounts of American slaves telling their stories and jokes to other slaves, and those that exist are usually vague, describing blacks laughing but not detailing what prompted them to do so.[71] Lewis W. Paine recalled that the slaves "tell stories, and joke and laugh awhile" as they sat about the "evening campfire."[72] Similarly, J. K. Paulding described slaves on Saturday night congregating "at their cabins to laugh, chat, sing, and tell stories, with all imaginable glee." He went on to add that "it would grieve an abolitionist to hear their free and joyous peals of laughter,"[73] but all it would have taken was just a little more imagination and those peals could have sounded strangely threatening rather than joyous. In his autobiography, James Weldon Johnson, the African American author and activist, commented memorably that "for the grim white man in the backwoods of the South this deep laughter of the Negro should be the most ominous sound that reaches his ears."[74] Johnson was writing about the end of the nineteenth century, but his observation was certainly as true, if not more so, of the long years of slavery. Landon Carter, one of the great Virginia planters of the eighteenth century, kept the most extensive diary of any southern slave owner, but in his recent brilliant recovery of the worlds of Landon Carter's plantation, Rhys Isaac finds a curious omission. "How," Isaac asks, "could [Carter] not suspect that the sounds of merriment coming up on the night air from the quarters often included laughter at his expense?" And yet if he did, then, as with so many slave owners (and most were nowhere near as literate as the diarist of Sabine Hall), he certainly did not record this suspicion on any piece of paper that has survived. In microcosm, this is both the problem and the challenge of writing African American cultural history, particularly of writing about sound, and most particularly about laughter. Even as the cantankerous old curmudgeon composed his narrative of the day's events in his diary, a few hundred paces away, almost within earshot, Carter's slaves fashioned their versions of the same occurrences, performances that ranged from burlesque to high drama, and that often elicited raucous peals of knowing laughter. There are thousands of pages of Carter's ink scratchings on the blank pages of his copies of the *Virginia Almanack*, on scores of carefully fashioned stitched booklets, but the only traces of the laughter of the Virginia planter's slaves are the tracks left in the minds of twenty-first-century historical ethnographers.[75]

Perhaps in the end, then, we are saying something as simple as that the speech, voices, and even laughter of most slaves sounded different from those of their owners and that wherever there were substantial numbers of slaves in America those sounds saturated the landscape. In the plantation South, whites were bombarded with the sound of black voices, from the time they were in their crib, listening to their slave nanny telling stories and singing lullabies, through their working life, almost invariably spent directing slave labor, to their old age and death, at which point they were tended to by black servants, and inevitably this constant contact would have had its effect. At the turn of the nineteenth century, the traveler John Davis noted that "each child has its *Momma* whose gestures and accent it will necessarily copy, for children, we all know, are imitative beings."[76] Almost three decades earlier, the disapproving New Englander Josiah Quincy had similarly commented on the way in which South Carolinian white children had "contracted a negroish kind of accent, pronunciation, and dialect." Quincy thought that these speech characteristics would be gradually leached out of the children as they became adults, but it was still the case that parents talked to their children "as though they were speak[ing] to a new imported African."[77] In the same decade, Ebenezer Hazard, another traveler, thought that "the common country people talk very much like Negroes, and indeed many of the better sort use a little of that dialect."[78] As is well known, the result was the incorporation of a few African words and some grammatical innovations into the American way of speaking, something that is apparent to this day to outsiders who spend time in some parts of the South, but whose more deep-seated impact remains uncharted, and is probably now unknowable.

And yet the most important implications of the fact that most slaves sounded different from whites when they spoke had little to do with the white population. To a large extent African American slave culture was made to be heard, and it was heard in an English that had been transformed by the fact that the slaves brought with them an African heritage. Whether it be Brer Rabbit stories told to children in the slave huts at night, a hymn being deaconed out and used as a work song, a slave sermon whose power compelled some in the congregation to faint, or merely the conversation between slaves in the quarters on a Saturday night, all these things were told in a language that, for all of the borrowings, still sounded noticeably different from that of slaves' owners. And that difference was both reassuring and a matter of some pride. In the twentieth century such authors as Langston Hughes, Zora Neale Hurston, Sterling Brown, and later Alice Walker would revel in the distinctive sounds of African American culture, making the speech of ordinary black men and women the very center of their writing. But this was merely an acknowledgment of the way in which many slaves themselves had felt about their speech. In the 1930s, the former slave Lorenza Ezell made clear to his WPA interviewer how he wanted his words put down on paper: "Be sho' and put it 'becase' insteder 'because,' 'cause us didn' say 'because,' us said 'becase.' Us didn' say 'then' us said 'den.' Us said 'dem' and 'dose' and 'dese' and 'wid' and 'hab' and 'an' and 'uster' and 'gwine' and 'gwinter' and all like dat."[79] And of course he was right to insist on this correction. For outsiders such as Higginson, and indeed us, as well as for the slaves themselves, the way slave speech sounded was a crucial part of the power and fluency of African American culture itself.

CHAPTER 6

"Boots or no boots,
I gwine shout today!"

While walking through "a rather mean neighborhood" of New Orleans one Sunday morning in the late 1850s, the northern journalist Frederick Law Olmsted was attracted by the sounds of "loud chorus singing" coming from the doorway of a large African American church. As he entered the church a young black minister rose to begin his sermon.

Having announced that he would speak on the biblical text: "I have fought the good fight, I have kept the faith; henceforth there is laid up for me a crown of glory," the minister presented, as it seemed to Olmsted, an accurate account of some of "the customs of the Olympic games," and made "a proper and often eloquent application" of these ideas to the lives of members of the congregation. He did so in language that was often "highly metaphorical," employing figures "long, strange, and complicated, yet sometimes . . . beautiful." At times, to be sure, he used "vulgarisms and slang phrases," misconstrued the meaning of words, or used grammar and pronunciation that rendered his ideas incomprehensible to Olmsted, but if members of the congregation were aware of such lapses, there was nothing to indicate that they were perturbed by them.

Nor did the preacher seem at all disconcerted by the increasing volume of noise issuing from his hearers. No sooner had he started to speak than an old man seated near Olmsted "began to respond . . . with such cries as 'Oh, yes!' 'That's it, that's it!' 'Yes, yes—glory—yes!'" From that time onward, whenever the preacher's tones were "unusually solemn, or his language and manner eloquent or excited," other church members cried out in equally loud and enthusiastic fashion. As the sermon proceeded, not merely articulate verbal responses, but "shouts, and groans, terrific shrieks, and indescribable expressions of ecstasy—of pleasure or agony," as well as the sounds of foot stamping and hand clapping, echoed through the building. Caught up in the rising torrent of emotion, Olmsted was surprised to find "my own muscles all stretched, as if ready for a struggle—my face glowing, and my feet stamping—having been infected unconsciously... with instinctive bodily sympathy with the excitement of the crowd." Yet, as the journalist reflected, "the basis of this excitement" had been "wholly unintellectual," Olmsted having been unable, once he had collected his thoughts, to "find any connection or meaning in the phrases of the speaker that remained in [his] memory." It had been the preacher's "action," Olmsted decided, by which he meant, presumably, the drama of the man's performance, that had so aroused the large African American assembly.

In the record he made of the young minister's address, Olmsted transcribed sections of the sermon, interpolating congregational responses. Invoking the spectacle of an Olympic boxing match, the preacher had asked his hearers to imagine that the more determined of the combatants had first boldly confronted his opponent, and then, protecting himself with one hand, had struck the opponent a fearful blow with the other. What, the black preacher then asked rhetorically of his audience, would the aggressive boxer do after that?

> Would he stop, and turn away his face, and let the adversary hit back? No, my brethren, no, no! he'd follow up his advantage, and give him another lick; and if he fell back, he'd keep close after him, and not stop!—and not faint!—not be content with merely driving him back!—but he'd persevere! (yes, glory!) and hit him again! (that's it, hit him again! hit him again! oh, glory! hi! hi! glory!) drive him into the corner! and never, never stop till he had him down! (glory, glory, glory!) and he had got his foot on his neck, and the crown of wild olive leaves was placed upon his head by the lord of the games. (Ha! ha! glory to the Lord! etc.)

These rousing words brought the sermon to its first emotional peak. There followed a brief period of relative calm, as the preacher explained that sometimes the lord of the games was corrupt, and instead of honoring the winner would award the crown to his own favorite. But, the speaker then triumphantly declared, beginning a sequence that would propel the sermon to its highest dramatic and emotional pitch, that was a situation his listeners need never confront:

There ain't no danger of that with our fight with the world, for our Lord is throned in justice. (Glory!—Oh, yes! yes!—sweet Lord! sweet Lord!) He seeth in secret, and he knoweth all things, and there's no chance for a mistake, and if we will just persevere and conquer, and conquer and persevere (yes, sir! oh, Lord, yes!), and persevere—not for a year, or for two year, or ten year; not for seventy year, perhaps; but if we persevere—(yes! yes!)—if we persevere—(oh! Lord! help us!)—if we persevere unto the end—(oh! oh! glory! glory! glory!)— until he calls us home! (frantic shouting.) Henceforth there is laid up for us a crown of immortal glory—(Ha! ha! HA!)—not a crown of wild olive leaves that begin to droop as soon as they touch our brow (oh! oh! oh!) but a crown of immortal glory! That fadeth not away! Never begins to droop! But is immortal in the heavens!

These words produced a "tremendous uproar," with "many of the congregation on their feet...uttering cries and shrieks impossible to be expressed in letters."

After the commotion had subsided, the young minister again spoke calmly, offering members of the church "sensible and pertinent advice." Soon, however, his judicious remarks were interrupted by the actions of a woman who rose from her seat in the gallery and began to dance, clapping her hands and shouting all the while. When others joined in, the noise became so great that the minister had to stop speaking altogether, bringing to premature conclusion "much the best part of his sermon," in Olmsted's estimation. Eventually, "a voice in the congregation struck up a tune, and the whole church members rose and joined in a roaring song," effectively drowning out the woman's cries and bringing the first preacher's sermon and role in the service to a close.

A second African American minister now addressed the people, declaring that he would draw further meaning from the Pauline text. Despite the uproar that had attended the first speaker's words, that young minister had seemed to Olmsted relatively restrained, his "voice and manner generally quiet and impressive." Not so the new man. Having begun in "a low, deep, hoarse, indistinct and confidential tone," he "soon...struck a higher key, drawling his sentences like a street salesman, occasionally breaking out into a yell with all the strength of extraordinarily powerful lungs." He also adopted "a striking attitude[,] ... gesturing in an extraordinary manner" and assuming a boxing pose as he demolished the arguments of an imaginary opponent. This dramatic posturing created "a frightful excitement in the people, and [was] responded to with the loudest and most terrific shouts." Olmsted had been able to follow sections of the first preacher's address well enough, but he found the second preacher's language "in great part unintelligible." Yet the congregation "seemed to enjoy [the sermon] highly, and encouraged and assisted [the preacher] in his combat with 'Sir' Knight of his imagination most tumultuously." The sermon ended in a cacophony of sound.

When the noise had died down, a hymn was sung, one of the preachers reciting the words, two lines at a time (again to the accompaniment of shouts) for the congregation to sing. Olmsted found the "collective sound" "wonderful," but thought some aspects of the performance unusual. "The voices of one or two women rose above the rest," he recorded, "and one of these soon began to introduce variations, which consisted mainly of shouts of 'Oh! oh!' at a piercing height." And all the while, many of the singers stamped out the time with their feet. As the singing wound down, the preacher "raised his own voice above all, ... clapped his hands and commenced to dance" in a vigorous fashion. Finally, the commotion having subsided, some formal announcements were made and "the congregation slowly passed out, chatting and saluting one another politely as they went, and bearing not the slightest mark of the previous excitement."[1]

To Olmsted, the New Orleans church was full of unfamiliar sounds. The shouts and groans, the "terrific shrieks," the "indescribable expressions of ecstacy," the noisy congregational interjections, the clapping of hands, the stamping of feet, the weird intonations, the piercing yells—all these would have been jarringly out of place in the churches with which the northern journalist was familiar. Not merely the nature and volume of such sounds, but the indiscriminate way in which they were mixed seemed inappropriate. In services to which Olmsted was accustomed, sound was carefully controlled. Preachers preached, congregations listened. Sermons were not interrupted (or even terminated) by recurrent interjection or ecstatic audience response. Hymns did not emerge spontaneously from the congregation, but were selected beforehand and sung at predetermined times. They were neither prolonged by repetition, nor amended by embellishment—as individual voices soared above the rest, for example, or shouted " 'oh! oh!' at a piercing height." In white churches with which Olmsted was familiar, appropriate boundaries were respected and things were done "decently and in order, unto edification," as the scriptures enjoined, God being "not the author of confusion, but of peace."[2] In this black church, by contrast, boundaries seemed blurred, indiscriminately transgressed.

Olmsted wrote without hostility, as one surprised but not seriously affronted by unaccustomed religious sounds. So, also, in the main, did George Hepworth, another northerner, who had been sent by the Union government in 1863 to inspect conditions in a large contraband camp at Carrollton, Louisiana. Hepworth, who had previously held black religion to be, in many cases, "not always quite reasonable; ...a kind of nervous spasm," was struck by the peculiar, yet somehow compelling, sounds he heard when he attended a church service there. On entering the makeshift building, he was surprised to find the gathering of about one hundred blacks completely silent. Soon, however, "a single voice... began a low, mournful chant," in which, increasingly, the congregation joined. To Hepworth, the sound was of "a strange song," with "little rhythm," sung in a minor key; "not a psalm, nor a real song," but "more like a wail, a mournful, dirge-like expression of sorrow." Initially, he had been "inclined to laugh," as the song seemed "so far from what I had been accustomed to call music," but he soon became "uncomfortable, as though I could not endure it, and half rose to leave the room." As the "weird chorus rose a little above, and then fell a little below, the key-note," however, Hepworth was suddenly "overcome by the real sadness and depression of soul which it seemed to symbolize." Later, he recalled, at the conclusion of a prayer delivered by an old man, "the whole audience swayed back and forward in their seats, and uttered in perfect harmony a sound like that caused by prolonging the letter 'm' with the lips closed. One or two had begun this wild, mournful chorus, but in an instant all joined in, and the sound swelled upwards and downwards like waves of the sea."[3]

Part of what Hepworth described here—the "mournful, dirge-like expression of sorrow"—was probably a type of congregational moan-

ing, a very deep form of worship, in which it was felt that words were
no longer needed. Some slaves clearly believed that moaning, as well
as shouting, was a prerequisite for redemption. Former Louisiana slave
Elizabeth Ross Hite testified that her master "didn't want us shoutin'
and moanin' all day long," but, she declared emphatically, "you gotta
shout and you gotta moan if you wants to be saved."4 A faint echo
of the contrabands' "mournful chorus" probably formed part of the
mix of sounds that accompanied Reverend Henry Ward's prayer at
the Johnson Place Baptist Church near Livingston, Alabama, in the late
1930s (track 12).5 Reverend Ward delivered his prayer as a chant,
whose rhythmic cadences elicited voiced responses from the congregation, and as he continued to pray, members of his congregation set up
a supportive, collective moaning, bearing up their minister as he
brought his and their supplications to their God.

Other whites, unaccustomed to black religious noise, were less
sympathetic to it than were either Olmsted or Hepworth. Attending a
service at a Philadelphia African American church in 1820, the English
traveler William Faux was surprised when, at the conclusion of the
sermon, members of the congregation boisterously sang themselves to
the point of exhaustion. They sang " 'Oh! Come to Zion, come!' 'Hallelujah, &c,' and 'O won't you have my lovely bleeding *Jasus*,' a thousand times repeated in full thundering chorus," Faux reported, and
as they did so "they were clapping hands, shouting, and jumping, and
exclaiming, 'Ah Lord! Good Lord! Give me *Jasus!* Amen.'" The din,
which continued for an hour, seemed, to Faux, "like Bedlam let loose."6
The English actor Charles Mathews was equally scathing. Observing
an African American congregation's reaction to a sermon delivered by
a black preacher in Boston in 1823, he concluded that "the pranks that
are played in the 'nigger meetings,' as they are called, are beyond belief—yelling, screeching, and groaning, resembling a fox-chase much
more than a place of worship."7 And in the judgment of the English
barrister Godfrey Vigne, both minister and congregation of a black
Methodist church in Washington, D.C., which he visited in 1831, were
"ranters," the preacher, in particular, having "talked the most incoherent nonsense, and worked himself up to such a pitch of frenzy, that his
appearance was almost that of a maniac." At times, Vigne lamented, "I
was nearly stunned by the noise he made."8

The English clergyman Ebenezer Davies was another who reacted badly to his first visit to a black church. In the late 1840s Davis heard a black minister in Baltimore preach a sermon to some five or six hundred African Americans on the text "Behold, I come quickly." The man had begun uncertainly, speaking in a "scarcely audible" voice, but had soon "worked himself and his audience into a tremendous phrenzy." As he developed his ideas (ideas that Davies considered largely nonsensical), "the laughing, the shouting, the groaning, and the jumping were positively terrific." So "shocked and grieved" was Davis by "this ranting exhibition" that he walked out of the meeting, feeling it "unwarrantable to remain."9 The schoolteacher Elizabeth Kilham, too, had been appalled, when she attended "Old Billy's" Sea Island church just after the Civil War, by the unexpected eruption of wild, earsplitting sound. Following the minister's sermon and a prayer, Kilham wrote, there began "one of those scenes, which, when read of, seem the exaggerations of a disordered imagination; and when witnessed, leave an impression like the memory of some horrid nightmare—so wild is the torrent of excitement, that, sweeping away reason and sense, tosses men and women upon its waves, mingling the words of religion with the howlings of wild beasts, and the ravings of madmen." Those church members who gave their "experience" (their personal testimony) to the rest of the congregation "always talk[ed] in a scream, and as if crying; a natural tone of voice not being suitable for such occasions"; meanwhile, other members clapped, danced, and shouted. When hymns were sung, the noise of stamping feet became "deafening." Kilham granted the sincerity of these blacks, but believed that "the majority of them were ignorant as heathens of the objects and foundation of our faith." "Is noisy excitment," she asked, "a proof of religious feeling?"10

Another to speak out against "inappropriate" black noise was the Presbyterian minister Charles Colcock Jones, a leader in the slave missions movement in Liberty County, Georgia. "Public worship should be conducted *with reverence and stillness on the part of the congregation*," Jones reminded fellow ministers in 1847 (italics in original). Those who preached to African Americans must set their face against "demonstrations of approbation or disapprobation, or exclamations, or responses, or noises, or outcries of any kind," practices which, Jones conceded regretfully, "prevail[ed] over large portions of the Southern country," and were "not confined to one denomination, but appear to some extent in all." "Ignorant people," Jones warned, becoming "easily excited," could mistake "the sound for the substance; feeling in religious worship, for religion itself." Jones even wanted these prohibitions to apply to the space around the church, perhaps against the possibility that members of the congregation would perform the religious dances they called ring shouts there.[11]

Some black churchmen, too, set their faces against "excessive" congregational noise. Ebenezer Davies, the Englishman who had been horrified by the behavior of the black preacher in Baltimore, came across one such minister when he attended service at a "coloured" Congregational church in New Haven, Connecticut, in the late 1840s. This black minister's church, Davies noted approvingly, was "exceedingly neat and clean," and the prayer with which the preacher had begun the service was "very judicious, sensible, and pious." The meeting took place in the midst of a revival, during the course of which many claimed to have been converted, but "such were the care and caution exercised" that "none of them had [yet] been admitted into the fellowship of the church." Here was religious life as it was meant to be, orderly, reverential, affording opportunities for thoughtful contemplation of the divine word. There would be no place in this black church for the frenzied shouting and laughter that Davies had earlier encountered, no chance that emotions could run wild, finding expression in undignified yells and screams. So "prudent, unassuming, and devout" was the church's African American pastor that Davis "could not resist the inclination to go up, introduce myself, and give a short address." Invited to preach on the following Sunday, he did so, enjoying the (obviously uninterrupted) service "very much."[12]

But in all probability this New Haven pastor was merely one of a long line of black ministers who, influenced by white religious practices, took a stand against what they regarded as disruptive sound. As far back as the mid-eighteenth century, the black preacher "Uncle Jack," of Nottaway County, Virginia, had not hesitated to upbraid his congregation for giving full and public vent to their feelings. Jack had been brought from Africa to Virginia, where he had learned English at an early age and, in due course, having been converted to Christianity, was licensed by the Baptists to preach. He won the confidence of slave-holders, who allowed him to address their slaves. But Jack distrusted extravagant displays of emotion, and, as Mechal Sobel has pointed out, was "appalled" by black noise. "You noisy Christians remind me of the little branches (of streams) after a heavy rain," he told his black church members on one occasion. "They are soon full, then noisy, and as soon empty. I would much rather see you like the broad, deep river, which is quiet, because it is broad and deep."[13]

Nor, of course, did whites uniformly shun ecstatic displays of emotion and effusive religious sound; proceedings at some white churches and religious gatherings, especially camp meetings, resembled those in the black church that Olmsted visited. But the practices that Olmsted and others described, or some variant of them, were sufficiently widespread among black churches, and the African American voices raised in defense of those practices sufficiently bold and defiant, to indicate that the battle over religious noise reflected quite profound cultural differences.

The emphatic comments of two women not long out of slavery effectively make this point. Addressing a black religious meeting on the Sea Islands soon after the Civil War, one "sister" expressed her regret that when she visited certain churches she saw "all de folks settin' quiet an' still, like dey dunno what de Holy Sperit am." Yet, the woman continued, "I fin's in my Bible, that when a man or a 'ooman gets full ob de Holy Sperit, ef dey should hol' dar peace, de stones would cry out; an' ef de power ob God can made de stones cry out, how can it help makin' us poor creetures cry out, who feels ter praise Him fer His mercy." "Not make a noise!" the woman declared, with some impatience. "Why we makes a noise 'bout ebery ting else; but dey tells us we musn't make no noise ter praise de Lord. I don't want no sich 'ligion as dat ar."[14] No less forceful were the remarks of the former slave Old Jenny, on her return from a camp meeting. "Why Missus," Jenny told the white woman for whom she worked, "you hab no idea how dem ministers did preach, and how de people did pray and sing dar! 'Pears like dey was clar gone up to de mount dat was touched wid fire!" Jenny went on to explain in what respects the religious practices in her employer's church were deficient. "*You* neber hear de like in your church. . . . Yous so chained up wid' spectability dat yous feared to hab de Sperit work, les' dere some noise wid it. You's willing to hab Him come, if he always come wid de still, small voice; but you'd rader hab Him stay to home, den to come wid de earthquake and de fire. We's glad to git Him *any way*." White people may have been willing to forgo the blessings of the Spirit in order to preserve the good order and decorum of their meetings, Jenny was asserting, but black believers were not.[15]

As WPA testimony clearly shows, it was often restrictions on exuberant religious sound that made slaves' attendance at white churches an unsatisfying experience. Sarah Fitzpatrick recalled that the blacks on her Alabama plantation were at first required by their owners to go to the Baptist church in Tuskegee, but eventually, she explained, " 'Niggers' commence'ta wanna go to church by de'selves, even ef dey had'ta meet in de white church." "Ya'see," she elaborated, " 'Niggers' lack'ta shout a whole lot an' wid de white fo'ks al' round 'em, dey couldn't shout jes' lack dey want to."[16] Ex-slave Minerva Grubbs, too, had felt inhibited in white-controlled religious space. "Us went to de white folks' Church, an' sit on back seats, but didn't jine in de worship," she told her interviewer. "You see," she explained, "de white folks don't git in de spirit, dey don't shout, pray, hum, and sing all through de services lak us do."[17] It was unusual for blacks who attended white churches to transgress customary boundaries, but on occasions they did. The former slave Lizzie Davis remembered her father telling her about an old man named Tom, who regularly disturbed white congregation members with his shouting. Eventually, in an effort to keep Tom quiet, his master promised him a new pair of boots if he would desist. The slave agreed, but as the sermon delivered on the following Sunday proceeded, "he keep on drinkin in" the preacher's words "till he overflowed," at which point Tom jumped up and hollered, "Massa, boots or no boots, I gwine shout today!"[18]

Such sharply differing perceptions as to the role of sound in religious performance challenge us to discover more about the aural universe of African American slaves, to understand what they understood to be the meanings of the sounds they created, to invest those sounds with something of the significance they once possessed. For a start, we need to strip away Western assumptions as to the appropriateness of various types of sound in various contexts. It was clearly the case, for instance, that cultural expression in African societies was more fluid than in the Euro-American world. We have seen that, in their endeavors to "render emotions and desires as naturally as possible," to "translate everyday experiences into living sound,"[19] African singers freely interpolated shouts, yells, and moans into their music, sounds that whites would have placed well beyond the bounds of acceptable musical performance. In the same way, when their stories required it, African orators broke easily into song. As J. H. Kwabena Nketia explains, in African cultures "a narrator may change from speech to song and back again, according to the requirement of the story.... His audience may interrupt him here and there with song interludes, for now and then a song may suggest itself to a member of the audience because of the action of the story."[20] Clearly, boundary transgressions of this type were permissible in Olmsted's New Orleans church, where sermons were "interrupted" by singing (or dancing), and where shouts of encouragement accompanied and even drowned out the preachers' words. Religious meetings such as the one Olmsted happened upon (and, of course, those held secretly by plantation slaves) were communal, interactive events, in which the preacher's "calls" were answered by enthusiastic congregational "responses," responses that pushed sermons to a higher emotional pitch and could even alter their course. In the strong oral tradition of African Americans, a slave preacher's sermon was not a sequence of words on paper, an inviolate text, but an unfolding conversation that, precisely because it was a conversation, was impossible to script in advance. Whites who urged blacks to desist from their role in such "conversations," to keep still, to avoid making a noise, were unknowingly disrupting cultural practices with deep and particularly tenacious roots. It is probable too that West African beliefs in spirit possession, and the ecstatic sounds (as in shouting) and movements (as in dancing) that gave expression to those beliefs, lived on in some fashion in the slaves' distinctive form of Christianity. Through their responses to their preachers' calls, black members of Olmsted's church were not merely bearing up their ministers; they were, in effect, entreating the Spirit to come among them, whose presence would be confirmed by a prolonged outburst of ecstatic congregational sound.

The battle over religious sound was played out on plantations as well. It was certainly the case that some slaveholders tolerated the sounds of slave religion and even, under certain circumstances, encouraged them. The great South Carolinian planter R. F. W. Allston constructed a prayer house for his slaves and claimed that their attention to religious matters and general behavior improved greatly as a result.[21] Marriah Hines's owner held family prayers each night to which he invited any persons on the plantation who might wish to come, but if the slaves preferred to pray by themselves they were free to do so.[22] Slaves on Uncle Henry Barnes's plantation "sho' did hab plenty singin' o' hymns an' shoutin' at night in de cabins," presumably with their master's consent.[23] "We didn't have no place to go to church," former Arkansas bondsman George Kye explained, "but Old Master didn't care if we had singing and praying."[24] Slaves on Lina Anne Pendergrass's plantation went each Saturday night to a praise house that her grandfather had built, where, after prayers, they would "git to singin' and shoutin'," and "de Spirit done come down and tuck hole of dem."[25] Each Sunday, Mose Hursey attended religious meetings in the quarters, during which slaves would "preach and pray and sing—shout too." Hursey had often heard them "git up with a powerful force of the spirit, clappin' they hands and walkin' round the place. They'd shout, 'I got the glory. I got that old time 'ligion in my heart.'"[26] But other owners showed no such leniency, and, fearing that they would be punished for what their masters or overseers considered to be excessive noise, and dissatisfied with white religious observances, many slaves held their meetings secretly in the woods. "On Sundays," ex-Mississippi slave Emily Dixon recalled, "us would git tergether in de woods" where they "could sing all de way through an' hum 'long an' shout, yo' all know, jist turn loose lak."[27] Even in such locations, however, "excessive" noise could invite retribution from the dreaded slave patrols. To avert that threat, Becky Ilsey testified, whenever slaves in secret locations sang spirituals "an' de spirit 'gin to shout some de elders would go 'mongst de folks an' put dey han' over dey mouf an' some times put a clof in dey mouf an' say: 'Spirit don talk so loud or de patterol break us up.'"28

Slave shouting could prove a particular offense. Slaves might shout when touched by the Spirit, something that could happen when they met for worship or even as they worked in the field. Julia Cox, born into slavery in Mississippi in 1850, remembered that slaves on her plantation "done deir shoutin' and worshipping" in the fields, where they would "sing, shout and pray to deir hearts content."29 Baptisms, too, could be accompanied by tumultuous shouting. Slaves on Virginia Harris's plantation attended a black church, where they were preached to by a white minister, and when baptizings were held, "there would be hundreds at a time to go into the water." On such occasions, the slaves "would shout till it most shook the town down."30 Some slaves also shouted, "in a easy way," as Maggie Wright expressed it, when sitting up all night with a slave who had died.31 And when a slave was buried, Henry Barnes asserted, those who were present at the graveside "sometimes shouted an hollered."32 "I still shouts at meetin's," ex-Texas slave Ellen Payne informed her interviewer. "I don't have nothin' to do with it. It hits me jes' like a streak of lightning, and there ain't no holdin' it."33 But many whites heard in these seemingly wild, uncontrolled sounds a dangerous loosening of planter control, and punishment for persistent offenders could be severe. "My old masta was good," the former slave O. W. Green declared, "but when he found you shoutin' he burnt your hand."34 Even "if the Lord converted your soul," Squire Irvin testified, the master "wouldn't so much as let you shout in the fields." Irvin had seen his mother being whipped for doing just that. No sooner had the whipping ceased, however, than the mother began to shout once more, declaring that she was "going to praise the Lord Jesus, and she don't care what they do to her and she sure did do it."35 Former Mississippi and Louisiana slave Sol Walton testified that he had "seed my mother whipped for shouting at the white fo'ks meeting. Old Master stripped her clothes down to her waist and whipped her with a bull whip."36

There was significant planter opposition too to slave prayer. "As fo' to go to chu'ch," former Texas slave Annie Row scornfully informed her interviewer, "shunt dat f'om yous head. W'y, weuns warnt even 'lowed to pray."[37] "Marse Tom didn't mind us singing in the cabins at night," William More testified, "but we better not let him ketch us prayin'." To forestall punishment, More and the others sent one of their number outside to keep watch, at which point those inside the cabin would begin to pray and before long would "get to moanin' low and gentle, 'some day, some day, some day—this yoke going be lifted off'n our shoulders.'"[38] Mingo White remembered that, when their day's work was done, "de slaves would be foun' lock in dere cabins prayin' for de Lawd to free dem lack he did de chillum of Is'ael." But such activity could be dangerous. When the drivers caught "old Ned White" praying they staked him to the ground with four pegs and "whipped him 'twell de blood run from him lack he was a hog." The rest of the slaves, who had been forced to watch the whipping, were warned that, if they were caught praying, the same thing would happen to them.[39] "We was scart of Solomon," the plantation's black driver, Mary Reynolds recalled. "We'd set on the floor and pray with our heads down low..., but if Solomon heared he'd come and beat on the wall with the stock of his whip. He'd say, 'I'll come in there and tear the hide off your backs.'"[40] Former Virginia slave Silas Jackson told how the master's father, eavesdropping on a secret prayer meeting, overheard a slave "ask God to change the heart of his master and deliver him from slavery so that he may enjoy freedom." By morning, Jackson stated, that man had disappeared, and no one ever saw him again.[41]

Ex-slave Lucindy Hall Shaw explained to her interviewer that, to avert discovery, slaves on her plantation would fetch a large iron pot and hold their prayer meetings around it.[42] Shaw's testimony reflected the widespread slave belief that if large pots, such as might be used for cooking or washing clothes, were upturned and elevated slightly from the ground, they would absorb sound. When Mariah Barnes and other slaves gathered in one of the cabins to pray, "dey turned a big wash pot over close to de door, a little off'n de floor, so it'd ketch all de sound." Once that precaution had been taken "de slaves'd shout and pray all dey pleased." Every so often a member of the group would go outside to make sure the pot was catching all the sound. If it were not, those making the most noise would be thrown onto a bed, with blankets over their heads.[43]

Many owners found the sounds of slave religion unnerving. Slave prayers, with their subtext of deliverance, must often have seemed subversive, as striking at planter ideology and control. But beyond these planter concerns, the slaves' shouts and "wild," ecstatic cries, must have seemed to confirm for some whites the ineluctable "otherness" of their human property, waking dark, subliminal fears. These apprehensions must have come closer to the surface whenever whites observed the slave religious dance known as the ring shout.

Greatly loved by slaves, the ring shout was an African American cultural creation that fused the biblical teachings and powerful imagery of the Old and New Testaments, and oftentimes secular lyrics, with the sounds and rhythms of West African music and dance. (Nicely illustrating this syncretic process, the ex-slave Vinnie Brunson explained to his interviewer that "de Bible tells how de angels shouts in heaven, so dat is where dey get de scripture' fer de dance dat is called de 'Shout.'"[44]) Participants in the ring shout danced counterclockwise in a circle, maintaining a steady beat with their feet, but moving their bodies freely as the mood took them. At the same time, the song leader's embellished calls were answered by the basers (members of the chorus), whose heterophonic singing and polyrhythmic clapping added further layers of culturally resonant sound.[45] Sylvia King described a ring shout that took place after she and some other slaves had stolen away into the woods at the conclusion of the morning service in a white church. "De Folks git in er ring an' sing an' dance, an' shout," she explained. "De dance is jes' a kinder shuffle, den hit gits faster, an' faster as dey gits wa' amed up; an' dey moans an' shouts; an' sings, an' claps, an' dance." Eventually, "some ob em gits 'zausted an' dey drop out, an' de ring gits closer. Sometimes dey sing an' shout all night."[46]

Although ring shouts were often staged secretly, many whites must have known of these odd-seeming slave dances, which were sometimes held, for example, at the conclusion of plantation praise meetings,[47] and wondered at the meanings of their strange "wild" sounds. That was certainly true of "M. R. S.," who described a ring shout that she witnessed at an African American school in Beaufort, South Carolina, in 1866.

> After school the teachers gave their children permission to have a "shout." This is a favorite religious exercise of these people, old and young. In the infant schoolroom, the benches were first put aside, and the children ranged along the wall. Then began a wild droning chant in a minor key, marked with clapping of hands and stamping of feet. A dozen or twenty rose, formed a ring in the centre of the room, and began an odd shuffling dance. Keeping time to this weird chant they circled round, one following the other, changing their step to quicker and wilder motion, with louder clappings of the hands as the fervor of the singers reached a climax.

As M. R. S.'s reference to the sights and sounds of the shout—the singers' "wild droning chant," the ever louder clapping of hands, the incessant thumping of feet, the "wilder motions" of the dancers, and the rising fervor of those taking part—suggests, she found the performance alienating. Reviewing what she had heard and seen that day, she would write of "little barbarians... circling round in this fetish dance."[48] Likewise, the schoolteacher Laura Towne, who watched her Sea Island pupils performing a ring shout, detected in their performance "the remains of some old idol worship," and declared that she had never witnessed "anything so savage."[49]

The ring shout "Run, Old Jeremiah" (track 13), "called" by Joe Washington Brown and Austin Coleman, which John and Alan Lomax recorded at Jennings, Louisiana, in 1934, is characterized by the rough-voiced fervor of the lead singers' calls, the antiphonal singing, the fast-paced tempos, the repetitive lyrical sequences, and the complex rhythmic patterns beaten out by the basers' hands and feet. Apart from occasional references to "Old Jeremiah," the lyrics are mostly secular (as they sometimes were in slavery times) rather than sacred, but in parts of this very long shout, parts which, for technical reasons, the authors were unable to include on the CD, sacred and secular lyrics follow closely on one another. For example, at one point in the longer version of "Run, Old Jeremiah," the first leader calls:

> I've got a rock.
> You got a rock.
> Rock is death.
> O my Lordy.

O my Lord.
Well, well, well.
Run here, Jeremiah.
Run here Jeremiah.
I must go
On my way.
On my way.
On my way.
On my way.
Who's that ridin' the chariot?
Who's that ridin' the chariot?
Well, well, well...

Later on, a new song leader having taken over, we find the words

Old number 12
Comin' down the track.
Comin' down the track.
Comin' down the track.
See that black smoke.
See that old engineer.
See that engineer.
See that engineer.
Tol' that old fireman
Ring his ol' bell
With his hand.
Rung his engine bell.
Rung his engine bell.
Well, well, well.
Well, well, well.
Jesus tell the man,
Say, I got your life
In My Hand;
I got your life
In My Hand...[50]

It was nonsequential lyrics and surprising juxtapositions such as those illustrated here that had prompted William Francis Allen, one of the compilers of *Slave Songs of the United States*, to observe that, when

Sea Island blacks performed the ring shout, the lead singer "carries on the song, stringing verse after verse of the most absurd stuff, which he often makes up as he goes along."[51]

One genre of black religious sound to which owners seldom objected was the slave spirituals.[52] Whether sung at plantation praise houses—where, as the slave preacher James L. Smith recalled, the enthusiastic singing and handclapping could cause the "old house" to ring with the singer's "jubilant shouts"[53]—or in cabins in the quarters, or while working in the field, the sounds of spirituals often impacted significantly on plantation soundscapes. They did so, however, in ways that masters generally found agreeable, or at least nonthreatening to any significant extent.

Indeed, these communally created slave songs sometimes provided opportunities for a mutually satisfying social exchange. The former slave Aunt Clussey, for instance, remembered how slaves would gather behind the Big House, where "young massa played his fiddle an us'd sing, 'Swing Low Sweet Chariot.'"[54] Ex-slave Gus Feaster told of a pleasant interlude that took place as he and other slaves were returning one night from a camp meeting. Inevitably, the slaves had begun to sing, and before long "de air soon be filled wid the sweetest tune as us rid on home and sung all de old hymns dat us loved." As the wagons carrying the slaves approached the Big House, the singers would "soften down to a deep hum dat de missus like!" at which point, the mistress of the plantation would often raise her window and ask the slaves to sing "Swing Low Sweet Cha'ot" for the entertainment of her guests and herself. Thus encouraged, Gus Feaster related, "us open up and de niggers near de big house ... would ... come out to de cabin door and jine in de refrain," after which the slaves "would swing on into all de spirituals dat us love so well and dat us knowed." According to Feaster, the mistress of the plantation "often 'low dat her darkies could sing wid heaven's 'spiration (inspiration)."[55]

One cannot miss here the sense of pride that infuses Feaster's account, the unalloyed enjoyment he derives from his recollection of the slaves' communal singing all those years ago. Those returning from the camp meeting loved the spirituals, he tells us, but so also, significantly, did the plantation mistress, she whose people "could sing wid heaven's 'spiration." But this plantation owner's wife was hardly the only one who found black religious singing enjoyable. "To hear at night... the songs of Zion, at a distance, caroled in tones of sweetest melody by many co-mingled voices, when native harmony outvies instructed skill," wrote Alexander Dromgoole Sims in 1834, "such is the melody with which night after night the Negroes charm the ear."[56]

In constructing their religious songs, slaves drew most freely on the stories of the Old Testament rather than those of the New. They sang proudly of David, who defeated the giant Goliath, of Samson, who brought down the temple of his enemies, of the Hebrew children who were delivered from the fiery furnace, but much less frequently of the New Testament followers of Jesus, who often suffered persecution for their faith. This Old Testament bias in the spirituals had been discerned by Thomas Wentworth Higginson. After listening to his black troops' songs, the colonel decided that the Bible from which they drew their religious music was largely restricted to the books about Moses in the Old Testament and the book of Revelation in the New. Everything "that lay between," Higginson declared, "even the life of Jesus, they hardly cared to read or to hear."[57] Higginson exaggerated. Jesus often appeared in the spirituals—slaves sang "I'm going to walk and talk wid my Jesus,"[58] "Jesus rise from de dead, happy morning,"[59] "In the morning when I rise, / Tell my Jesus huddy oh,"[60] "See how they done my Lord, / An' He never said a mumblin' word" (a reference to Christ's fortitude on the cross)[61]—but, as Lawrence Levine has observed, "it was not invariably the Jesus of the New Testament of whom the slaves sang, but frequently a Jesus transformed into an Old Testament warrior whose victories were temporal as well as spiritual."[62] That transformation became evident in the spiritual "No Man Can Hinder Me," when "sweet Jesus," who had miraculously brought Lazarus back to life, suddenly became a more conventionally warlike figure.

> Walk in, kind Saviour,
> No man can hinder me,
> Walk in, sweet Jesus,
> No man can hin'der me.
> . . . .
> Rise, poor Lajarush, from de tomb,

No man can hinder me,
Rise, poor Lajarus, from de tomb,
No man can hin'der me.

. . . .

King Jesus ride a milk-white horse,
No man can hinder me,
King Jesus ride a milk-white horse,
No man can hin'der me.[63]

A chaplain to one of the Northern armies even suggested that it was not Jesus, but Moses who was the slaves' ideal "of all that is high, and noble, and perfect, in man," whereas Christ was regarded "not so much in the light of a *spiritual* Deliverer, as that of a second Moses," a fighting saint.[64]

Keenly attentive to Old Testament stories, slaves found little space, in their religious songs, for New Testament injunctions to labor honestly and diligently, and to "be subject to [their] masters with all fear."[65] Resentment against such coercive instructions ran deep. As a child, Howard Thurman used to read the Bible to his grandmother, a former slave, who, however, always forbade him to read from the Epistles of Paul. When Thurman finally asked why this was so, the grandmother explained that the white minister who used to visit her plantation had always preached from Paul's letters, urging slaves to obey their masters in all things. This had led her to vow that "if freedom ever came and I learned to read, I would never read that part of the Bible!"[66]

It was the Old Testament that spoke more directly to the slaves' situation. Identifying strongly with the Israelites of old, they, too, they had come to believe, were a chosen people, held captive in an oppressive Egypt (the slave system), waiting for a Moses figure to lead them across the River Jordan (the Mason–Dixon Line), into the land of Canaan, the Promised Land (the North). This epic tale of Jewish deliverance supplied the richest material for the spirituals. The slaves sang "To the promised land I'm bound to go,"[67] "O Canaan, sweet Canaan, / I am bound for the land of Canaan,"[68] "I want to go to Canaan, / To meet 'em at de comin' day,"[69] "Pharaoh get lost, get lost, get lost … in the Red Sea,"[70] "My army cross over, / O Pharaoh's army drownded,"[71] "Jordan River, I'm bound to go, / And bid 'em fare ye well."[72] And because the slaves' situation so closely resembled that of the children of Israel, many of the spirituals had a sharp, contemporary pointedness. "O my Lord delivered Daniel," the slaves sang. "O why not deliver me, too?"[73] Or, in the emphatic words of another spiritual:

> He delivered Daniel from de lion's den,
> Jonah from de belly ob de whale,
> And de Hebrew children from de fiery furnace,
> And why not every man?[74]

These and many other spirituals were replete with double meanings. Ex-slave Frederick Douglass wrote that "a keen observer might have detected in our repeated singing of 'O Canaan, sweet Canaan, / I am bound for the land of Canaan,' something more than a hope of reaching heaven. We meant to reach the *north*—and the north was our Canaan." In much the same way, Douglas declared, the spiritual containing the following lines "had a double meaning":

> I thought I heard them say,
> There were lions in the way,
> I don't expect to stay
> Much longer here.
> Run to Jesus—shun the danger—
> I don't expect to stay
> Much longer here

The aspiration here is not for a quick translation to heaven but escape to a free state and "deliverance from all the evils and dangers of slavery."[75] The testimony of former slave Wash Wilson was similarly instructive. "When de niggers go round singin' 'Steal Away to Jesus,'" Wilson explained, "dat mean dere gwine be a 'ligious meetin' dat night."[76]

Where veiled meanings were too easily decoded, retribution could be swift. Colonel Thomas Wentworth Higginson, who listened to the spirituals his black troops sang around their fires at night, recorded in his diary that, for singing one of their spirituals, "We'll Soon Be Free," some slaves had been jailed in Georgetown, South Carolina, at the outbreak of war. The slaves had sung:

We'll soon be free
We'll soon be free
We'll soon be free
When de Lord will call us home.

. . . .

We'll fight for liberty
We'll fight for liberty
We'll fight for liberty
When de Lord will call us home.77

On another occasion, when Joseph Farley and a group of other slaves were singing the spiritual "Ride on King Jesus, No Man Can Hinder Thee," members of a slave patrol warned them that if they persisted they would quickly discover "whether they could be hindered or not."78

Recordings made in the 1930s recall something of the sounds and lyrical content of the slave spirituals. "Job, Job" (track 14),79 which Mandy Tartt, Sims Tartt, and Betty Atmore sang for John and Ruby Lomax, celebrates the patience of the Old Testament figure Job, who despite all manner of misfortune being visited on him remained faithful to his God.

Job had patience
Job had patience
Job had patience
In the morning

O Job O Job
Your wife is dead
And what you reck[on]
That Job he said
Lord He giveth
And God take away
And blessed be
The name of the Lord...

The verses of the song have a call-and-response format, the response to the lead singer's calls in each line of each verse simply being the recurring "hum, hum" sounds made by others in the group. Choruses are sung in unison. "Job, Job" illustrates once again the African American tradition of parallel statement, which allowed the singers to prolong their song merely by altering a word (in this case, "gal," "God," "wife"). In "Sometimes I Feel Like a Motherless Child" (track 15),[80] sung by Clifford Reed, Johnny Mae Medlock, and Julia Griffin at the State Farm, Raiford, Florida, the keening quality of the singers' voices, the drawn out, plaintive cries of "Lord, Lord," the progressive slowing of tempo in each stanza, and, of course, the song's melancholy lyrics, evoke feelings of helplessness and loss. But to a greater extent than is usual with songs collected in the 1930s, the trio's rendition of this spiritual seems very much an artifact of the recording situation. Probably because members of the group wished to present the Lomaxes with a "good performance," there is little vocal ornamentation in their singing and the usual raggedyness of African American vernacular music is missing. Had the group sung before a black audience, voices may well have overlapped, and the silences in the song would have been filled, as members of the gathering moaned, cried out, and added vocal embellishments of their own. In "Have Mercy, Lord" (track 16),[81] a "morning spiritual" sung by Mary Tollman and the congregation of the Johnson Place Baptist Church, near Livingston, Alabama, in 1939, moaning sounds can be heard issuing from the congregation, and the singer ornaments her song with vibrato effects and melismatic variations.

Although slave owners must sometimes have found the lyrics of spirituals provocative, many seem to have been prepared to ignore the double meanings, to see these subterfuges as part of the ambivalences and ambiguities that were always inherent in the plantation system, and, as the mistress of Gus Feaster's plantation had done, to enjoy the music their slaves made. Undoubtedly, slaves did encode veiled meanings in their spirituals, but that was hardly the main purpose of these African American songs. As Christianity took a powerful hold on the slave community in the decades before the Civil War, slaves, through their spirituals, sang a different world into existence, a syncretic world that subtly blended Anglo-American and African religious belief and practice and gave promise of a deliverance that transcended human time.

CHAPTER 7

"When we had a black preacher that was heaven"

Black preachers had begun to emerge by the mid-eighteenth century, following the conversion of significant numbers of blacks in the Great Awakening, and over time some of these preachers, both slave and free, were licensed by the Baptists and Methodists. In North Carolina, a slave named Peter preached regularly at slave funerals.[1] In Nottaway County, Virginia, "Uncle Jack" was a licensed Baptist preacher, whom planters were happy to have instruct their slaves.[2] In Westmoreland County, Virginia, in the 1780s, Lewis, a slave, preached to crowds of as many as four thousand persons.[3] A number of Virginia masters who advertised for the return of runaway slaves described the absconders as preachers.[4] In one South Carolinian parish in the mid-1770s, as many as fifteen slaves were known to preach "to great crowds of Negroes...very frequently...in the woods and other places."[5] In Virginia in the 1790s, the racially mixed congregation of the Portsmouth Baptist Church hired Josiah Bailey, a black man, to preach to them.[6] From the late eighteenth century, and especially from the 1830s onward, Christianity spread rapidly among the slaves, and by the outbreak of war in 1861 it was pervasive.[7] Reflecting this expansion, the number of black preachers multiplied.

Some black preachers preached at African American churches in or near urban areas, which often attracted impressively large congregations. The Scottish traveler William Thomson noted that the black church he attended in South Carolina in 1842 had "about twelve or fourteen hundred negro members belonging to it, partly house servants, but mostly slaves from the cotton plantations in the neighbourhood."[8] Sometimes slave preachers were permitted to preach in white churches as well, but only after the conclusion of the main service, and usually with white oversight. "We had some colored preachers," the former Maryland slave Henry Clay Bruce stated, "who...preached every Sunday afternoon in the white people's church, but there was always some leading white man present to take note of what the preacher said." If the preacher ventured onto dangerous terrain, he would be interrupted and lectured, and in some cases would lose his license. Henry Bruce recalled an incident involving the slave preacher Uncle Tom Ewing, who, having "got warmed up" during a prayer that followed one of his sermons, had boldly declared: "Free indeed, free from death, free from hell, free from work, free from the white folks, free from everything," whereupon Ewing's master warned him that he would lose his license if he ever used such language again.9

The activities of slave preachers sometimes caused public alarm. In the wake of the Nat Turner slave revolt in Southampton County, Virginia, in 1831, which resulted in the death of some sixty whites, James Spare and others petitioned the Delaware General Assembly to the effect that "the public tranquility" of New Castle County and other areas had been "much disturbed by rumours of intended insurrectionary movements." Many of the black preachers who came to Delaware from other states were, the petitioners claimed, "regular and constant preachers of sedition, to our slaves and free blacks at their night meetings, where no whites are present." In 1842 the commissioners of Raleigh, North Carolina, drew the North Carolina General Assembly's attention to the law that "forbids slaves and free persons of Color, under any pretence whatever to preach or exhort or to act as preachers or teachers in any prayer meeting or association for worship where slaves of different families are assembled." The spirit of that law, the petitioners lamented, was "daily violated in many sections of the State particularly in the Towns and villages where it is less difficult for them [slaves] to congregate in large numbers." Fifteen years later, citizens of Hardeman County urged the Tennessee Assembly to outlaw black preaching completely, since its effects were "baneful, to the negro, and dangerous to the public weal & safety."10 Clearly, at different times and in different places in the antebellum South, the authorities did enforce the letter of the law and clamped down on slave preachers, if only for short periods of time. But it was impossible to maintain the degree of vigilance required to outlaw them totally and, in fact, for much of the last decades of slavery, white authorities turned a blind eye to the slaves who, whether licensed or not, continued to preach the word.

In general, slaves had scant regard for white churchmen who, having conducted plantation services for whites, dispensed religious advice to members of the slave community. The white preacher who came regularly to Lucretia Alexander's plantation would simply instruct the slaves to "serve your masters. Don't steal your master's turkey. Don't steal your master's chickens. . . . Do whatsomever your master tells you to do." It was, she said, the "same old thing all the time."[11] Emma Tidwell spoke scathingly of the white preacher who, on Sunday evenings, would call her and her fellow slaves together under a tree and repeat there his invariable text: "Mind yo mistress. . . . Don't steal der potatoes; don't lie bout nothin an don' talk back tuh yo boss; ifn yo does yo'll be tied tuh a tree an stripped nekid." That, Emma Tidwell declared, was "de kind uv gospel we got."[12] With black preachers, however, it was a different matter.

Former slaves, interviewed for the Federal Writers' Project, spoke loudly of their preference for black preachers. Louis Fowler told of a preacher named Allen Beaver who used to preach to the slaves on Fowler's Texas plantation. "Allen am not educated," Fowler stated, "but he can preach a pow'ful sermon. O, Lawd! He am inspire from de Lawd and he preached from his heartfelt."[13] Former Alabama and Mississippi slave Clara Young remembered that "de mos' fun we had was at our meetin's," which were held most Sundays and "lasted way into de night." The preacher she liked best was Mathew Ewing, "a comely nigger, black as night." Ewing could not read but "he sho' knowed his Bible an' would hol' his han' out an' mek like he was readin' an' preach de purtiest preachin' you ever heered."[14] Anthony Dawson's master, "a fine Christian," allowed his slaves not only to "have preachings and prayers," but also to travel ten miles or so to camp meetings, religious gatherings that sometimes lasted for several days. "Mostly we had white preachers," Dawson recalled, "but when we had a black preacher that was Heaven."[15]

Blacks who preached in urban churches, or in more remote locations, sometimes won praise from whites for their eloquence, for the power of their imagery, for their understanding of the spirit (if not their mastery of the letter) of religious teachings, for their ability to relate scriptural precepts to the circumstances of church members' everyday lives. The historian John Abbott was deeply impressed by a sermon he heard in an African church in New Orleans in 1859. Although the black preacher who delivered it was, to Abbott's way of thinking, "entirely without culture," he had "clearly understood, and touchingly unfolded the plan of salvation through faith in Jesus Christ." Abbott was particularly struck by the man's "beautiful adaptation of Christianity to the wants of the world." (He was less comfortable with the congregation's singing, which seemed to him "an extempore wail, without articulate words, such as I never heard before from earthly voices.")[16] That same ability to relate scriptural events to his hearers' immediate circumstances was possessed by the black preacher to whom an English woman, Barbara Leigh Smith Bodichon, listened in Louisville, Kentucky, in 1860. Having told "very vividly the whole story of the resurrection," the man continued:

And what has he [Jesus Christ] done? Why, he nailed our *paper of freedom* on his cross. And he, the same, the same good kind King, Friend, Father, Saviour, will receive us all. Not another Christ, but our own Christ. And all who know him, who have been *borned* again are gwine to him, the old Friend. Now, my brothers and sisters, suppose a gentleman gave you a pass..., and you are out and taken up, aint you glad if the magistrate is the same gentleman as signed your pass...? Now, my dear friends, it is always so with us. It is before him who signed the pass that we shall go.[17]

Attending a religious meeting at a contraband camp in the South in 1863, George Hepworth, too, had been much taken by the "thrilling, oratorical effect" achieved by one of the black preachers, and the great beauty and grandeur of some of the man's phrases.

He spoke of *"the rugged wood of the cross,"* whereto the Saviour was nailed; and, after describing that scene with as much power as I have ever known an orator to exhibit, he reached a climax, when he pictured the earthquake which rent the veil of the temple, with this extremely beautiful expression: "And, my friends, *the earth was unable to endure the tremendous sacrilege, and trembled.*" He held his rude audience with most perfect control.[18]

Again, the Swedish traveler Fredrika Bremer was struck by the eloquence of a preacher to whom she listened in a black Baptist church in
Savannah, Georgia, in the 1850s. The man's theme was the manner of
Jesus's appearance on earth and the Savior's purpose in coming. Speaking "extempore with great animation and ease," the preacher con-
trasted the arrival of the president of the United States in Savannah,
some time before, with the coming of Jesus.

> I remember what an ado the people made, and how they went out in
> big carriages to meet him [the president]. The clouds of dust were ter-
> rible, and the great cannon pealed forth one salute after another. Then
> the president came in a grand, beautiful carriage and drove to the best
> house in the whole town.... And when he came there he seated him-
> self in the window. But a cord was drawn around the house to keep us
> negroes and the other poor folks from coming too near. We had to
> stand outside and only get a sight of the president as he sat at the win-
> dow. But the great gentlemen and the rich folks went freely up the
> steps and in through the door and shook hands with him. Now, did
> Christ come in this way? Did he come only to the rich? Did He shake
> hands only with them? No! Blessed be the Lord! He came to the poor!
> He came to us, and for our sakes, my brothers and sisters!

At this point, ecstatic cries of "Yes, yes! Amen! He came to us! Blessed
be His name! Amen! Halleluiah!" rang out, and members of the congregation "stamped their feet, and laughed and cried, with countenances beaming with joy."[19]

But often such favorable assessments tended to be drowned out by
the chorus of negative white criticism. Much of that criticism related
to a perception that, although impassioned and deeply affecting, black
sermons, for a variety of reasons, lacked substantial meaning. Some
whites believed that the words of slave preachers were rendered meaningless by "faulty" pronunciation, odd-sounding dialects, grammatical
failings, or screeched delivery. Some combination of these factors may
have prompted Frederick Law Olmsted to declare the address of one
of the black preachers to whom he had listened in the New Orleans
church to be "in great part unintelligible,"[20] or led the English traveler
Godfrey Vigne to conclude that a black preacher in Washington, D.C.,
had "talked the most incoherent nonsense."[21] Again, slaves' illiteracy
and limited knowledge of the Bible often persuaded whites to dismiss

their sermons as meaningless. Ebenezer Davies' suspicion that an African American preacher in Baltimore could not read the book he was holding in his hand was quickly "confirmed by the amount of nonsense that he soon uttered." Davies deplored the fact that "between 500 and 600 people were listening to this ignorant man, giving as the pure and positive word of God what was of very doubtful authority, intermingled with the crudities of his own brain."[22] (There is, of course, a special kind of irony in the fact that whites, who had mandated black illiteracy, then criticized slaves for misquoting biblical texts and mistaking the meaning of words.)

Other critics, a majority, attributed the meaninglessness of black sermons to their structural frailty, their lack of logically ordered, coherent thought. Fredrika Bremer, so admiring of the black preacher in Savannah, complained that an African American preacher in Charleston had "poured forth his eloquence for a good hour, but said the same thing over and over."[23] Elizabeth Kilham could not recall the text on which "Old Billy" had based a sermon delivered in his Sea Islands church, but suggested that "almost any thing would answer the purpose, being sure to fit some one of the numerous subjects embraced in that discourse, which went entirely through the Bible, from the Creation to the last chapter of Revelation."[24] Charles Carleton Coffin, a war correspondent for the *Boston Herald*, described the sermon that a black minister, the Reverend Abraham Murchison, preached to a congregation of recently freed slaves at Port Royal as "a crude, disjointed discourse, having very little logic, [and] a great many large words, some of them ludicrously misapplied."[25] George Hepworth, who marveled at the eloquence and power of the slave preacher who had addressed the contrabands in Louisiana in 1863, had listened earlier on that day to an African American preacher who "lost all self-control," and "produced logic which brought tears—of laughter—to my eyes."[26]

Charles Raymond, a white minister of religion, had made something of a study of African American sermons, to many of which he had listened, not only in a courthouse town in South Carolina in which he resided for several years, but in such cities as Savannah, Charleston, Richmond, and New Orleans. Thus, when asked to attend the "funeral preaching" of the slave woman "Sis Sally Green," who had died two years earlier, he readily agreed. Drawn from surrounding plantations, the congregation that gathered for the event was a large one, numbering about three hundred, two hundred of whom were slaves. The oration was to be delivered by Uncle Phil, a famed slave preacher.

Raymond had listened to Uncle Phil preach a number of times and nothing that he heard on this occasion changed his mind as to the fundamental character of this slave's and, indeed, of most slaves' addresses. "In their general want of outline, and in their jumble of thoughts and use of remarkable adjectives," Raymond decided, Uncle Phil's sermons "were like the sermons of all other negro preachers in the country. Exposition was not attempted. Description, exhortation, appeal formed the warp and woof." Intellectually, Phil's orations were "mere trash," as were "the sermons of nearly all negro preachers." The address Phil had delivered, Raymond pointed out, had not contained anything "peculiarly appropriate to a funeral, and...would have answered for any other occasions as well." On an earlier occasion, Raymond had tried to improve the slave's technique. He had presented Phil with a book of sermon skeletons, or outlines, hoping to encourage in the black man a more structured presentation of ideas. Phil, however, had merely been nonplussed, reacting with incredulity to the notion that sermons could be planned and delivered in this way.

Other things puzzled the white churchman. He noticed that Phil's congregation seemed to be unusually affected by the very sounds of words rather than simply their sense, by "the merest word-jinglings," even when the phrases in question were "destitute of meaning." Phil himself appeared to share this love of word sounds, seeming, for all the undoubted power of his performance (power that Raymond freely acknowledged), to be most proud of "the brilliancy of his quotations," by which Raymond meant phrases supposedly taken from the Bible, but made nonsensical in translation. Thus, Phil's "favorite pyrotechnic," the rhetorical flourish with which he often concluded his sermons, was

Oh my dyin' hearers, you don't know de feelin's of Jesus—you nebber will know the feelin's of de precious Jesus—when he was in the garden, where he sweat de big drops ob blood—when dey took him up afore de Pontius Pilate, and put de thorny crown upon dat blessed brow—and when he hung upon de cross, and when he cry, "Elias!! Elias!! Elemi!!! BETHANI!!!!"

To Raymond's knowledge, Phil had never translated for his hearers the meaning of those concluding words, a "corruption" of the Aramaic sentence "Eloi, Eloi, lama sabachthani," in Mark 15:34 of the King James Bible. (The full text of the verse reads: "And at the ninth hour Jesus cried with a loud voice, saying, Eloi, Eloi, lama sabachthani? which is, being interpreted, My God, my God, why hast thou forsaken me?") He had failed to do so, Raymond surmised, because of a reluctance to "mar by any less classical language" the "profound impression" the sound of those words had created.

Raymond may have thought Phil's sermon "wholly ridiculous," but he himself had been deeply affected by it. "To hear [Phil] with his broad, genial, honest face, his eyes full of mildness and suppressed tearfulness, his deep chest tones wonderfully sweet in their modulations,...His visions of 'de pearly gates ob shinin' gold.'...His gazing on 'dat bressed Lamb dat died for Phil,'" Raymond conceded, was "to rouse and stir all the tenderest depths of your nature."[27]

Time and again, white observers of slave religious practice would display this kind of ambivalence. When, in the early phase of the Civil War, Mary Chesnut heard Jim Nelson, the black driver on her husband's South Carolina plantation, deliver a prayer, she was struck by the tonal power and subtlety of a voice that "rose to the pitch of a shrill shriek," yet was "strangely clear and musical, occasionally in a plaintive minor key that went to your heart." But, Chesnut decided, the man's performance had been "all sound...and emotional pathos." "There was literally nothing in what he said. The words had no meaning at all."[28] As we have seen, similarly dismissive comments had not infrequently been made about the lyrics of slave religious songs, which were described variously as "nonsensical," "absurd," and "meaningless."[29] Yet these can hardly have been the judgments of the African Americans who heard these prayers or sermons, or sang these songs. Clearly, there were messages in these forms of religious expression that whites could not hear, cultural imperatives they were unable to discern.

Whites' understanding of black religious expression was often obscured not only by differing ideas as to the appropriateness of various types of sound in various contexts, but by a distrust of emotionalism and a reliance on reason as an important (though not wholly sufficient) path to religious truth. As Bruce Rosenberg has noted, a theology that privileges reason and the intellect as the path to truth "equates emotionalism with hysteria and hysteria with the negation of reason." For those who accept such theological premises, "the ideal sermon mode is exposition."³⁰ It was in the interests of well-ordered exposition that the Reverend Charles Colcock Jones, a leader of missions to slaves, advised his fellow ministers in 1847 to write out their sermons beforehand and read them to black audiences, rather than speaking extemporaneously. Manuscript sermons, Colcock Jones further advised, should be read in a "dignified and simple" manner, "free from levity, coarseness and vulgarity." Nothing could more directly "impair [a minister's] influence and render his efforts fruitless, than to descend to the use of their [black preachers'] corrupt expressions and broken English."³¹ But sermons of this type, if delivered to a slave audience, were probably doomed to fail. There were tonal and rhythmic effects, absent from such a discourse, that slaves needed to hear, aesthetic expectations that a sermon of this kind could never fulfill. Only occasionally, and then obliquely, were these elements of the slave sermon alluded to by former slaves, or by whites who actually listened to slave addresses. Those elements have, however, caught the attention of more recent inquirers into the nature of African American sermonic practice.

In his study of old-time black preachers, the African American writer James Weldon Johnson emphasized the importance of tonal qualities to their performance. Old-time preachers, Johnson wrote, "often possessed a voice that was a marvellous instrument, a voice he could modulate from a sepulchral whisper to a crashing thunder-clap." The "intoning" practiced by such men was "a thing next to impossible to describe; it must be heard." It was "always a matter of crescendo and diminuendo in the intensity—a rising and falling between plain speaking and wild chanting." Often, Johnson went on to say, "a startling effect [was] gained by breaking off suddenly at the highest point of intensity and dropping into the monotone of ordinary speech." Johnson told of going to a church in Kansas City in order to hear a "famed visiting preacher" speak. The circumstances in which the man delivered his address were unpromising. It was late at night when his turn finally came and the audience had grown tired, having already listened to several other addresses. The famous preacher commenced "to preach a formal sermon from a formal text," but the congregation did not respond, remaining listless and inattentive. Suddenly, however, the man abandoned his script, stepped forward, and began "intoning [an] old folk-sermon." The transformation was wonderful: the preacher became "a changed man, free, at ease and masterful." The congregation "instantly came alive." During the rest of his sermon the old-time black preacher "brought into play the full gamut of his wonderful voice, a voice—what shall I say—not of an organ or a trumpet, but rather of a trombone, the instrument possessing above all other the power to express the wide and varied range of emotions. He intoned, he moaned, he pleaded, he blared, he crashed, he thundered. I sat fascinated; and more, I was, perhaps against my will, deeply moved; the emotional effect upon me was irresistible."[32]

Back in the world of antebellum America, Charles Raymond, too, had been moved by the funeral preacher Phil's "peculiar pathos of tone and expression,"[33] by the "deep chest tones, wonderfully sweet in their modulations."[34] He had marveled at the "wonderful sympathy" that existed between black preachers and their audiences, sympathy that "finds expression in those peculiar tones which are inimitable by a preacher of any other race, and which, in their influence upon the negro hearers, are unequalled."[35] Raymond himself had been emotionally affected by these "inimitable" tones, but, as he realized, the effect of such sounds on Phil's black audience had been more profound. It was as though the black audience "heard" something far more significant. In Phil's audience's attraction to the musical intoning of clusters of words, to mere "word jinglings," Raymond "heard" an absence of intellectual content. Phil's audience, by contrast, "heard" a culturally resonant play of deeply evocative sound. As James Weldon Johnson pointed out, the "old-time Negro preacher loved the sonorous, mouth-filling, ear-filling phrase because it gratified a highly developed sense of sound and rhythm in himself and his hearers."[36]

Slaves needed to hear the changing tones of the preacher's voice, the sweet, solemn, harsh, or impassioned sonorities that registered the speaker's sincerity and conviction, expressed his varying emotions— sorrow, elation, anguish, joy—and echoed, however distantly, the tonal characteristics of African speech. To a much greater extent than was true of white preachers, black preachers conveyed meaning in this way.

Johnson's reference to the "highly developed sense of . . . rhythm" in both black speaker and audience is also instructive. "The old-time Negro preacher," Johnson wrote, ". . . knew the secret of oratory, that at bottom it is a progression of rhythmic words more than it is anything else." Johnson pointed to "a decided syncopation of speech" in the sermons of such men, "the crowding in of many syllables or the lengthening out of a few to fill one metrical foot."[37] Whites who described the preaching style of African Americans during slavery or just after emancipation tell us virtually nothing about the rhythmic patterns of black speech. Clearly, however, slave preachers, like slave singers, were able to fit their words to the rhythms of their sermons' "songs." In so doing, they set in train the rhythmic cadences that fired the emotions of the people, called forth increasingly impassioned responses, and propelled sermons toward their dramatic and emotional climax.

What, then, of the almost invariable complaint that the slave sermon was so structurally weak, the ideas contained in it so jumbled, that the words of the preacher conveyed little coherent meaning? In part, these criticisms reflect not cultural differences, but the requirements of extempore as against scripted speech. It is not surprising that extempore preachers, who were, after all, engaged in spontaneous composition, sometimes made associational leaps that were difficult to follow, or strayed intermittently from the point. It is not surprising that they repeated themselves, or copiously and, as whites often felt, "excessively" illustrated their ideas. As Walter Ong has pointed out, repetition and amplification allow orators time to move from one idea to another, so maintaining the flow of speech. They also give hearers a chance to consider an idea before the speaker moves on. For these reasons, oral cultures do not manifest the same impatience at the sort of repetition and verboseness that literate cultures find distracting and pointless.[38] It is not surprising, either, that extempore preachers, who, like slave singers, needed artfully to select and set alongside one another biblical texts and stories from their memory store, fitting their words to the sermon's metric patterns, often presented their ideas in a nonsequential, nonlinear form. Somewhat in the manner of slaves who created their own hymns, hymns that often seemed to whites to have a mosaic-like structure, slave preachers drew their texts and stories from many parts of the scriptures, as well as from everyday life, and combined them in often surprising ways.

This was especially the case after the point of "elevation" in the sermon. At this juncture, the preacher's voice moved "from a conversational to a poetic mode," as the words of the preacher "pattern[ed] themselves into short, cadenced phrases," taking on the tonal contours of chant. Exposition may or may not have occurred earlier in the sermon; it certainly had no place here. Here, both preacher and congregation believed, the preacher's words were being impelled by the Spirit, and as the Spirit's hold over the meeting increased, some members of the congregation would shout, or weep, or take part in the holy dance.39

Extracts from a sermon entitled "The Unusual Task of the Gospel Preacher," delivered by the Reverend Harry Singleton at Sandy Island, South Carolina, in January 1972 (track 17), illustrate some of the processes described above. On the occasion in question, Singleton, a visiting preacher, directed his remarks at Reverend Green, the minister of the Sandy Island church at which Singleton had been invited to speak. The visitor's message was that, having been called by his God to preach, Reverend Green must faithfully continue in that calling until, his task on earth being done, he made his final journey to "the other side," that is, to heaven. In the chanted part of the sermon, Singleton drove home this all-important message, sampling, in the main, verses from the King James Bible to suggest what it was that their God wanted his faithful servant to say.

In the following transcription, texts that Singleton drew from the King James Bible (his wording is approximate), the hymn "Amazing Grace," and the *Anglican Book of Common Prayer* are italicized, and the locations of those texts are indicated. Except for "lines" consisting of only one word—a long, drawn-out "and"—each line of the sermon evoked from the Sandy Island congregation a volley of affirmative sound, a chorus of "yesses," intermingled with clapping, occasional shouts of "preach it," and other supportive cries. Here and there, throughout the sermon, we hear also the rhythmic tapping of feet. We pick up the sermon just beyond the point at which the preacher has begun to chant.

> O Green
> I know you say some time "Lord
> why is it me?"
> "Lord, why did you call me?"
>
> Yes
> I don't know
> And I'm not here to question God
> But I believe
> I believe
> That God looks
> On the inside
>
> O brother Green
> God saw something in you
> And
> He laid his hands on you
> Yes
> And I want to tell you tonight
> I want you to preach
> Like the Lord told you to do
>
> O Green
> I want you to preach
> Until *the world*
> *is turned upside down* (Acts 17:6)
>
> O Green
> I want you to preach
> *Until justice*
> *roll down like water*
> *and righteousness*
> *like a mighty stream* (Amos 5:24)

O Green
I want you to preach
And tell Sandy Island
That *the wages of sin is death
and the gift of God
is eternal life* (Rom. 6:23)

O Green
I want you to preach
That Jesus
Is the Son of God
And
He said *"I am the way
the truth and the life
no man
cometh to the father
but by me"* (John 14:6)

O Green
I want you to preach
Until hate
Give way to love

O Green
I want you to preach
Until poverty
Give way

O Green
I want you to preach
*Until corruption
Becomes incorruption* (1 Cor. 15:54)

O Green
I want you to preach
Until men
Fall out with the wicked ways
And come cryin'

"What?
What
must I do
to be saved?" (Acts 16:30)

O Green
I want you to preach
Until hell
Get disturbed

O Green
I want you to preach
Until heaven
Get disturbed

There is a cut in the recording at this point. When Singleton's sermon resumes, the words he uses to begin his "verses" have changed, and the volume of affirmative sound has increased. He speaks now of Green's journey to "the other side."

O after while
And by and by
You gonna have to
Close up the book

After while
And by and by
You gon' hear
"amazing grace
how sweet the sound
that saved a wretch like me" ("Amazing Grace")

After while
Yes
And by and by
The war is gon' be over

But Jesus

Jesus
"I am a rock
in a weary land" (Isa. 32: 2)
He said *"I'll be with you*
to the ends of the earth" (Mark 28:20)

O Green
He said *"be thou faithful*
unto death" (Rev. 2:10)
I have paradise
On the other side

One day
You gonna have to cross the river
And it's not gonna be Waccamaw

One day
You're going for the last time
Over yonder

Yes
There is a paradise
Over there

The angels
cry holy holy (Isa. 6:3)
Cause God wants
Heaven and earth is full of thy glory (Communion
    Service, Anglican Book of Common Prayer)

By and by
Yes
Tell of the love
The love of God
Preach and moan
I want you to come on
On the other side

I been looking ...

At this point, the preacher's voice was drowned in an outburst of ecstatic sound, following which, the congregation launched into a song ("Meet You on the Other Shore"), to the accompaniment of foot stamping and polyrhythmic clapping.[40]

In this chanted section of the sermon, Reverend Singleton (whose words, both he and the congregation would have believed, were being impelled by the Spirit) makes free associations around the sermon's unifying idea (that Reverend Green must continue, faithfully, to preach the gospel), mixing verses from the Old Testament and New Testament, the opening lines of the hymn "Amazing Grace," and the words "heaven and earth are full of thy glory," from the Communion Service in the Anglican Book of Common Prayer. Yet Singleton's sermon is anything but a mere jumble of thoughts, as Charles Raymond had taken the sermons of virtually all slave preachers to be. Around his sermon's central theme, Singleton, playing, as it were, the ventriloquist, offers Green and members of the Sandy Island congregation not an orderly, sequential discourse, but a freely associative and newly powerful reiteration of uncontested religious truths.

Not only this, but for Singleton's audience the scriptural texts, hymn lines, and so forth, that are woven into his sermon would have carried with them a whole web of associations. The folklorist Michael Taft points out that the formulaic expressions—which is to say, familiar blues lines—drawn upon by blues singers "are recognized, whether consciously or unconsciously, from other blues contexts," and, as a consequence, "gather thematic and psychological associations around themselves." The cumulative impact of such newly recollected expressions can therefore be considerable. As Taft states, "With each new singing of a formula [that is, a formulaic expression], the audience becomes aware of all its past lyrical contexts and of all the other formulas with which it was juxtaposed. The formula, therefore, gains meaning and significance beyond its immediate semantic components." Moreover, "by his realignment of commonplace elements," his use of new and original combinations of well-known expressions, the blues singer "shocks us with the familiar," making "the old newly meaningful."[41] Like other oral communicators, slave preachers undoubtedly used language in this way, and with similar effect, calling up familiar, metrically based expressions drawn from the scriptures, or spirituals, or black vernacular expression, and combining them in artful and unexpected ways. Such language, with its accretions of meaning and provocative juxtapositions, could be powerful, even when the various ideas expressed through it were not tidily arranged. Singleton's sampling of the scriptural texts with which his sermon is suffused—"I am a rock in a weary land," "I'll be with you to the ends of the earth" and so forth—would have called those texts, with all their associations, vividly and surprisingly to mind.

In her study of the language of religious rituals in the Sea Islands of South Carolina, Patricia Jones-Jackson draws on similar ideas. In black sermons, Jones-Jackson writes, "the words are everything," by which she means not that they build into a well-ordered and coherent sequence of thought, but that they call up powerful images and associations from scripture and contemporary life. To illustrate this point, Jones-Jackson quotes not from a sermon, but from a closely related cultural form—the prayer of a Gullah woman, lyrically beautiful and powerful in its associations:

> Dear Massa Jesus, we all uns beg Ooner [you] come make us a call dis yere day. We is nutting but poor Ethiopian women and people ain't tink much 'bout we. We ain't trust any of dem great Massa, great too much dan Massa Linkum, you aint shame to care for we African people.
>
> Come to we, dear Massa Jesus. De sun, he hot too much, de road am dat long and boggy [sandy] and we ain't go no buggy for send and fetch Ooner. But Massa, you 'member how you walked dat hard walk up Calvary and ain't weary but tink about we all day way. We know you ain't weary for to come to we. We pick out de torns, de prickles, de brier, de back-slidin' and de quarrel and de sin ut of yor path so dey shan't hurt Ooner or pierce feet no more.[42]

As Jones-Jackson points out, "Aunt Jane" speaks, here, "in the language of the community":

> The "boggy" roads attest to the tortuous path that many congregation members have traveled to make it to the morning services; the briars and thorns attest metaphorically to the pricks and stabs that most of

the members have received not only in their feet but in their daily lives as well.... The words...touch the listeners' lives and give them temporary solace from the outside world. So when the members of the congregation scream out their despair in unison to the speaker's call, they are doing more than practicing an ancient African ritual; they are replying to the words of a speaker who is gifted in a rhetorical technique, who knows how to "join the words" to provide the kind of emotional release that members of African American congregations go to church to experience.

But Aunt Jane summons associations that are even more compelling. When she speaks of her regret that no buggy can be sent to fetch Jesus, the same Jesus who "walked dat hard walk up Calvary," she draws associations from the many contexts in which, we might suspect, the formulaic expression "walked dat hard walk up Calvary" had been used, and these associations, as well as the references to cruel thorns and pierced feet, irresistibly evoke the passion and drama of the Crucifixion. With her expression of regret that no buggy is available now to transport Jesus, "Aunt Jane" has also surprisingly juxtaposed two ideas, thereby collapsing time and achieving a kind of immediacy and intimacy that makes her hearers' religious experience newly "real." As Jones-Jackson has remarked, "In most European-derived religious services and rituals, the congregation sits quietly and thinks of the Divine in abstract terms. To worshippers on the Sea Islands, however, the Divine is a concrete entity whose presence can be created by a master rhetorician and a responsive audience."[43] Similar observations have been made across time. Writing in the 1930s, the historian Arthur Raper remarked that a traditional black preacher "talks to his congregation about Moses and Daniel at mid-day as though he had eaten breakfast with them."[44] In his discussion of the religious perceptions of slaves, Lawrence Levine quotes slaves as making such declarations as "I saw God sitting in a big arm chair"; "I seen Christ with His hair parted in the center."[45]

In the course of their 1930s study of African American folk beliefs in the coastal regions of Georgia, members of the Georgia Writers' Project attended a service in a black church at Silver Bluff on Sapelo Island. As these researchers pointed out, African Americans on this sea island, located in a region once dense with slaves, lived "an isolated existence," a circumstance that had allowed them to preserve "many customs and beliefs of their ancestors, as well as the dialect of the older coastal Negro." In this small community, perhaps as well as anywhere else in the South, we might expect the past to be present, the religious practices of slavery to be maintained in something like their earlier form.

The sermon at the Silver Bluff church was delivered that day by an itinerant minister, Preacher Little. As Patricia Jones-Jackson explains, such a person would need to make sure that he spoke "the language of his congregation," choosing "imagery unique to the[ir] environment." In Jones-Jackson's irresistible example, a visiting preacher might "ask a blessing that the Holy Spirit 'touch each and every heart so that their spirits shine like a crab's back in the rain.'"[46] Having established the necessary rapport with the congregation, the preacher could begin his address.

Preacher Little announced that he would speak on the biblical passage: "You ah the salt of the earth; but if the salt has lost its savory, wherewith shall it be salt; it is then no good and should be trompled intuh earth."[47] It soon seemed to the Georgia writers, however, that the sermon itself had little relationship to the text.

Preacher Little divided his sermon into three parts and lectured his congregation on "straying frum duh paat." What he said was not really coherent. Words stood out, phrases rang in our ears, quotations from the Bible resounded at random but that was the beginning and the end. The impelling element was the sound of Preacher Little's voice.

In each part he began slowly, quietly, persuading and reasoning with his congregation. His voice would carry a pleading question to them and they would answer, "Huh." As he progressed, the quiet reasoning diminished; he shouted to his listeners. The "Huh-Huh's" became loud, guttural, vibrating grunts that echoed through the little building. Regular stamping of the feet began; the vibration penetrated into every corner. It was impossible not to think of the beating of the drum. The regular rhythmic, swelling noise was deafening. It meant agreement with Preacher Little. It urged him on to greater heights

until his shouting voice not only seemed to fill the church but to re-
verberate from wall to wall. This climax was reached three times, at
the end of each of the three parts of the sermon. Each time it seemed
to act as a great emotional purge to the listeners and leave them hap-
pily exhausted.[48]

There is no animus in these words of the Georgia writers, but there is
the same sense of difference that many of those whites who once listened to slave sermons often convey, the feeling that the people whose
religious practices they are observing inhabit another cultural world.
Separated in time though it is from accounts of slave sermons given by
those who actually heard them, the authors' brief description never-
theless picks up many of the points that those earlier writers made.
There is an apparent lack of connectedness in Preacher Little's remarks: his sermon's text seems to bear little relationship to what fol-
lows. The sermon is "not really coherent," which is to say that it lacks
organization, a linear structure. As was often the case in descriptions
of slave sermons, the imagery is vivid ("words stood out"), and there is
a liberal, if seemingly unsystematic, sampling of biblical texts, which,
we are told, "resounded at random" throughout the sermon. There is
also the fact that the preacher's words evoke a crescendo of ultimately
deafening congregational noise, as feet stamp rhythmically, and cries
of "Huh-Huh" endorse those words and help fix the rhythm of the sermon's chant. Again, the sound of Preacher Little's voice (the writers
identify changes in volume but allude also to variations in tone) is
"the impelling element" in the sermon, all-important to the preacher's
success. Unlike contemporary observers of slave preachers, the Georgia writers recognized, to some extent, the importance of the tones and
rhythms of the preacher's voice. Like earlier observers, they showed
little appreciation of the cumulative associational power of his words.

Far away from the Sea Islands, on Easter Sunday in 1934, the Reverend Sin-Killer Griffin, an African American prison chaplain, delivered a sermon at Darrington State Farm, Sandy Point, Texas. Its title
was, appropriately enough, "The Man of Calvary." The section of the
Lomax recording of this sermon included on the CD (track 18) begins
about midway through Griffin's address and proceeds almost to the

end.[49] To begin with, the preacher had described, in a vivid and highly dramatic fashion, the events leading up to the crucifixion of Jesus. He had told how, while on the cross, Jesus had been cruelly wounded by a spear thrust into his side; how the mountain on which the crucifixion was taking place had begun to tremble; how "as soon as the sun recognized its Maker, ...it clothed itself in sack clothing and went down ...in mourning!"; how, when the moon saw Jesus on the cross, it "took with a judgement hemorrhage and bleed away"; how the little stars "remembered Jesus when he struck on the anvil of time"; how, as Christ neared death, darkness covered the land; and how, after Jesus had died, a Roman centurian cried out, "Sholy, sholy, this must be the son of God."

With Griffin's surprising announcement: "I seen the horse come steppin' on Calvary's brow," however, there is a sudden change in direction. Hitherto, the preacher had been concerned to convey to his prison audience the dramatic events leading to Jesus's death. Now, in a series of audacious leaps across time, he begins to draw into his narrative the powerful, apocalyptic imagery of the Revelation of Saint John the Divine, the last book of the King James Bible, with its ominous prophecies and intense spiritual visions. The rider of the horse that arrives at the crucifixion scene, the preacher tells his hearers, is Death, and when one of the thieves who is being crucified with Christ looks upon Death he also sees, written on the side of the horse, the words "Death and Hell followeth him." (The passage in Revelation on which Griffin has drawn for this part of his discourse is: "And I looked, and behold a pale horse: and his name that sat on him was Death, and Hell followeth him" [Rev. 6:8].) At this point, no longer doubting Jesus's divinity, the dying thief, who is being crucified with Jesus, implores Jesus to remember him when he comes into his kingdom. (This episode in the preacher's unfolding story is drawn from Luke 23:42: "Lord, remember me when thou comest into thy kingdom.") The preacher then reminds his congregation that, whereas neither Elijah, nor Job, nor Moses the great lawgiver had been able to take hold of the horse, "the incarnated Son of God caught the horse by the bridle and held him still." Which is to say that Jesus, by seizing the horse on which Death rode, stopped death, that through his own death on the cross he defeated death. "Pay no attention to death," Reverend Griffin has Christ say to the dying thief, for "This day thy parting spirit will be with me in heaven." (Griffin borrowed these words from Luke 23:43: "And Jesus said unto him [the dying thief], 'Verily I say unto thee, Today shalt thou be with me in paradise.'") Surprising at first, the metaphor of the horse is strikingly poetic, making Griffin's account of the Crucifixion vastly more powerful.

Now, in a classic mode shift, Griffin leads the prisoners in a slow-meter hymn—"I'm Not Ashamed to Own My Lord"—lining out the words and embellishing the melody with melismas and gliding tones, around which members of the group also improvise. Then, drawing again on the prophecies of Revelation, the preacher describes how God "fastens the great dragon," binding him "for so many thousand years" (words that are based on Rev. 20:2: "And he [an angel] laid hold on the dragon, that old serpent, which is the Devil, and Satan, and bound him a thousand years.") God, Griffin declares, "twisted the stinger away from Death" (he is referencing here the First Epistle to the Corinthians, 15:55: "O death, where is thy sting?"), with the result that Death no longer has any dominion over the people of God.

From here until the end of his sermon, Griffin returns to events that took place after Jesus's death—how the angels rolled back the stone guarding the entrance to the sepulchre; how Jesus rose from the grave; how the angels told Jesus's followers that he would come again—while continuing to work into his narrative images drawn from Revelation. For instance, picturing for his audience a scene in heaven, Griffin states that "three and twenty elders left their seats, each one cryin', 'Ho-ly, ho-ly, holy!'" (an image based on Rev. 11:16: "And the four and twenty elders, which sat before God on their seats, fell upon their faces, and worshipped God.")

Griffin's sermon calls to mind several recurring features of black sermonic style: the power of the preacher's imagery; the lavish use of biblical texts; the rhythms and tonal contours of elevated speech; the incessant call-and-response; the grainy tautness of the preacher's voice (signifying intensity); the surprising juxtapositions, most notably, in this case, the sudden appearance of the fourth horse of the Apocalypse on Calvary's hill, but more generally in the free mixing of verses from

Revelation with the accounts of the Crucifixion as found in the four Gospels.

Suppose, now, that we return to Uncle Phil's funeral sermon (a sermon also marked, as it seemed to Charles Raymond, by unconnectedness: its thoughts loosely arranged; its content apparently unrelated to the person whose death was being commemorated) and attempt, using insights drawn from the preceding discussion, to view it, however partially and inadequately, through a broader and more sympathetic cultural lens.

We can better understand now that if Charles Raymond felt alienated by the apparently jumbled content of Uncle Phil's sermon and the lack of temporal connection between the death of Sis Sally Green and the preaching of her funeral, Phil must have found the expectations of the dominant culture equally strange. Raymond had wanted Phil to work from a basic script, to structure his ideas in a methodical way, but as the slave preacher well knew, his address would be judged by different standards. His audience would be concerned not merely with the semantic content of his words but with the aesthetics of his performance, with his ability to fit metrically based and easily recalled expressions, whether spontaneously created or drawn from the scriptures or everyday black speech, into his own rhythmical style. Steeped in the traditions of an orally centered culture, Phil would have stored in his memory a vast repertoire of biblical texts and phrases awaiting artful use, expressions with which, in many cases, his audience was familiar, but which, imaginatively placed in new contexts, would provoke in his hearers the shock of recognition. Phil's sermon would be measured, therefore, not simply for the poetic fit of the expressions sampled (and mixed together), but for their connotative referencing, for the world of memories and associations those words had conjured, their effectiveness in bringing meanings from other contexts to a particular moment in his address. Under such circumstances, expressions such as "dat bressed Lamb dat died for Phil" and "de pearly gates ob shinin' gold" must have had powerful cumulative effects. In the context within which Uncle Phil operated, controlled linear organization, secured through the explication of a predetermined text, was far less important than were enthusiastic congregational involvement, imaginative sampling, and cumulative associational effects. To this funeral preacher's African American congregation, it was far less important than were the tonal cadences, speech rhythms, and impassioned invocations that fired the people's emotions and brought the Spirit of their God into their midst.

CHAPTER 8

Soundtracks of the City: Charleston, New York, and New Orleans

He had begun his first letter to the *South Carolina Gazette* in late August 1772 by pointing out that his initial impression of the province had been one of surprise "at the Number of *Black Faces* that everywhere presented themselves." Indeed, on his arrival in Charleston, the surprise of "the Stranger," as the anonymous author of an oft-cited series of letters would become known, had been "so greatly heightened" that, had he not, by his travels through other colonies, already acclimated himself in some way to the sight of blacks, he would have suspected that his guide "had conducted me to Africa, or *Lucifer's Court*." Even at this early date, the literary pose of the naive European shocked at the presence of black slaves in the American colonies was becoming a cliché: two years later, Patrick M'Robert, another traveler, would scribble in his diary the observation that "it rather hurts an Europian eye to see so many negro slaves upon the streets"—and M'Robert was describing not a southern city, but New York. What particularly struck the Stranger was the "great Difference in Appearance as well as Behavior, between *the Negroes* of the Country, and *those* in Charles-Town." The former were "generally clad suitable to their Condition, *contented, sober, modest, humble, civil,* and *obliging*"; indeed, "*their* whole Deportment" excited a degree of empathy. The latter, though, were "in all Respects, the very *Reverse*": Charleston blacks were "abandonedly *rude, unmannerly, insolent,* and *shameless,*" and, moreover, many of the city's female slaves were "far more *elegantly dressed*" than all but the city's white elite.[1] Hiding behind the Stranger's language was the suggestion that the sounds emanating from Charleston's slaves as they traversed the city's thoroughfares among whites were most decidedly not appropriate to their condition.

What the Stranger deplored, of course, was precisely what made Charleston and every other urban center in mainland North America immensely attractive to slaves. In these places, it seemed, the traditional restraints of the institution were loosened and many slaves achieved surprising degrees of autonomy. Some hired out their own time and lived away from their owners. In Savannah, just before the Revolution, 10 percent of the adult black population were said to "live by themselves & allow their master a certain sum p. week," and, as Philip Morgan has suggested, that figure was probably much higher in Charleston.[2] But even when they were not able to come to such an arrangement with their owners, the ease with which urban slaves were able to slip away for at least a few hours, and the allure of social contact with what whites probably regarded as the city's underbelly, must have seemed an enthralling prospect to many a slave laboring on a plantation. Urban slavery was different and that difference attracted slaves like a magnet. Frederick Douglass, who was a slave both on a Maryland plantation and in Baltimore, put the matter succinctly: "A city slave is almost a freeman, compared with a slave on the plantation." A few years later, on further reflection, he concluded that "slavery dislikes a dense population."[3] Douglass was writing about the nineteenth century, near slavery's end, but a litany of white complaint about the degree of latitude accorded to urban slaves clearly shows that right from the beginning of urban slavery in British mainland North America the authorities struggled to keep slaves orderly—and suitably deferential.

Charleston was a case in point. As early as 1712, when the city's population was scarce two thousand, legislation was passed to try to prevent slaves from loitering on Sundays and holidays in order to "drink, quarrel, fight, curse, and swear and profane the Sabbath... resorting in great companies together."[4] Two decades later on a November Sunday evening "nigh 200 Negroes met together on the Greene," a gathering that made the pages of the *South Carolina Gazette* because of the stabbing of a slave.[5] In 1744 the Charleston grand jury complained about "the great Insolence" of Charleston slaves, and in particular about their "Gaming in the Streets and caballing in great Numbers through most parts of the Town, especially on the Sabbath Day." The following year the jurors were concerned about the "pernicious Practice of the Negroes in Charlestown playing at dice and other Games," and at the "ill consequences" of allowing "great numbers" of blacks to assemble "at their burials and on the Sabbath Day."[6] Year after year the grand jury decried similar aspects of African American behavior, but on the eve of the Revolution little had changed, apart from the fact that the city's African American population had increased. In 1773 Josiah Quincy, a disapproving New Englander, was shocked by the "great numbers playing pawpaw, huzzle cap, pitch penny and quarrelling around the doors of the Churches in service time." The following year the grand jury felt compelled to conclude that the "Negroes in Charles-town are become so obscene in their language, so irregular and disorderly in their conduct, and so superfluous in their Numbers" that more legal sanctions were urgently needed to control their behavior.[7]

What was needed, however, was not new laws but the desire or interest on the part of the authorities to enforce the ones already on the books. It was, for example, illegal to sell alcohol to slaves, but as complaint after complaint in the presentments to the grand jury show, there were always one or two whites running "pernicious dramshops" who were quite willing to do so. In 1768 Edward Johnston kept a "disorderly house" in Elliot Street and retailed "spirituous liquors without a licence, and to Negroes." Similarly, William Manning sold liquor to blacks near St. Michael's church.[8] Laws designed to control slave behavior were openly flouted by whites who made "in a few years considerable fortunes." The owner of one runaway slave was in no doubt as to the cause of his human property's recalcitrant behavior: it was the result of "sundry persons paying him freight and the keeper of dram-shops selling him liquor." In 1769 Philopolis wrote to the *South Carolina Gazette* demanding a reduction in the number of dramshops as "it is at those places that they [slaves] meet and form schemes for defrauding their masters or others of money or goods to pay for the liquid fire they guzzle at them."[9] Inevitably there was an ebb and flow to the way the laws governing slaves were enforced: sporadic convulsions, often induced by panic about slave unrest, in which the letter of the law was rigidly upheld, would be followed, on the part of most whites, by a slackening and a willingness to turn a blind eye. Individual dramshops may have come and gone, but at most times in the city's history there were sly establishments in back alleys and the like where a few slaves could gather and buy alcohol.

The most flagrant examples of the type of unruly behavior that the Stranger bemoaned, however, were not to be found squirreled away in the city's nooks and crevices. Right in the very heart of Charleston, at the corner of Broad and Meeting Streets, stood the city's public market. If the mere presence of black faces in South Carolina suggested "Africa" to some travelers, then this site should have prompted more specific comparisons to the great West African markets at Cape Corse in Guinea or at Wydah in the kingdom of Dahomey. The Charleston market, as the Stranger noted in 1772 with some incredulity, was dominated by "a great number of loose, idle, disorderly negro women," constantly hovering and keeping their eye open for the main chance, who were allowed to "*buy* and *sell* on *their own accounts*, what they please." These slaves exploited their connections with "country negroes," who brought their and their owners' produce to the market, in order "to obtain whatever they may chuse, in preference to any white person." Thus market women were able to "*forestall* and *engross* many articles" that a few hours later they could resell at a hefty premium.[10] In much the same way as occurred in West Africa and the Caribbean, women monopolized the occupation of huckster. Occasionally, someone commented on the sheer number of such women. One day in early 1778, an observer "counted in the market and different corners of this town, sixty-four Negro wenches selling cakes, nuts, and so forth." Most comment, though, focused on the demeanor often displayed by these women as they boisterously hustled their supposed masters and mistresses. The Stranger, for one, had "known those black women to be so insolent, as even to wrest things out of the hands of white people," claiming that they were already bought and then reselling them an hour or two later for a handsome profit.[11]

But this was hardly new—whites had been complaining about slave behavior in the market for decades, in fact, ever since the slave ships had begun disgorging the large numbers of Africans who would transform South Carolina into the richest colony in mainland North America. According to the clerk of the market in 1741, slaves frequenting the venue evinced such an "insolent abusive Manner" that he was "afraid to say or do Anything in the Market"; indeed, he was left to be made "a Game of."[12] Only a few years later, several whites petitioned the assembly, complaining that some owners were giving their slaves "all imaginable liberty, not only to buy and sell those commodities, but also . . . to forestall the markets of Charles Town." As long as slaves paid their owners the agreed-upon sum, irresponsible whites "seldom or never enquire how they came by the same." Consequently, some slaves used quite large sums of money to purchase foodstuffs, which they then resold to the city's inhabitants. These slaves, then, were essentially "free from the government of their masters."[13] In 1763 the city's market commissioners bemoaned the fact that "Negroes and other slaves . . . have of late raised the price of almost every necessity of life beyond anything hitherfor to known."[14] Less than a decade later, with slaves still behaving in much the same manner at the markets, the Stranger, exasperated to the point of italics, expostulated to his Charleston audience that "*they* are *your slaves*, who fix the exorbitant prices."[15]

In short, then, Charleston's slaves, whether milling around the church on the Sabbath, frequenting dramshops, or hustling on the streets or in the markets, were noted for behaving in an unruly and not infrequently an insolent manner. What is almost completely missing from the litany of white complaint about slave behavior, however, is any sense that slaves were particularly noisy, although, of course, we might expect that they were. It is always difficult to sound convincing when arguing for an absence, a silence if you will, in the historical record, but we would suggest that, in eighteenth-century Charleston, whites were paying very little attention to the sounds of the city's slaves. Partly, the explanation appears to be that the slaves deliberately muted the amount of noise they made. Indeed, for all the complaints about the demeanor of Charleston blacks, there was still something deferential about their behavior. What appears to have been the case is that, for the eighteenth century and at least the early years of the nineteenth, rather than slaves from the surrounding countryside slipping away into Charleston in order to attend dances, denizens of the city spread out into the hinterland to mingle with those who toiled on the plantations. On a Saturday night in the summer of 1772, the

Stranger closely observed a "Country-Dance, Rout, or Cabal of Negroes" that occurred about five miles outside Charleston. About sixty blacks, fifty from the city, bringing with them all manner of luxurious foods and bottled liquor, joined in the entertainment, which began with "the men copying (or *taking off*) the manners of their masters, and the women those of their mistresses." Later the motley crew *"danced, betted, gamed, swore, quarrelled*, [and] *fought"* until well into the night. The Stranger had also learned that "such assemblies *have been* very common" and that as many as two hundred slaves had attended some of these dances that were barely a mile out of town.[16] For all of this observer's innuendo and mutterings about secret councils that also took place at these gatherings (and doubtless some did), what now seems remarkable is that when Charleston slaves felt the urge to raise hell they went and did it out of the earshot of whites. Three decades later they were still behaving in much the same fashion. Early one Sunday morning in 1804, a visitor to Beale's Wharf in Charleston was "astonished to see about forty negroes, men and women, arrive in one boat from Sullivan's Island." Curious, he inquired as to what they had been doing, and learned that "they had been dancing and carousing from Saturday night, until near sunrise the next morning, to the number, [he] was informed, of about one hundred."[17] By the 1850s urban slaves and free blacks would be rather less shy about making a din, indeed would often be deliberately noisy, and in American cities, certainly from a white perspective, things would seem very much louder.

But clearly white Charlestonians' apparent indifference to the sounds of black life cannot be accounted for merely by the evident desire of eighteenth-century slaves to hold their entertainments beyond the earshot of whites. Almost everything Charleston slaves did that whites complained about involved the making of noise, yet such noise, in and of itself, was not the focus of white censure. What marked out Charleston slaves, according to the Stranger, was their aggressive demeanor. These slaves were accustomed to the ways of white folks, or highly acculturated, and arguably their most prized possession was their voice—and those voices could be heard all over town arguing with or hustling whites in the market and street as they attempted to sell goods or their labor. In a similar fashion, tumults, riots, and drinking in dramshops are not usually carried out quietly. Whites complained endlessly about this kind of behavior, indeed often felt threatened by it, but not on the grounds of its noisiness. It is as though white Charlestonians were simply not attuned to the sonic frequency on which their human property was operating. At times, it almost seems as if they were wandering around their city wearing the eighteenth-century equivalent of earplugs. Perhaps what was happening was not that they were deaf to what was going on; it was more a case of noise being an accepted part of everyday life, something barely worthy of comment.

What was true of Charleston was also the case elsewhere. In Savannah, Georgia, during the Revolution and the quarter of a century following it, the authorities complained of slave behavior but paid little attention to the sounds slaves made. In 1776, just as the fighting was about to start, Archibald Bulloch, governor of Georgia, felt the need "to conciliate the divine favour and protection," an urge that required "taking proper notice [of] the tumultuous meetings of Negro Slaves, in and about the Town of Savannah, & their practice of buying & selling [on] the Lord's Day." Three decades later, the Savannah grand jury was still complaining about the "Assemblages of Drunken & riotous negroes" that took place on most Sundays. Similarly, in 1808, the grand jury suggested that, while the "higher orders of Society" passed time on Sundays, "in our Churches [being] taught to reverence God," the less refined were "crying Small wares about our Streets." Indeed, according to the jurors, the "Market is filled with Boys and Negroes engaged in different kinds of games, forgetful alike of the laws of God and of their Country."[18] Here again were the complaints about slave riotousness, drunkenness, and general unruliness, but with barely any reference to the sounds that undoubtedly accompanied such behavior.

This silence in the sources about slave noise eerily echoes the more general silence about eighteenth-century slave music. For all of our intentions in this book to include the colonial period—and we have done so whenever possible—material is almost impossible to come by. Others, too, have ruminated about this puzzling omission.[19] Most recently, Ronald Radano has commented that there is an uncanny "sense of quiet about eighteenth-century slave music, given the likelihood that its qualities and character would have been so discernible, so palpable, so loud." The most extensive and expansive source for examining slavery in colonial Virginia is the surviving volumes of Landon Carter's diary, a document that is hundreds of manuscript pages in length and describes in detail all manner of aspects of slave life. But as Rhys Isaac has noted in his recent brilliant study of the moody and idiosyncratic Virginian and his world, in not one entry does Carter mention the singing of his slaves.[20] It would not be until the New Nation had been established for some years that white writers, both American and foreigners, would pay close attention to the music, indeed the whole panoply of sounds made by slaves. Certainly by the middle decades of the nineteenth century, noise, particularly that made by urban blacks, seemed to contemporaries to have become more noticeable and more discordant.

In the colonial period, slaves in northern cities seemed as quiet as did those in Charleston, even quieter given that there were far fewer of them, but in the years after the Revolution there were, for the first time, substantial numbers of free blacks living in towns and cities, with the result that things would never again sound the same. The changed tenor of life was palpable enough in some of the smaller urban centers. A citizen of Newark began her complaint to the local newspaper, the *Centinel of Freedom*, in May 1798, by stating that "I am a widow and have no husband to protect me." She and her small children lived in town and she had "had no sleep for several nights" because of "noise in the streets." The cause of her troubles was Newark's black population: indeed, several times she had suddenly "lift[ed] up my windows" and "surprised negroes peeping around the house." A decade later, what the whites saw as similar problems were still besetting the town. In late September 1809 a notice in the *Centinel of Freedom* announced a public meeting to consider measures "to suppress the riotous and disorderly meetings of the Negroes in our streets at night." These constant disturbances had "grown to a very great pitch—and call loudly for the vigorous application of the law."[21] Here, even the language used to outline the problem of black behavior was infused with an awareness of sound.

But of course the changes were most obvious in large centers such as New York. It was not just the fact that from the 1790s onward there were, for the first time, a significant number of free blacks living in New York, but also the way in which these former slaves had attained their freedom that made a turning up of the volume in the city's public spaces such an attractive proposition. Early in 1809, Amos Broad, an upholsterer by trade and a well-known evangelist who had established his own church, and his wife, a milliner, were sent to trial for brutally "assaulting and beating" Betty, their slave, and her daughter Sarah. During the course of their well-publicized trial the Broads "voluntarily" manumitted Betty, Sarah, and one other slave whom they owned, a tactic whose feigned magnanimity impressed neither jury nor judge. Both husband and wife were found guilty: Amos Broad was fined $1,000 and sentenced to 120 days in the city prison; his wife was fined $250. This case, notorious at the time, has remained a staple adduced by historians writing on blacks in New York: its sequel, however, is less well known. According to the compiler of the pamphlet version of the Broads' trial, the court's punishment of Broad gave "the most universal satisfaction." But as it turned out, this was not so: far from being grateful for the outcome, Betty believed that, considering what Broad had done to her daughter and herself, he had escaped far too lightly. She began noisily to harass the evangelist at his church in Rose Street, creating, as often as not, an unwanted, raucous antiphony. On one occasion when Broad was preaching to "a considerable number" who were "quietly sitting and listening," Betty burst into the church, started talking, and "interrupted them in their worship." On another, she came in and "walked about the church" all the while talking "loudly." She also, according to Broad, arranged for some of her friends to throw stones and "other substances," most likely horse shit scraped up from the street, through the church windows during worship. Eventually, the evangelist was forced to resort to the law and have Betty indicted for rioting in church, a charge that, ironically, was most commonly used against white rowdies who disrupted African American religious services.[22]

The details of Betty's story were unusual, but in many ways the case was emblematic of the ways slaves entered freedom. In its concern for property rights, the New York State legislature was as grudging as Amos Broad had been in his "voluntary" manumission of Betty. In

1799 the legislature had passed a bill ending slavery, but the measure was a compromise. On the one hand, it was now clear that slavery was going to end, but on the other, the legislature had ensured that abolition would occur at a pace that could only be described as glacial. Under the terms of the act, all children born to slave women after July 4, 1799, were to be free, but males were to remain in a form of indentured servitude until they reached the age of twenty-eight, and females were to be so bound until they were twenty-five. Those who were still slaves on July 4, 1799, were abandoned to their fate; not until 1817 would the legislature finally agree to free such persons and even then that was not to occur for another decade, until July 4, 1827. In the event, many slaves took things into their own hands and negotiated individually with their masters. Implicit in every negotiation was the threat that if some arrangement were not agreed upon—usually some combination of money and a period of "faithful service"—the owner would be left with either a sullen, refractory slave or, if his or her property ran away, nothing at all. To a large extent, then, the details of slavery's demise in and around New York City were worked out on an individual basis and it was only through their own efforts that New York slaves advanced the legislature's lackadaisical timetable.[23]

It was a grudging process, and while few former slaves were quite as aggressive as Betty had been in her loud shaming of her former owner, there was, on the part of African New Yorkers, a widespread and noisy indifference to white sensibilities. The early decades of the nineteenth century were the liminal years of slavery's gradual withering and of slaves' final freedom, and black life in these awkward transitional decades possessed a distinct edge, a particular kind of restless vitality. Not only did recently liberated slaves incorporate exuberant signs of their freedom into the performances of everyday life, but prompted by their memories of slavery, they also brought with them an impatient aggressiveness that decisively influenced the black culture forged in these years on the streets of the metropolis.

In the early decades of the nineteenth century, white New Yorkers' concern over the presence and behavior of blacks in the city seemed wildly out of proportion to their numbers. According to city censuses, the percentage of African Americans in the population in the early decades of the nineteenth century was not only low but was even diminishing; in the 1800s and 1810s the figure was about 10 percent, in the 1820s and 1830s, as the city's total size soared to over two hundred thousand people, the black share hovered around 7 percent. The most important explanation for the disparity between white perceptions and the actual demographic reality was blacks' visibility and audibility: most African New Yorkers were forced to live not only a public but also a very noisy existence.

For many blacks, the street became the place of employment. Here they helped feed the city's white inhabitants, cleared the snow from their paths, and cleaned up after them. Much of the work done by blacks was of a casual nature (typically unskilled manual labor), so that besides working on the streets, blacks often spent a lot of time on the streets seeking employment, often to the inconvenience of whites. Black men jostled and crowded around as the steamboats docked near the Battery, importuning passengers to hire them to carry bags, undercutting the licensed porters; in winter, sawyers, most of whom were black, hustled for custom on the street and then occupied the sidewalks to cut the wood.[24]

Black petty entrepreneurs of all sorts were also an obvious and irritating presence. Among a whole list of complaints arising from a walk he took in the Bancker Street area in 1820, "Humanitas" drew attention to the "oyster stands and numerous tables of eatables" that rendered passage along the sidewalks all but impossible. But most visible, and audible, were the street peddlers, those "smutty vendors who," as one querulous white observed, "roll out the long words—Cha-a-a-r-r Co-a-a-le...in varying tones upon each syllable as long as an Anaconda." From early in the morning until late at night—far too late by many accounts—their distinctive cries could be heard all over the city. Hollers such as "he-e-e-e-e-er's your fine Rocka-a-way clams" and, most famously, in the autumn months, the ubiquitous "h-a-u-t corn," "h-a-urt ca-irr-ne," became a recurring and often disconcerting part of the city's soundscape.[25] It was the distinctiveness of the African American criers that made it clear that, even if a book such as *The Cries of New York* (1809) was inspired by a centuries-old English genre, its content was undoubtedly drawn from an American city.[26]

In the latter part of 1824, Samuel Jenks worked for several months as a newspaper editor in New York. Originally from Nantucket, he was, judging by the entries in his diary, particularly sensitive to the barrage of sound that constantly assailed his ears as he traversed the metropolis. At four o'clock on an August morning he was awoken by "incomprehensible and barbarous outcries" coming from the street below. On peering out of his window he discovered that the noise came from four blacks "armed with besoms" (brooms made of twigs) and "iron instruments resembling a short hoe." The adult, "wrapped in an immense mahogany-coloured shawl," was urging on three children, garbed in "ragged cloaks of the same hue": "Come, wy de debble don't you hollar?"—"Yes, missee—Ek ho! Yaw, ak hikko yek! E oh! Yekko kik aw!" "The long character in the shawl," Jenks observed, "was a strapping, she-negro chimney sweep; and the smaller imps were her apprentices, thus compelled to proclaim their vocation in accents more dismal and appalling than those of Orpheus."27

Late at night, too, an army of blacks, the tubmen, swarmed over the city. The job of emptying the privies, which is to say, carrying the tubs down to the nearest dock and dumping the contents into the Hudson or the East rivers, was virtually a black monopoly. Not only was the work hard, unpleasant, poorly paid, and nocturnal, but whites constantly complained about the way in which it was done. In 1817 twenty-two inhabitants of the First Ward petitioned the city in an attempt to curb the "detestable cries" of the "vagabond negroes" vying for this business. Nor was excessive noise the whites' only complaint. As soon as they earned some money, the black sanitary workers bought rum, presumably to try and anesthetize themselves, and a few hours later were in such "a state of intoxication" that invariably tubs were dropped in the streets, accidents that, for hours the next morning, left pungent reminders of the workers' passage. Mostly, though, it was the din they made that irritated. Black tubmen usually worked in pairs, an arrangement that resulted in raucous duets cutting through the night air, and any request for quiet was greeted with "a torrent of clamarous abuse." Indeed, it was not just their "savage yells" that offended, but their "habit of bawling out such expressions as are most shockingly indecent." A person standing in Franklin Square could "often hear a dozen or twenty of them at once."28

Any unoccupied space in the city, but particularly the sidewalk, became a potential site at which African New Yorkers could spend their hours away from work; miserable housing conditions hardly induced them to stay unnecessarily inside. The years in which African New Yorkers finally gained their freedom were also those during which the sociability of the street, activities associated with what would later be called the "stroll," became established as a key element in an emerging and distinctive northern urban black culture. As the *National Advocate* noted in August 1821, "their modicum of pleasure was taken on Sunday evening, when black dandys and dandizettes, after attending meeting, occupied the sidewalks in Broadway, and slowly lounged towards their different homes." In May 1815 there were bitter complaints about black women on the streets using "obscene and infamous language," particularly "profane oaths and vulgar epithets," and the aggressive way they conducted themselves, "crowding and jostling" white citizens. A little more than a decade later the *New York Evening Post* reported a minor incident in which a stout black man "was lately heard to exclaim, in a peevish tone, as he elbowed a lady out of the way, *'Damn these white people, there's no getting along for them.'"*[29] Everywhere about white New Yorkers were signs that the older deference had crumbled under the sheer weight of black volubility, and that the world had truly been turned upside down.

And what nagged at white New Yorkers was their awareness that free blacks were behaving in this fashion deliberately. This was particularly clear in the numerous African New Yorker parades, usually held contrary to the advice of generally well-meaning whites, that crisscrossed the city in the early decades of the nineteenth century. Not all black parades met with white disapproval. When, in March 1827, the *New-York Enquirer*'s editor accidentally happened upon a parade of black masons on one of the streets branching off Broadway, he was pleasantly surprised. Not only had these marchers "conducted themselves with propriety, obedience and intelligence," but most importantly they were also "well dressed, silent and decorous."[30] But there of course lay the problem. Not many African New Yorkers were much interested in marching silently along a backstreet. Most of the parades they organized would be loud and lengthy affairs—the annual parades celebrating the end of slavery took at least three or four hours—

traversing all the major and many of the minor streets of the city. Bands usually accompanied the marchers; in the case of the first parade to celebrate the end of New York slavery in 1827, there were, according to the *New York American*, as many as "four or five bands, comprising a great variety of instruments, played with much skill." The African American doctor James McCune Smith remembered that march vividly. "That was a celebration!" he wrote, "A real, full-souled, full-voiced shouting for joy, and marching through the crowded streets, with feet jubilant to songs of freedom!"[31] Anyone out and about on the city streets would have to have been stone deaf and blind to have missed these proud African New Yorkers celebrating their freedom.

In the years before emancipation began in earnest, New York slaves had been an accepted part of city life, attracting for the most part surprisingly little comment. Once freed, however, and with numbers swollen by fugitives and migrants, the city's blacks were marked off as a separate group and increasingly demonized. This process was often expressed in terms of blacks' bodies, African Americans being an affront not merely to whites' eyes, but to almost the full range of senses. If the look of "dandified" blacks strolling on Broadway caused offense, so too did the touch of the black body that shouldered whites from the sidewalk, the "savage" sounds of black street cries, and somewhat less frequently, the smell that black bodies were believed to emit. In June 1823 one letter writer, protesting bitterly to the *National Advocate* about black behavior on the streets, concluded by pointing out that "they are so rude, and talk so loud, and smell so bad, what are we to do —to whom shall we apply, Mr. Editor, to keep them more orderly?"[32] In large part, such unhappiness was caused by the deliberate actions of free blacks who declined any longer to remain quiet and unobtrusive. Whites were also developing new ways of perceiving the city's black inhabitants, but it was the assaults on their sense of hearing that seemed to bother them the most. Many whites considered the noise of everyday black urban life as an intimation of the chaos and lack of control that they saw as the almost inevitable accompaniment to the ending of slavery.

They were certainly right in thinking that things were completely different from the way they had been under slavery. Slaves in eighteenth-century Charleston may have left the city limits to hold their dances, but the newly liberated African New Yorkers in the 1820s and 1830s were doing no such thing. Newly freed blacks by the hundreds attended formal balls and danced cotillions and waltzes until dawn, but the most frequent dancing occurred in the underground dance cellars that sprang up all over town in the years of slavery's slow demise in New York. These black spaces were usually cramped, crowded, smoky, and hot, especially in summer, with the result that patrons often spilled over loudly into the street; inevitably we mostly hear about these places from the records of police intervention in the wake of white complaints. On a Tuesday night in December 1834, the police heard that a dance was planned in what was known as "Ogilvie's buildings." Early in the evening, police entered the premises, broke up the dance, and "civilly" told the blacks to go home. As soon as the officials left, however, everyone poured back into Ogilvie's, restarted the music, and "soon made the house shake, the welkin to ring, and night to be terrible with their revelry and noise." About one o'clock in the morning, a group of police officers along with some of the watch descended on the black revelers and caused a "wild affright": "The fiddle and the tambarine were soon hushed," and twenty-six African New Yorkers were carted off to the watch-house.[33] Far from trying to slip off and do things away from the prying eyes and keen ears of whites, these blacks ignored a gentle police warning and continued to raise hell right in the middle of the city.

And then there was the music itself. In the early decades of the nineteenth century, black musicians and dancers in the urban crucibles of New York and Philadelphia, and to a lesser extent Boston and some of the smaller northern cities, took from what they found around them and created something that was new. The result was a dynamic, unruly music and dance form constantly developing and responding innovatively to the changing environment. George Foster, a journalist, visited one of the better-known of New York's dance cellars on a Saturday night in the late 1840s. The three-piece band was playing the familiar enough instruments of the fiddle, the bass drum, and trumpet, but Foster believed his readers would have little chance of even beginning to conceive of how the music sounded:

> You cannot see the red-hot knitting-needles spirted out by the red-faced trumpeter, who looks precisely as if he were blowing glass, which needles aforesaid penetrating the tympanum, pierce through and through your brain without remorse. Nor can you perceive the frightful mechanical contortions of the bass-drummer as he sweats and deals his blows on every side, in all violation of the laws of rhythm, like a man beating a baulky mule and showering his blows upon the unfortunate animal, now on this side, now on that.[34]

This was the relentless beat to which black New York moved, and its echoes can be heard in American culture down to today.

It was not only African American music that permeated every corner of the city. To quite an extraordinary extent, and this was a complete reversal of what had happened under slavery, black voices decisively influenced the way in which the city was rendered. Newspaper stories about the parade of humanity at the police office, about court cases, or even just about the goings on in the city, were filled with accounts of blacks speaking, often including verbatim lines of dialogue.[35] In late 1832 Dennis Brink, a police marshal, was doing his nightly rounds along Anthony Street, near the notorious Five Points. Near number 52, a house occupied by three black families, his attention was "arrested" by two black women in the backyard who were loudly arguing about a gold ring. Brink intervened and one of the women fled through a doorway. On trying to pursue her, Brink was confronted by another black woman and "warm words ensued." The hullabaloo quickly attracted a crowd including a Mrs. Stivers, a white woman married to the owner of the premises, and she, on attempting to sort things out, was roundly abused by Brink with "some harsh and indelicate epithets" and "a warm strife of words was the consequence." Stivers brought suit for damages. Brink's defense was that he was endeavoring to enforce the law by preventing "noise and disorder," and that the scene was so dark that he had thought Stivers was a mulatto. Some aspects of this case were slightly unusual—Stivers was awarded $25 damages against the police marshal—but the details of the way in which loud and strident voices of black women traveled over city back fences certainly had a broader application.[36] In the 1830s, papers such as the *Transcript* and the *Sun* filled column inches with what their reporters and sources had overhead about town, detailing black urban life in all its noisy garrulousness.

Freedom had changed everything in New York. Slaves had always had a pretty good idea of what being free would be like—and, doubtless, some African New Yorkers could almost taste its sweetness as the last months and days of their negotiated terms of "faithful service" dragged by—but most whites were totally unprepared for what would happen once the city's blacks were no longer slaves. It was not, after all, as though white New Yorkers had before them many examples of slave-owning societies that had successfully ended the institution. Most whites probably unthinkingly assumed that things would go on much as before, or just hoped that blacks would quietly go away. They were completely mistaken. With the ending of slavery, African New Yorkers became a loud and unavoidable presence, noisily enacting on the city's streets and public spaces their own version of what freedom meant.

Cyrot Gentes, an inhabitant of New Orleans, would doubtless have sympathized with some of the bemused white New Yorkers. In July 1858, he appeared before Recorder Long to make what the *Daily Picayune* in the "Police Matters" column labeled "a sad complaint" against William Hubert, a free man of color and a neighbor. According to the irritated, indeed almost despairing, litigant, Hubert lived "with the most opstreperous negro girl, who has a gang of the most abandoned negro children, who, with their mother, continually insult deponent and knock at his door and windows, in order to disturb him, breaking panes of glass." By Gentes's reckoning, they were "maliciously making such a noise that deponent cannot neither read, write, nor take some rest when sick." Although "the rules of society, the laws of the State, and ordinances of the city so guaranty him peace and quietness," his black neighbors were making his life a misery, rendering his house "uninhabitable." Gentes went on to inform the recorder that "these free niggers are the most terrible plague which may desolate society" and "that an abandoned free negro, with his mother, shall make more disturbance than 1000 little negro slaves" who were "properly managed" by their owners. He concluded, according to the newspaper's police reporter, by giving a long list of occasions on which he had "suffered at the hands, tongues and other unruly members of his aforementioned colored neighbors."37

New Orleans did in fact have legislation specifically designed to mute black noise. A somewhat taken aback Henry Fearon, an English traveler who visited the city in 1817, even thought it worth recording in his published narrative that a municipal ordinance decreed that any slave found "guilty of whooping or hallooing any where in the city or suburbs, or of making any clamorous noise, or of singing aloud any indecent song" would receive twenty lashes. But such legislation revealed more about official intent, even wishful thinking, than the way the city sounded.38 For most of the antebellum years, New Orleans had the largest black population of any city in the United States. According to the 1830 census there were, among its inhabitants, 26,038 blacks, constituting about 56 percent of the population, living there, and slightly less than one in three of those blacks was a slave.39 And as everyone who lived in the city must have been aware, New Orleans was saturated with the sounds of African Americans going about their daily lives.

Black noise may have been most obvious in and around Congo Square, where, as we have seen, the percussive throb of drums, clapped hands, and dancing feet stamping into the dirt often seemed to invade whites' aural space, but it was also apparent, if often less spectacularly, on every one of the city's streets. While wandering home to his lodgings in New Orleans, early in the evening of May 4, 1819, Benjamin Latrobe, the famous architect, happened upon some two hundred African Americans taking part in the funeral procession of a very old Congo-born woman. Curious, and with time on his hands, the Frenchman tagged along to the cemetery and secured a vantage spot very close to the grave. The chanting, the prayers, and even the "very loud lamentations" of the "great croud of women press[ing] close to the grave" were all familiar enough rituals to Latrobe, even if they were performed differently. They were the sort of sounds to be expected on an occasion such as this. But what followed soon after was completely alien to the visitor's experiences. The deceased's grandsons and great-grandsons picked up bones and even skulls lying around the graveyard and pelted them at the simple casket, making "a loud report on the hollow Coffin." By the time the service was completed the "noise and laughter was general" among the mourners. For Latrobe, the funeral had degenerated from tragedy into "a sort of farce." But the raucous sounds that so shocked him meant something very different to the black participants. What had horrified the traveler was in fact a ritual moment now known as "cutting the body loose," a process which, as Joseph Roach has pointed out, "joyously affirm[ed] the continuity of community" and triggered a "wave of lively music and motion."[40] As far as the blacks who attended the burying were concerned, it was perfectly appropriate to bury the African-born matriarch in this way.

Black funeral processions often crisscrossed southern cities, particularly on Sundays. Most were probably not as raucous or as alien as the one Latrobe observed, but they were still markers of the extent to which African American lives and deaths shaped the urban soundscape. In September 1835 a citizen complained to the *Charleston Patriot* that, several times a week, "there are Funerals of Negroes, accompanied by processions of 3, 4, and 5 hundred Negroes and a tumultuous crowd of other slaves who disturb all the inhabitants around the burying Ground."[41] Some two decades later, as he was traveling through the South, Frederick Olmstead stumbled across a black funeral in Richmond and followed a few dozen blacks out of town to the cemetery. Once there he was disconcerted by the singing of a "wild kind of chant" and by the "ludicrous language" of the man who led the service. For all his disdain, however, Olmstead admitted to having been moved by what he saw and heard.[42] In Savannah in late 1856, the Reverend Andrew Marshall, a colored minister over a hundred years old, was buried with considerable ceremony. Not only had his body been sent down from Richmond, but a huge gathering of blacks and whites turned out for the funeral. Hundreds, unable to fit into the church, spilled over into the grounds outside. After the service, the procession, led by deacons and the members of various societies, and followed by some fifty carriages and a "multitude of pedestrians," made its way through town to the cemetery. According to a press report it was a "most solemn and imposing spectacle," a form of wording suggesting that this particular, and probably fairly unusual funeral procession, was characterized by restraint and quiet.[43]

In the antebellum years more and more African Americans converted to Christianity, but their memories of Africa changed and embellished the way their religion was practiced. To an extraordinary degree those embellishments, be they banging on a coffin or adapting a white hymn, were in the sonic realm. Some whites loved watching and particularly hearing the way blacks had transformed religious services; others, particularly if they lived close to churches where blacks worshipped, were rather less enamored of African American religious enthusiasm. In 1840 in Mobile, for example, seventy-four citizens petitioned the city council regarding the behavior of black worshippers. "From a very early hour in the morning until after dark," they complained, "those residing in the neighborhood of the meeting house are annoyed and disturbed by the noise and outcries of the assembled negroes—so that it has become a perfect nuisance."44

If funeral processions or the sounds of Sunday worship provided the occasional crescendo of black noise, it was the black street hawkers and petty entrepreneurs who supplied the constant hum that was a backdrop to street life in New Orleans and every other southern city, and indeed to many northern cities as well. According to a writer in the *New Orleans Bee* in 1835, "almost the whole of the purchasing and selling of edible articles for domestic consumption [is] transacted by colored persons."45 From dawn until often well past dusk, free blacks and slaves traipsed the streets calling out chants that advertised watermelon, strawberries, charcoal, coffee, and all manner of other foods and pastries. What gave New Orleans cries their distinctive flavor was that, because of the city's past, they were often infused with French words and phrases. Vendors of cala, a thin fritter made with rice and yeast sponge created by African Americans, called out:

Belles calas,	Beautiful rice fritters,
Madame, mo gaignin calas	Madame, I have rice fritters,
Madame, mo gaignin calas	Madame, I have rice fritters,
Madame, mo gaignin calas	Madame, I have rice fritters,
Mo guaranti vous ye bons	I guarantee you they are good
Beeelles calas . . . Beeelles calas.	Fine rice fritters . . . fine rice fritters.

Not only were such cries accepted as part of New Orleans' life, but it was also the case that many whites, both locals and travelers, developed a real affection for their plaintive sounds. When the Louisiana Writers' Project came to publish a selection of the folklore they had collected in *Gumbo Ya-Ya* (1945), predictably the first chapter was devoted to Mardi Gras, essentially a postbellum creation, but the second was entitled "Street Criers."[46]

Probably the best known of these street vendors was Old Corn Meal, an aged black man who took his name from what he sold. According to a young Englishman, Francis C. Sheridan, who visited New Orleans in 1840, Old Corn Meal rode the city streets "in an old cart drawn by an older horse, & pulling up in front of the Exchanges—generally a little before dinner time when the rooms began to fill, he commences his performances." His popularity was such that in 1837 he was enticed onto the stage, along with his horse and cart, to sing his cornmeal song in "Life in New Orleans." It was supposed to be a one-off event, but Old Corn Meal "met with such a warm reception" that an encore performance was arranged the following week, during which his horse unfortunately fell onstage and was killed. Again, on at least two occasions in 1840 he performed at the Camp Street Theater in what was billed as the "eccentricities of the original Corn Meal." According to Sheridan, this black street performer sang "in a manner as perfectly novel as it is inimitable, beginning in a deep bass & at every other 3 or 4 words of his song, jumping into a falsetto of power." The Englishman likened it to "one of our street duets" where a man and a boy sang alternately, but as he readily admitted, Old Corn Meal's songs were much livelier and, of course, he sang the duet by himself. When Corn Meal died in May 1842, the *Bee* noted his passing: "Never again shall we listen to his double toned voice," his obituarist wrote, "never again shall his corn meal melodies, now grumbled in a bass—now squeaked in a treble, vibrate on the ear."[47]

The greatest concentration of vendors was found at the marché, or market. "Our butchers are negroes; our fishmongers negroes, our vendors of vegetables, fruits and flowers are all negroes," the writer for the *Bee* exclaimed in 1835, and "the only purchasers that frequent the market are negroes; and generally slaves."[48] He exaggerated, of course; local whites did go there and so did tourists. Only a few months previously, Joseph Ingraham, a self-confessed Yankee, sojourning in the

South and considerably taken with the huge varieties of physiognomies on display in New Orleans, recommended an early morning visit to the market house where blacks "in all their variety and shades of colouring...may be seen and *heard*." Indeed, he continued, "If a painting could affect the sense of hearing as well as that of sight, this market multitude would afford the artist an inimitable original for the representation upon his canvass of the 'confusion of tongues.'"

What is fascinating in Ingraham's account of New Orleans is that it was centered around the black sounds of the city. On his early morning sightseeing trip to the market he could not help but notice the "Black women, with huge baskets of rusks, rolls and other appurtenances of the breakfast table,...crying, in loud shrill French, their 'stock in trade,' followed by milk-criers, and butter-criers and criers of everything but tears." Not only were these black peddlers loud, but "they all seemed as merry as the morning, saluting each other gayly as they met, 'Bo'shoo Mumdsal'—'Moshoo! adieu,' &c. &c, and shooting their rude shafts of African wit at each other with much vivacity and humor." When he arrived at the marché, he had to walk "through a dense mass of negroes, mulattoes and non-descripts of every shade, from 'sunny hue to sooty,' all balancing their baskets skilfully upon their heads, [and] my ears were assailed with sounds stranger and more complicated than I ever imagined could be rung upon that marvellous instrument the human tongue." In the half hour Ingraham spent wandering around the market, he estimated that there was only one white for every fifty blacks, but he was impressed by more than just the volume of black sound that he had heard. "The 'lange des halles'—the true 'Billingsgate' was not only here perfected but improved upon; the gods and godesses of the London mart might even take lessons from these daughters of Afric, who, enthroned upon a keg, or three-legged stool, each morning hold their *leveé*, and dispense their esculent blessings to the famishing citizens."49

From at least the time that the Stranger first set foot in Charleston, some observers, and later on some historians, have seen in the way urban slaves comported themselves, signs that, in the cities at least, the peculiar institution was collapsing in on itself. This perception was certainly understandable—slavery in American urban centers was about as different from slavery on a big cotton or sugar plantation as it was possible to be—but it underestimates the flexibility and adaptability of the institution. The scion of the De Boré family, who owned a huge sugar plantation on the outskirts of New Orleans, sent some of his slaves, particularly the older, less useful ones, out onto the city streets every day to peddle his surplus foodstuffs, a practice that was said to have "produced at least six thousand dollars per annum."[50] Far from being under the close supervision of their owners, these blacks, and others like them, as long as they turned over the requisite amount of cash each evening, had a considerable amount of control over what they did during their workday and undoubtedly had the opportunity to do at least a little trading on their own account. For all that, though, they still returned their owners a very good profit and, at the end of the day, they were still slaves, the property of someone else.

And yet regardless of the institution's flexibility, by mid-century if not earlier, there clearly was considerable strain in the cities in relations between black and white. With the benefit of hindsight, it is almost impossible not to hear the clamor of urban black life in slavery's last years as a tocsin, warning whites of the changes to come after the institution was abolished. Although the black experience under slavery was predominantly rural and southern, much of the African American story in the twentieth century would be located in urban settings, not only in places such as Charleston and New Orleans, but also in Chicago's South Side and Harlem, where, as Richard Wright so memorably put it, "the noise of our living, boxed in stone and steel, is so loud that even a pistol shot is smothered."[51] But in the 1850s of course that was not yet known. In the final chapter of this book we shall examine the sounds of black living in one city, Richmond, a locale picked almost at random, in slavery's final years.

CHAPTER 9

Soundtracks of the City: Richmond in the 1850s

At about eight o'clock on a Monday evening in early November 1852, an informant brought word of a black subscription ball to the somewhat improbably named Officer Trueheart of the Richmond police. It was not as though the occasion was a clandestine affair. Far from quietly slipping off to Sullivan's Island or some such destination well outside the built-up area, as Charleston blacks had earlier done, the organizers of the Richmond dance had rented out the cellar, basement, and dining hall of the Washington Hotel, right in the heart of the city. Acting quickly, Trueheart secured a warrant from the mayor, rounded up a "posse of watchmen," and headed across to the hotel. According to the *Daily Dispatch*, a "supper had been prepared for the company, and dancing was about to commence" when the authorities descended on the establishment, causing a "tremendous stampede of the negro aristocracy." A few dozen of those present escaped, but some ninety blacks, forty-seven men and forty-three women, all "adorned in full ballroom dress," were arrested. The newspaper writer was unable to resist livening up his account with the sort of humor that inevitably accompanied such a story: he wrote of the "ebony sprigs of youth and beauty" spending the night in the "cage" and then, the following morning, being "marched in mournful procession, amid a large concourse of grinning, sympathizing friends to the Mayor's Court." Outside the court, nearby streets were unlawfully blocked by parents and relatives who "wore very *dark* and rueful countenances." Inside, it was even more crowded, as irritated owners and hirers of the slaves, come to fetch their human property, filled the courtroom to overflowing. All but three of the police's haul of African Americans were slaves: the fact that the next issue of the *Dispatch* printed both the names of the slaves and their owners probably did little to improve anyone's temper. It turned out that only one slave, an "unfortunate ebo" named Robert Harris, as the newspaper had it, did not have a pass from his master or mistress to go to the ball. The luckless Harris's back "was mulcted in damages to the amount of 10 lashes"; the rest of the blacks were discharged. According to the *Dispatch*, the proprietors of the Washington Hotel had made themselves liable for a fine of one dollar for each slave at the dance.[1]

If the *Dispatch*'s reporter treated the whole affair with a certain amount of levity, another writer for the newspaper a few days later took a less sanguine view. Moving the arrested blacks to court had prompted "thousands of idle slaves" to pour out onto the streets, to everyone's inconvenience. Not only had these slaves been "permitted to leave their homes at a busy hour in the morning," but hundreds of them had loitered around city hall for hours. The writer of this piece thought that this behavior "was equally as unlawful and reprehensible as the gathering at the Washington Hotel the evening before," and concluded that "that race have more idle time, and really see more pleasure than do the whites generally."[2]

For white Richmonders, what was most disconcerting about the whole incident of the black ball was probably not the amount of noise that such an event was likely to create. Had the black band been allowed to play, perhaps, in the early hours of the morning, the music may have become what we might anachronistically term "hot," and the ball might have become somewhat raucous, but generally the event was hardly going to be much louder or any more of a nuisance than were the elite white balls that dotted the social calendar. Similarly, in the case of the crowd scenes around city hall, there may well have been an element of threat or menace in the air, but if the gathered blacks were unduly loud, that circumstance was not mentioned in the *Dispatch*. Richmond blacks who attended the curtailed ball or who watched proceedings at city hall the next morning were behaving in an almost indistinguishable fashion from whites. And there was the rub. Only a few months previously, a Mr. Mayo, in his charge to the grand jury, condemned "the assumptions of equality exhibited by blacks" in both their "dress and deportment" and in "riding in carriages contrary to law."[3] In the case of the black ball, then, the vexing issue was not the volume of noise that would have emanated from the ball but by whom it would have been made: slaves dancing the night away at a ball at one of the city's big hotels would not necessarily have made an extraordinary amount of noise, but they certainly would have created what can be termed "sound out of place."4 Maybe New York blacks could attend balls, mill noisily around the streets, and think of themselves as the equal of any man or woman in the city—hardly a comforting thought for whites contemplating black behavior in Virginia's capital, or indeed any southern city—but there was a widespread feeling among whites in Richmond in the 1850s that things were getting more than a little out of hand. That over a hundred slaves thought nothing of attending a ball at the Washington Hotel—and, hardly less worrying, that most of their owners had given them permission to do so—was about as good a sign as any that things were awry.

Of course, Richmond was hardly typical of the urban South, but then nothing was. By the 1850s, Richmond was the most important city in the upper South, a regional center for processing and manufacturing, a slave market, and the capital of the state of Virginia. According to the 1850 census, 44.6 percent of the total population of 27,570 were black, and of those blacks 9,927 were slaves and 2,369 were free.5 What made southern slavery different in Richmond was the extent to which slaves lived away from their owners, the extent to which many slaves were able to hire themselves out and to negotiate the conditions of their employment, and the extent to which slaves could elude white supervision. But for all its idiosyncrasies, a close analysis of the city still reveals much about the urban South, in particular the degree to which African American sound, be it the "sound out of place" of a black ball, the sound of slaves singing as they worked, or the noise of everyday black life, saturated the streets of southern cities.

One of the features that made Richmond distinctive was the scope of slave hiring. Typically, slaves were hired for the calendar year and many individual slaves were given the freedom to bargain with potential masters, allowing a slave, as a writer in the *Dispatch* complained bitterly in December 1852, to chose someone who would indulge him, or "grant him many privileges and a good deal of time for himself." As a result, in the week between Christmas and the New Year, Main Street became "one vast unroofed intelligence office," with numerous slaves clamoring to secure their future for the next twelve months.6 A few days later, another writer to the *Dispatch* noted that on the Saturday after Christmas, "the streets were thronged with negroes, hirers, owners and buyers, as is the annual custom," and that "thousands of dollars exchanged hands, [and] thousands of negroes changed homes and masters." From experience, he predicted that for the rest of the week "the streets will be filled with negroes brought in from the country for hire."7 Any white Richmonders in the vicinity would be confronted by a sea of black humanity thronging Main Street and would have to endure the sound of innumerable importuning black voices washing over them as they made their way through the crowd. One week before Christmas in 1855, a writer in the *Dispatch* forlornly reminded readers that "*Hiring Time* is at our doors, and with it will come all the harassing incidents necessarily attending the hiring of servants."8 Everyone was out for a bargain or a good deal and, inevitably, occasional disputes and raised voices could be heard above the general hubbub of intense bargaining.

The week after Christmas was hardly the only occasion on which black voices impinged upon the consciousness of whites. Indeed, snippets of black speech, occasionally comic but more often worrying, were continually reported in the press. Sometimes it was the content of the utterance that attracted attention. In 1852 Jane Williams, a slave, used a hatchet to kill her mistress, a Mrs. Winston, and her mistress's nine-month-old child, a frightening incident that shook white Richmond to its core. A few days after Williams's execution an outraged white reported in the *Dispatch* some of the comments he had overheard from the large number of blacks who had attended the gruesome ritual. One had pronounced that "She has gone home," another, that "She is in glory," and a third had opined that "her seat is far higher in Heaven than that of Mrs. Winston."9

In other cases it was the language and tone of voice with which African Richmonders addressed whites that was shocking. A constant stream of anything-but-deferential slaves and free blacks was hauled in front of the mayor on charges of insolence and then soundly flogged. In August 1852, a Dr. Hunt angrily marched off to the house of his washerwoman, Elizabeth Clarke, a free black, in search of his new shirt collars. Clarke claimed that the collars had already been delivered and responded to Hunt's demands in a "very insulting" fashion. Things quickly escalated, with the angry washerwoman ordering two black women who were also in the room with her to shut the door and to "kill the d—d white s— of a b—." After a scuffle, Hunt managed to slip out of the door and escape from "the black tigresses." Clarke and one of the other black women each received ten lashes.[10] In the following month, a Mr. Bartholomew was walking along Franklin Street one evening when his attention was attracted by the din being made by two black men urging their dogs to fight. When the white man approached the loiterers to tell them to move along, one of the blacks, Reuben Baker, a slave, demanded "to know what the h—l he had to do with it, and swore he would whip any white man that interfered with him." He was only stopped from carrying out his threat by the intervention of another passerby. Baker was sentenced, "very properly" according to the *Dispatch*, to thirty-nine lashes.[11]

If, for Richmond's whites, the insolence of individual slaves and free blacks was alarming enough, their collective behavior was even more worrying. In the 1850s the city's newspapers were full of complaints about free blacks and slaves jostling whites on the street, blockading the streets, and not allowing whites the wall, in short not conducting themselves in a deferential fashion. There were also innumerable complaints about blacks who, in their leisure hours, congregated noisily to drink, gamble, and dance. Sometimes slaves took advantage of an owner's temporary absence. In March 1852 nine or ten blacks gathered in the kitchen of the absent Mr. Sturdivant's apartment and "commenced dancing and singing, and holding a Mormon pow-wow." The racket disturbed a Mr. Gianini's nerves so much that he knocked on the door in order to discover why his neighbor "was allowing such a bubbery to be kicked up." Gianini managed to secure three of the offending slaves, who were taken by the watch and then duly sentenced by the mayor to a whipping.[12] More often, though, slaves gathered at various tippling and "disorderly" houses. In January 1852, for instance, the watch was called out to investigate the "considerable noise and confusion" emanating from a house near Eighteenth and Main kept by Eliza Wood, a free woman of color.[13] Similarly, five years later, the *Dispatch* called for special vigilance on Sundays when the myriad grocery stores selling alcohol on the sly "attract[ed] and create[d], through the medium of liquor, throngs of noisy, drunken negroes."¹⁴ But undoubtedly the most notorious establishment in Richmond was the Bird in Hand, run by Richard Weston, a white man, a venue that many found noisome and that consequently was regularly descended upon by the watch. In January 1852 one such raid netted a haul of thirteen slaves and free blacks, who were brought before the court for participating in an unlawful gathering. Seven blacks who were in the back room gambling received thirty-nine lashes each; four who were in the front room eating were given twenty lashes, and two others caught coming in while the watch "were arresting and tying the others, were only ordered ten lashes each."¹⁵

As far as Richmond blacks, both slave and free, were concerned, things had become noticeably worse by the 1850s. Not only were laws requiring slaves about town to carry passes enforced more regularly, but it was also the case that an increasingly jumpy white population seemed to be intent on passing a series of measures fettering black street behavior. In these attempts free blacks were lumped in indiscriminately with slaves. A new city ordinance passed in 1852, for example, prohibited "negroes" from entering the public squares, carrying canes, smoking, riding in hacks, and standing on the street in groups of more than five.¹⁶ In 1859 all the measures concerning Richmond blacks were codified into a twenty-seven-part ordinance that not only made it clear that whites wanted to regain control of the city streets but also emphasized that muting black sound was an important part of this process. African Americans were forbidden from using "provoking language," making any "insolent or menacing gestures" or a "loud offensive noise," or uttering "any blasphemous or indecent word" within earshot of whites.¹⁷

But, of course, passing ordinances was one thing, enforcing them something else entirely. What happened in Richmond, and indeed throughout the South during the entire period of slavery, was that a flurry of activity in which the letter of the law was enforced vigorously would be followed by a lull of weeks or months in which whites lost interest. Because too many people made too much money selling liquor illegally to African Americans, because it was much more convenient for whites to pay slaves small sums of money on the quiet to do things that slaves were not supposed to do, and because enforcing all of the laws required a considerable amount of effort, it was unusual for any crackdown to last too long.

For all that, though, there was a noticeable quickening of the pace in the 1850s, much more interest in quieting Richmond's blacks, and a diminishing time between police crackdowns. These crackdowns were sometimes prompted by a murder or some incident or other that re-awoke white fears. The *Dispatch* played a significant role in publicizing such incidents or in pointing out when law enforcement was lax. In November 1852, for instance, a correspondent to the paper pointed out that "crime is contagious," and that unless a moral atmosphere was maintained, Richmond's "streets will also become the scenes of daring and disgraceful deeds of lawlessness and crime." The writer referred to a "row between two negro women, at the corner of Cary and 10th streets, which continued, to the annoyance of the neighborhood, over half an hour," and which quickly attracted a crowd of black onlookers, as a case that not only disrupted the "peace and dignity" of the city, but was also a warning of "the approaching evil." The writer's solution was more and better-paid police, but in the meantime the warning, and others like it, prompted renewed police activity.[18] As well, Joseph Mayo, the mayor for much of the 1850s, often intervened, ordering the police to sweep the city looking for blacks illegally loitering; on one occasion Mayo ordered two policemen "to scour the by-streets, lanes, and alleys and break up the various gatherings of negroes who assemble every Sabbath day to pitch cents, bet at dice, drink and fight."[19] But then, inevitably, after a few score blacks had been made examples of and suffered the inevitable whippings handed out in the mayor's court, things would ease off for a while, until the next crisis occurred.

To talk of cycles, or ebb and flow, or even of ambiguity and ambivalence, in the way laws were enforced is to make it sound as if blacks were dealing with some abstract law of nature, rather than with white passions and whims. From the perspective of free blacks and slaves, it was a question of reading the mood of the city's whites, of knowing when the squeeze was on and when smart blacks should stay out of the way. And those who, because they were inept, or occasionally indifferent, or often just plain unlucky, misread the situation wore their mistakes on the skin of their backs, for even though slavery had only a few years left to run, it was still the most corporeal of institutions.

For some time in the early 1850s, according to the *Daily Dispatch*, the white citizens of Richmond had considered a free black named John Carter to be "partly deranged" and had tolerated what they viewed as his antics. When Carter had had a bit to drink, apparently a not uncommon occurrence, he would parade down the middle of the city's streets "*a la militarie.*" Carter would "then stop and mount some convenient barrel or stoop, [and] deliver an extemporaneous sermon upon the sin and frailties of mankind to an enchanted group of grinning 'sables,'" ending his preaching with a flourish by giving the crowd a "benediction," before turning on his heel and walking away, "swearing with the precision of a trooper and the fury of an anti-gospelist." This was loud, exaggerated, and edgy public theater that always threatened to get out of hand. As Carter's knowing black audience and the *Dispatch*'s writer were well aware—and probably most of Richmond's citizenry were at least dimly aware—white behavior was being parodied and satirized by the apparently drunk free black. Almost inevitably, the performance had to end. Perhaps Carter, emboldened by his compatriots' enthusiastic response, went too far—the *Dispatch* reported that things were escalating and that his recent conduct had been of "the most obscene and insulting character"—or perhaps the city's mood had changed in the wake of several violent incidents. From this distance, the motivation for official intervention is unclear, but the result is not. Carter was hauled in front of the authorities, sentenced to a biblical "thirty nine stripes," and then swallowed up in the legal system's maw, a free black man unable to produce the papers that could demonstrate his freedom.[20]

Not infrequently, then, individual blacks such as John Carter made obviously noisy incursions through the soundscape of southern cities and their impact was hardly negligible. But for all that, it was more the sounds of African Americans going about their daily lives that characterized those cities' sonic texture. Indeed, whether whites liked it or not—and as usual there was a range of opinion on the matter—it was impossible to be out and about in Richmond, or other urban centers, without hearing the sounds of slavery. African American culture—particularly in its musical expression—permeated southern cities just as effectively as did the scent of magnolia on a summer evening's breeze.

Take something as simple—or as complex—as whistling. Whistling, of course, was hardly the sole preserve of slaves, but in the early decades of the new nation the practice was particularly associated with African Americans. Alluding to the festival that was often the highlight of the year for slaves in New York City's hinterland, up the Hudson Valley and most especially around Albany, white New Yorkers sometimes referred to whistling as "Negro Pinkster music." Moreover, all manner of travelers sojourning in the South were struck by the variety of sounds slaves could make with their lips, and subsequently recorded their impressions of those sounds on paper. When Fanny Kemble, the famous actress and at the time wife of the southern planter Pierce Butler, arrived by boat in the town of Darien in the late 1840s, she was welcomed by several slaves in two boats, a greeting "accompanied with certain interjectional shrieks, whoops, whistles and grunts that could only be written down in Negro language." Three decades earlier and rather more appreciatively, James Kirke Paulding had listened carefully one evening to the black boatmen on the canal at Richmond and noted that "they whistle[d] as clear as the notes of the fife."[21]

The best account of slave whistling, though, comes not from Richmond but from nearby Lynchburg. It is a description through which, as happened more frequently than not, a white observer, in this case J. Alexander Patten, conveyed his own deep ambivalence about African American culture. Patten's comments were embedded in his complaint about Lynchburg's "very large negro population," who were mostly out of sight during the day, but who, in the early evening, were "unpleasantly numerous." As respectable citizens gingerly made their way along the "narrow and uneven" sidewalks, they did so under the watchful eyes of the city's blacks, hanging about on street corners and perched on fences and walls, who "keep up a continual whistling." All it took was a slight variation in the pitch or volume of the whistling to raise the hair on the back of white necks, especially those of women, to transform an evening stroll into an unpleasant lesson concerning the changing nature of race relations in the 1850s. Something ominous and threatening was in the air. According to Patten, Lynchburg's slaves and free blacks stood "with their backs to the pailings and walls, their hands in their pockets, and braced by their extended legs, whistle away their evening hours." This was an aggressive use of sound and, to a lesser extent, of the black male body (for the lounging whistlers were mostly male) to mark territory, signaling nothing so much as that all those indignant complaints in the newspapers were justified, and that unless something was done whites would indeed hand over control of the streets to a motley crew of free blacks and slaves.

And yet, for all his appreciation that the whistling blacks were passing contumacious messages between themselves, with an almost complete indifference to the angry glances of whites crowding the same sidewalks, Patten was also aware of the beauty of what he heard. As he readily acknowledged, "Lynchburg blacks have genius, as well as lips; and whistle in a manner well calculated to 'soothe the savage breast.'" They whistled, Patten noted acutely, "the tunes of the plantation where they were born, and hope to die" and those "of the factories, where the song lightens their labor" and, importantly, "each is given with an accuracy, and even sweetness" that an "instrument cannot always achieve." It is impossible to read Patten's words without gaining an idea of the pleasure—and it was often exhibited in the most exuberant of fashions—that Lynchburg blacks derived from their whistling. Individual blacks quietly whistling themselves to sleep on ketches moored to the riverbank, and groups of blacks who had "made wagers as to harmony and wind," all impinged on the soundscape in characteristically African American ways. Particularly interesting here were the groups of blacks performing what were essentially whistling cutting contests, a form that is familiar enough to us today from over a century of music history from jazz through rap, but that was worthy of note in slavery times. Patten carefully watched and listened to gangs of blacks going past on the street, "whistling their loudest and best," a performance "which incites the first to displays of their fullest capacity; and thus the concert goes on."²²

Black whistling was a commonplace of life in southern cities, even if it was not often commented on at length by travelers, diarists, and other chroniclers of everyday life; more memorable for whites, however, and hence more often mused over in writing, and ultimately more revealing of African American culture and its complexity, was the sound of slaves and free blacks singing. By the 1850s blacks and whites had been living cheek by jowl in the urban crucibles along the eastern seaboard for decades, indeed, in many cases, for well over a century. Inevitably, and regardless of whether either party liked it or not, black and white cultures mixed promiscuously, forming new patterns and changing the originals forever. Once slaves had incorporated white hymns into their musical repertoire—and it is important to remember that it was only in the last two or three decades of slavery that substantial numbers of slaves became Christian—those hymns would never sound the same again. Increasing numbers of whites went out of their way to listen to massed African American voices raised in song, and on Sundays in Richmond and other cities in the South, many became unabashed admirers of what they heard. Others, troubled by what they, against their better judgment, had come to enjoy, could only acknowledge their pleasure in the most grudging fashion. An anonymous correspondent of the *Daily Richmond Examiner* in 1861 noted that "some very fine vocal music" could be heard on Sundays "by listening to the choir of the First African Church." But the writer quickly went on to point out that "no extraordinary amount of *intellect* is required to make an excellent vocalist." However, the *Examiner's* correspondent conceded, "most of the Africans are naturally good musicians" and "with proper cultivation," the African church choir "would make the best vocalists in the world; yet the Africans are *radically* inferior in intellect to every other variety of the human species." From which he concluded "that music is not a highly intellectual art or accomplishment."[23]

Maybe the supercilious young man—he certainly seems sophomoric—was right in that the singing of hymns hardly demonstrated African American intellect. What is absolutely certain, though, is that the sounds of black religious music provided a soundtrack to which a range of the city's inhabitants, from white listeners sheepishly noticing their feet tapping in time, to Richmond slaves who used hymns as work songs, moved. In the cities, this casual exchange between what some have been misguided enough to see as discrete categories of the sacred and the secular, a mixing that is characteristic of African American music, and, indeed, culture, was if anything heightened. This was particularly the case in Richmond in the 1850s. Industrialization and urbanization are usually seen as noisily rendering work-songs redundant—there was good reason for the Lomaxes, in search of "authentic" work songs in the 1930s, to want to record black prisoners on the road gang rather than tractor drivers or factory workers—but in antebellum times most factories in Richmond processed tobacco, barely used machines, and were, if not silent, certainly quiet enough for slaves to use song to regulate the pace of their labor.

According to the *Boston Evening Transcript*'s correspondent, who visited Richmond in late 1860, if one went into any tobacco manufactory one would see from fifty to a hundred blacks working, and hear "their delightful voices" joined in "a flow of delightful harmony." As he explained to his Boston readers, "slaves work and sing as a matter of course," and in fact "could not well do the one without the other." He had visited "some twenty or more factories" in Richmond "where the same habit was observable."[24] When William Cullen Bryant visited a Richmond tobacco factory in which eighty black boys and young men were rolling leaves into plugs, which were cut into four-inch lengths and then run through a press, he noticed much the same thing. As he entered the room he "heard a murmur of psalmody... which now and then swelled into a strain of very tolerable music." Talking with the proprietor's brother, Bryant learned that "we encourage it as much as we can, for the boys work better while singing."[25]

What is particularly fascinating here is observing southerners, both white and black, striving to accommodate to a world that was changing, and doing so in ways most closely associated with the cities. Southern industrialization was still only in its most embryonic stage and older ways of behaving persisted for some time. Singing in factories did not occur just in Richmond. In a hemp factory in Lexington in the 1840s, one observer saw almost a hundred slaves "drown the noise of the machinery by their own melody." As far as he could make out, "the leader would commence singing in a low tone—'Ho! Ho! Ho!

Master's gone away.' To which the rest replied with rapidity, 'Ho! Ho! —chicken-pie for supper, Ho! Ho!—Ho! Ho!'" Even more surprising to modern sensibilities, some black factory workers managed to accompany their singing with a little jig. As they joined in the chorus, many of these Kentucky slaves "at the same time walk[ed] backward and forward about their spinning, with great regularity, and in some measure keeping time with their steps."[26] Here again we find blacks turning work into performance.

Richmond's slaves' practice of using spirituals as work songs reinforced the commingling of religion and industry. In his *Richmond in By-Gone Days* (1856), Samuel Mordecai wrote of the similarities between churches and tobacco factories. One of the latter had been built on the very spot on which a church had once stood: not only was the "tobacco factory large enough for a Cathedral" and capped by a belfry, but it was also the case that to passersby it sounded as if it were a religious establishment. As Mordecai commented, "It is a pleasure to listen to the sacred music with which they [the slave factory workers] beguile the hours of labour." Another building, first a Catholic church and then a Presbyterian church and now quadrupled in size, had also become a tobacco factory. "Here also fine psalmody may be heard, as of yore," Mordecai wrote, "and the organ loft is still occupied by a choir, but one whose music *ceases* on Sabbaths and Holy days."[27] Undoubtedly not all citizens of Richmond thought that the boundaries between religion and industry were blurred, but, regardless, the result was that on every day of the week in Richmond, people could stroll past imposing edifices and hear massed African American voices singing psalms, hymns, and spirituals.

It seems clear enough that more and more whites, both locals and visitors, enjoyed listening to this music—one traveler called it a "most celebrated tourist attraction"—but working out what it meant to the slaves themselves is, as usual, rather more difficult. The first thing to be said is that, for all the relative newness of a situation in which large numbers of slaves became Christians and sang hymns, the way they used the songs to pace their work and the way they sang those hymns were practices firmly embedded in African American culture. The *Boston Evening Transcript*'s correspondent explained to his readers that the black workers in the factories were singing hymns, "many of which are the same as are heard in the churches of Boston," yet for all that he called them "peculiar hymns" as well, a sure sign that melodies were being embellished, rhythms made more complex, tempos slowed or quickened.[28]

Interestingly, even in these white accounts—and they are the only ones we have—there is a strong suggestion that, on occasion, blacks carefully calibrated the volume of their singing to suit their own purposes. And those purposes, depending entirely on context, could have ranged from having a bit of fun, playfully ragging a white foreman or owner, or deliberately provoking an overseer into a desperate struggle of wills with his slaves. The *Boston Evening Transcript*'s correspondent reported that in several factories, "conversation with the proprietor was almost impossible, in consequence of the 'congregational singing' among the operatives." Doubtless a deliberate drowning out of the idle chat of gawking tourists gave slaves some satisfaction and not a little amusement, but the most effective black use of sound was the eerie silence that the slaves created when they refused to sing. The brother of one tobacco factory proprietor told William Cullen Bryant that the black factory workers "will sing all day long with great spirit," but that "at other times you will not hear a single note." Any sign of dissatisfaction with conditions on the factory floor, and usually this meant the behavior of the overseer, and the black workers clammed up. Bryant's informant went on to note that "they must sing wholly of their own accord; it is of no use to bid them do it."[29]

The situation was replete with irony, although not much of it was obvious to contemporaries. For the most part, our image of factory workers comes from later in the century and from the North. Serried ranks of young migrant women sitting at sewing machines in a New York sweatshop are both memorialized and rendered mute by the occasional photographs that survive. And, of course, nowadays we so often see them as young innocents, unaware of their rendezvous with the Triangle Shirtwaist Company fire of 1911, where 146 mostly teenage factory workers would die horrendously. When Richmond tobacco factories sounded the way we expect them to sound, when the only noise was from machines, was precisely the point at which things were most awry. Not only was the silence an unnerving contrast to the usual noisy scene on the factory floor but, as the proprietors well knew, that uncanny quiet was also costing them money. Silence signaled black solidarity, a lack of interest on the part of slaves in continuing to keep their fingers working in time, indeed a determination to upset the industrial rhythm and to cause production to taper off. At the conflict's end, the black workers would once again respond to one of their compatriot's call, the Lord's name would echo through the factory, and the money would start rolling in once more. William Cullen Bryant's informant thought it remarkable that "their taste is exclusively for sacred music; they will sing nothing else."[30] He certainly appreciated that slaves had no trouble at all with, indeed delighted in, using reconfigured hymns and psalms as work songs. But he exaggerated his case. Richmond slaves on occasion did sing songs in which the Lord's name was not invoked.

Late on a summer night in July 1852, Richmond's watch, doubtless responding to angry complaints from whites unable to sleep, managed to catch four miscreants, all of them free blacks. William Jackson Cash and Joseph Custols, both adults, and two small boys, Thomas Jenkins and Robert May, along with three others who slipped away too quickly, had been "engaged in serenading some black damsels." The mayor sentenced Cash and Custols to ten lashes apiece, while the two boys, who gave up the names of another three blacks who had participated "in the musical expedition," were "let off with five lashes each." The following night "two more 'negro serenaders,'" this time both slaves, were caught performing "with 'bones' and 'banjo' on Broad street," and sentenced to ten lashes apiece.[31]

For the *Daily Dispatch*, it was all an affair to be treated lightheartedly—fifty lashes were a drop in the ocean of floggings regularly handed out by the city officials, and, for the whites, were neither here nor there. The *Dispatch*'s editor, utterly incapable of resisting temptation, captioned the first story "A Barber-ous Serenade." And yet this minor incident was the product of well over a century of cross-cultural intermingling of black and white in the urban centers. The lyrics to the songs were rendered in English, probably in Black English; the serenade is not an African or an African American genre, although having a group, not an individual, perform it is. As well, the banjo and the bones were both instruments of African origin, although by 1852 they were well on their way to being widely recognized as vital parts of the quintessential American institution of the minstrel show. Working out exactly what was going on late on a summer night on Broad Street is well nigh impossible from such brief descriptions, particularly when they are freighted in the levity of a century and a half ago. What is clear, though, is that serenading was one more way that free blacks made the night "hideous" with their music, and what is particularly fascinating is that the following night a couple of slaves accepted the almost certainty of a flogging to ensure that the beat went on, and that the watch and courts were needed to secure quiet so that whites might sleep.

Apparently, serenading was relatively unusual—the authorities' approach hardly encouraged it—but the distinctive and often haunting cries of slave hucksters were pretty much accepted and a commonplace. As each fruit or food came into season, southern city streets became a cacophony of competing cries. In mid-July 1855 in Richmond, a writer in the *Daily Dispatch* noted that the first watermelons were beginning to come into market. "In a short time now," he continued, "the public ear will be greeted at every corner of the street, with 'red meat, black seed, so sweet, indeed.' "[32] In nearby Norfolk, Virginia, a few years after slavery had ended, William Wells Brown, the famous runaway slave and author, carefully listened to a black woman selling "some really fine strawberries" and then, unusually, wrote down her words. She sang:

> I live fore miles out of town,
> I am gwine to glory.
> My strawberries are sweet an' soun',
> I am gwine to glory.
> I fotch 'em fore miles on my head,
> I am gwine to glory.
> My chile is sick, an' husban' dead,
> I am gwine to glory.
> Now's de time to get 'em cheap,
> I am gwine to glory.

Eat 'em wid yer bread an' meat,
I am gwine to glory.
Come sinner get down on your knees,
I am gwine to glory.
Eat dees strawberries when you please,
I am gwine to glory.

What is immediately apparent here is the characteristic African American way in which this woman, probably an ex-slave, promiscuously mixed the sacred and the secular, unhesitatingly combining religious exhortation with entreaties to buy her strawberries. Brown's almost dismissive gloss on the lyrics—that "the interest, however, centered more upon the manner than the matter"[33]—suggests that she was also singing these words in a characteristically African American way, but of course these sounds are now long lost to us. If it was and is almost impossible to trap on the page just how these cries sounded, it is often easier to pick up something of the overall effect of scores of slaves noisily hawking their wares at full volume. In times of glut, the streets became a bedlam. "The city yesterday was uproarious with the clamour of the sable watermelon-venders," wrote one of the *Daily Richmond Examiner* correspondents in August 1861. "At every corner the inevitable mule-cart and the irrepressible negro were to be encountered." The superabundance would not last long though, "and negroes and carts will soon be a scarcity in our streets."[34]

From well before the sun rose until very late at night, the streets of Richmond echoed to the noise of black living. The sounds made by free blacks and slaves hawking their goods, singing, whistling, or humming, arguing, shouting, playing in the street, and merely going about their work were a part of the fabric of life not just in Richmond but, to a greater or lesser extent, in most American urban centers. White reaction to this development varied immensely. There were many whites who recoiled from every alarum and noisy disruption and who would try to insulate themselves from the city streets; others accepted such interruptions as part and parcel of living in an American city; and by the 1850s there was a significant minority who reveled in listening to examples of black cultural expressiveness. What is particularly intriguing is that the minstrel show, featuring white performers in black-face, became a sensation, the most popular form of entertainment in the country, at precisely the same time, and elicited a similar variety of reactions from its audience. In the late 1840s and 1850s, Americans, black and white, foreign and native-born, were attending minstrel shows in their droves. This was as true of Richmond as anywhere else. In 1852, for example, Kunkel's Opera Troupe came through the city several times to sellout crowds. At a performance on a Wednesday evening in early March, "the hall was filled to overflowing," and later in the year in September, according to the *Daily Dispatch*'s correspon-dent, "hundreds of visitors were obliged to return home, unable to ob-tain admittance."[35]

What did it mean that there was a good chance that the thousands of patrons, who queued up and paid to be spectators as a troupe of white actors with blackened faces performed in "black dialect," could, on their way home from the theater later that night, hear the "real thing," black cab drivers whistling, or the raucous duets of a pair of black tubmen emptying the privies? The answer is complicated be-cause undoubtedly Americans were attracted to minstrelsy for many reasons.

On the one hand, the theatrical representation on the minstrel stage leached out of black life most of its edginess and threat, taming African American culture for the entertainment of a mostly white audience. According to one member of the Richmond audience, the Kunkels' "songs and Ethiopian colloquies are chaste and witty, devoid of any-thing that could be exceptionable to the most fastidious taste."[36] Much of minstrel show humor depended on stereotypes of blacks, on pre-senting an exaggerated version of what many whites claimed to see every day around their own city. When the Kunkels put on a skit enti-tled the "Black Barber," in which one of the blacked-up cast members cavorted on stage "with his two foot razor, currycomb and blacksmith's shears," the performance "convulsed the audience with laughter."[37] But on the other hand, for some in the audience the appeal of the min-strel show lay precisely in its embrace of African American culture. For one enthusiastic Richmond patron, who wrote for the *Daily Dispatch*, the extraordinary appeal of the Kunkels was easy to explain. In other performances, by lesser companies, black "language and dialect [were] wofully travestied, often by persons who professed to be Ethiopian singers, but who knew nothing more of negroes than that their skin is dark." To attract the plaudits of a knowing audience, such as that in Richmond, rather more was involved than performers merely blackening their skin. The Kunkels, the *Dispatch* writer pointed out, "have studied the peculiarities of the African character with great success, and they speak the negro dialect as a real Virginia negro would do it."[38] In other words, the success of the Kunkels, at least in part, derived from the fact that they sounded very similar to performances from free blacks and slaves that could be heard throughout Richmond at virtually any time of the day or night.

Part of the minstrel show's staying power derived from its ability to embody these contradictory desires, to celebrate black culture and, at the same time, to repress it. From T. D. Rice down to Elvis and Eminem, a long line of white entertainers has stolen the sounds of black culture, becoming, thereby, famous and rich, certainly much more so than did the African Americans who inspired their performances. The Kunkels were pioneers, positioned early enough in this lineage to love as well as thieve, to pay careful attention to the particulars of what they imitated. And, of course, it has always been more than theft, not just imitation—the way in which the Kunkels and others transformed what they went out and listened to into something that could be staged successfully was no less a creative act than any of those performed by the African Virginians to whom the Kunkels apparently paid such close attention. By the 1850s the sounds made by African Richmonders, indeed more generally African Americans, were a familiar part of the soundscape. For all the scares and panics of the last years before America lurched into war, what was most noticeable was the extent to which, after decades of living together, it was finally obvious that the cultures of master and slave were entwined. This was a development deplored by some, welcomed by others, and scanted by many both black and white, but, regardless of that, the simple fact was that the sounds of slavery had penetrated the core of American culture, and the repercussions of that would be heard down to our own time.

The Sounds of Freedom

Fannie Berry would remember the day that Lee surrendered at the nearby Appomattox Courthouse for the rest of her long life. The Virginia plantation on which she had spent the first two decades or so of her life echoed to the sounds of joyous slaves:

Never was no time like 'em befo' or since. Niggers shoutin' an' clappin' hands an' singin'! Chillun runnin' all over de place beatin' tins an' yellin'. Ev'ybody happy. Sho' did some celebratin'. Run to de kitchen an' shout in de winder:

> Mammy, don't you cook no mo'
> You's free! You's free!
> Run to henhouse an' shout:
> Rooster, don't you crow no mo'
> You's free! You's free!
> Ol' hen, don't you lay no mo' eggs,
> You's free! You's free!
> Go to de pigpen an' tell de pig:
> Ol' pig, don't you grunt no mo'
> You's free! You's free!
> Tell de cows:
> Ol' cow, don't you give no mo' milk,
> You's free! You's free![1]

Emancipation in the South was a haphazard affair, occurring at different times and in different places during the Civil War, but whenever it occurred, the memories of the day of freedom were almost invariably vivid, and many of them were saturated with sound.[2] Hattie Sugg told her WPA interviewer that "I well 'member one night a calvary come through when it was rainin'. I could hear de bugle a long way off: toot—toot. De closer it come de louder it got: toot—Toot. I sho thought it was Gabriel a comin blowin his trumpet. It sounded like de prettiest music on earth."[3] Mittie Freeman had been fishing with her father on their Arkansas plantation when "all a-sudden cannons commence a-booming, it seem like everywhere." "Cannons," she explained, "was to roar every place when Richmond fell." Freeman's father had thrown his fishing pole up in the air, grabbed his daughter's hand and raced toward the house shouting, "It's freedom. Now we'se gwine be free."[4] Richard Carruthers, a twenty-one-year-old on a Texan plantation when freedom came, simply recalled, "That was the day I shouted."[5]

Hardly surprisingly, slaves reacted to their freedom in a variety of ways. A few even expressed sorrow—others were bewildered or simply disbelieving, but most were overjoyed.[6] Carrie Davis and her fellow slaves on a South Carolinian plantation had heard the news from their overseer. "Dat was a glorious day," she told her interviewer. "We shouted and thanked God and dat night de plantation folk gathered from miles around and we stayed up all night dancing and singing."[7] Charles Graham was very young when he was freed, but he could still remember that the other slaves on his plantation "were cutting up and clapping their hands and carrying on something terrible, and shouting, 'Free, free, old Abraham done turned us loose.'"[8] Another slave recalled that "everyone was a-singin'. We was all walkin' on golden clouds. Hallelujah!"[9] As soon as Molly Harrell, her mother, and the rest of the slaves on their Texas plantation were told they were free, they left—"We all walk down de road singin' and shoutin' to beat de band."[10]

In the ensuing months and years, the former slaves continued to insist loudly that things must be different now that they were free. In 1865, when one African Mississippian was greeted with a "Howdy, Uncle" from a planter, the former slave angrily retorted, "Call me Mister."[11] Another African American, on noticing his former master among a group of military prisoners, slyly greeted him: "Hello, massa; bottom rail top dis time!"[12] Unfortunately the former slave owner's response to this artful use of language was not recorded. Similarly, in the years after slavery, thousands of blacks would proudly and loudly march through the middle of such cities as Richmond and Charleston, celebrating major events in the black calendar, particularly Emancipation Day, in a way that was especially confronting for southern whites.[13] Mary Chesnut, the famed Civil War diarist, was horrified by the way former slaves behaved in nearby Camden, South Carolina. "Yesterday," she wrote in her diary in July 1865, "there was a mass meeting of Negroes, thousands of them were in town, eating, drinking, dancing, speechifying. Preaching and prayer was also a popular amusement." She then went on to raise the specter of the Haitian revolution of the late eighteenth century, which had haunted the South for decades, adding that "we are in for a new St. Domingo all the same. The Yankees have raised the devil, and now they cannot guide him."14 Of course, her fears were in the end misplaced. Southern whites would regain control and eventually replace slavery with the evil of Jim Crow, but for several years at least in the aftermath of the war the South echoed to the exuberant sounds of the recently freed slaves as they sang, danced, preached, and told their stories.

That the former slaves would celebrate their freedom in such a fashion should not surprise us. Over nearly two and a half centuries, several million African and African American slaves had fashioned a dynamic, unruly culture that was principally made to be heard. The insistent beat of black hands and feet patting juba, the haunting cry of a slave holler floating across the rice fields in the late afternoon, the massed singing of several score slaves returning from the funeral of one of their compatriots, the sound of Saturday night on a plantation, with a makeshift slave band's relentless beat driving the rollicking crowd of slaves toward a sweaty exhaustion, and the cacophony of black voices assailing potential customers in the city markets of a Charleston or a New Orleans—all these and much more helped African Americans suffuse the South with sound, making it a resonant place. All these and much more made it compellingly clear that there was rather more to slave culture than met the eye.

NOTES

1. Zora Neale Hurston, *Their Eyes Were Watching God* (Philadelphia: J. B. Lippincott, 1937), reprinted in Zora Neale Hurston, *Novels and Stories* (New York: Library of America, 1995), 175.
2. For a particularly insightful rumination on this problem of sources, see Alex Bontemps, *The Punished Self: Surviving Slavery in the Colonial South* (Ithaca, NY: Cornell University Press, 2001).
3. Our thanks to Alex Bontemps for pointing out to us the original source for this incident: John Spencer Bassett, *Slavery in the State of North Carolina* (Baltimore: John Hopkins Press, 1899), 92–93. Our account is drawn largely from David S. Cecelski, *The Waterman's Song: Slavery and Freedom in Maritime North Carolina* (Chapel Hill: University of North Carolina Press, 2001), 103–5. But see also Dorothy Spruill Redford, with Michael D'Orso, *Somerset Homecoming: Recovering a Lost Heritage* (New York: Anchor, 1989), 128–32; and Michael A. Gomez, *Exchanging Our Country Marks: The Transformation of African Identities in the Colonial and Antebellum South* (Chapel Hill: University of North Carolina Press, 1998), 119–20.
4. Edward C. Carter II, John C. Van Horne, and Lee W. Formwalt, eds., *The Journals of Benjamin Henry Latrobe, 1799–1820: From Philadelphia to New Orleans*, vol. 3 (New Haven, CT: Yale University Press, 1980), 203–4.
5. James R. Creecy, *Scenes in the South, and Other Miscellaneous Pieces* (Philadelphia: J. B. Lippincott, 1860), 20–21. On Congo Square, see also Joseph R. Roach, "Deep Skin: Reconstructing Congo Square," in Harry J. Elam Jr. and David Krasner, eds., *African American Performance and Theater History: A Critical Reader* (New York: Oxford University Press, 2001), 101–13.
6. C. G. Parsons (M.D.), *Inside Views of Slavery; or, A Tour among the Planters* (Boston: John P. Jewett, 1855), 159–61.
7. Quoted in Michael Wayne, *Death of an Overseer: Reopening a Murder Investigation from the Plantation South* (New York: Oxford University Press, 2001), 35–36.
8. [Joseph H. Ingraham], *The South-West. By a Yankee* (New York: Harper & Brothers, 1835), vol. 2, 126–27. On the "quietude" of the plantation land-

scape, see Mark M. Smith, *Listening to Nineteenth-Century America* (Chapel Hill: University of North Carolina Press, 2001), 67–91.

9. The WPA interviews with ex-slaves were conducted in the 1930s and published in several series in the 1970s. The full citation is George P. Rawick, ed., *The American Slave: A Composite Autobiography*, Series 1 and 2 (ser. 1 and 2), 19 vols. (Westport, CT: Greenwood, 1972); Supplement, Series 1 (sup. ser. 1), 12 vols. (Westport, CT: Greenwood, 1977); Supplement, Series 2 (sup. ser. 2), 10 vols. (Westport, CT: Greenwood, 1979). If the reference is to the supplements it is stated in the note. In this case the reference is Rawick, ed., *The American Slave*, sup. ser. 1, vol. 10, Mississippi Narratives, part 5, 2402.

10. Rawick, ed., *The American Slave*, sup. ser. 2, vol. 4, Texas Narratives, 103–4.

11. Rawick, ed., *The American Slave*, ser. 1 and 2, vol. 7, Oklahoma and Mississippi Narratives, Oklahoma Narratives, 308.

12. Ibid., vol. 12, Georgia Narratives, parts 1 and 2, part 1, 100.

13. "Diary of a Journey through the United States, 1821–24," vol. 3, August 28, 1823, New York Historical Society.

14. On this point and for a different view, see Smith, *Listening to Nineteenth-Century America*, 79–80.

15. Frances Ann Kemble, *Journal of a Residence on a Georgian Plantation in 1838–1839*, ed. John A. Scott (New York: Meridian, 1975), 162–64.

16. W[illiam] Faux, *Memorable Days in America: Being a Journal of a Tour to the United States* (London: W. Simpkin and R. Marshall, 1823), 95.

17. Quoted in Lawrence W. Levine, *Black Culture and Black Consciousness: Afro-American Folk Thought from Slavery to Freedom* (New York: Oxford University Press, 1977), 6.

18. Jane M. T. Turnbull and Marion Turnbull, *American Photographs*, vol. 2 (London: T. C. Newby, 1859), 42–43.

19. William Cullen Bryant, *The Prose Writings of William Cullen Bryant*, ed. Parke Godwin, vol. 2, *Travels, Addresses, and Comments* (New York: Russell & Russell, 1964 [orig. pub. 1884]), 25–26.

20. *National Advocate*, November 8, 1821.

21. Faux, *Memorable Days in America*, 84.

22. *Father of the Blues: An Autobiography by W. C. Handy*, ed. Arna Bontemps (New York: Da Capo, 1991 [orig. pub. 1941]), 74. See also Adam Gussow, *Seems Like Murder Here: Southern Violence and the Blues Tradition* (Chicago: University of Chicago Press, 2002), 66–119.

23. Frederick Douglass, *My Bondage and My Freedom* (1855), reprinted in *Frederick Douglass: Autobiographies* (New York: Library of America, 1994), 184–85.

24. Christopher Looby, ed., *The Complete Civil War Journal and Selected Letters of Thomas Wentworth Higginson* (Chicago: University of Chicago Press, 2000), 64.

25. Ibid., 59–60.

26. Ibid., 159.

27. For a particularly insightful article on slave songs, see Ronald Radano, "Denoting Difference: The Writing of the Slave Spirituals," *Critical Inquiry* 22 (1996): 506–44.

28. Quoted in Marybeth Hamilton, "The Voice of the Blues," *History Workshop Journal* 54 (2002): 133.

29. The Lomax quotes are taken from Benjamin Filene, *Romancing the Folk: Public Memory & American Roots Music* (Chapel Hill: University of North Carolina Press, 2000), 47–56; the chapter titled "Creating the Cult of Authenticity," on the Lomaxes and Leadbelly, was particularly influential in our account. See also Alan Lomax, *The Land Where the Blues Began* (New York: Pantheon, 1993).

CHAPTER 1   *"All we knowed was go and come by de bells and horns"*

1. Ira Berlin, Marc Favreau, and Steven F. Miller, eds., *Remembering Slavery: African Americans Talk about Their Personal Experiences of Slavery and Emancipation* (New York: New Press, 1998), 84–86.

2. On the Federal Writers' Project of the WPA and these interviews, see Paul D. Escott, *Slavery Remembered: A Record of Twentieth-Century Slave Narratives* (Chapel Hill: University of North Carolina Press, 1979), and Jerrold Hirsch, *Portrait of America: A Cultural History of the Federal Writers' Project* (Chapel Hill: University of North Carolina Press, 2003).

3. Jane Kamensky, *Governing the Tongue: The Politics of Speech in Early New England* (New York: Oxford University Press, 1997), 10.

4. The Works Progress Administration interviews with ex-slaves were conducted in the 1930s and published in several series in the 1970s. The full citation is George P. Rawick, ed., *The American Slave: A Composite Autobiography*, Series 1 and 2 (ser. 1 and 2), 19 vols. (Westport, CT: Greenwood, 1972); Supplement, Series 1 (sup. ser. 1), 12 vols. (Westport, CT: Greenwood, 1977); Supplement, Series 2 (sup. ser. 2), 10 vols. (Westport, CT: Greenwood, 1979). If the reference is to the supplements it is stated in the note. In this case the reference is Rawick, ed., *The American Slave*, ser. 1 and 2, vol. 14, North Carolina Narratives, part 1, 285–86.

5. Rawick, ed., *The American Slave,* ser. 1 and 2, vol. 12, Georgia Narratives, parts 1 and 2, part 1, 70–71.

6. Ibid., part 2, 73–74.

7. Rawick, ed., *The American Slave,* sup. ser. 1, vol. 10, Mississippi Narratives, part 5, 2233–34.

8. Rawick, ed., *The American Slave,* ser. 1 and 2, vol. 2, South Carolina Narratives, parts 1 and 2, part 2, 242.

9. Ibid., vol. 6, Alabama and Indiana Narratives, Alabama Narratives, 395.

10. Rawick, ed., *The American Slave,* sup. ser. 1, vol. 1, Alabama Narratives, 20–21.

11. Rawick, ed., *The American Slave,* ser. 1 and 2, vol. 6, Alabama and Indiana Narratives, Alabama Narratives, 109–10.

12. Alain Corbin, *Village Bells: Sound and Meaning in the Nineteenth Century French Countryside* (New York: Columbia University Press, 1998), 7.

13. Robin D. G. Kelley, *Race Rebels: Culture, Politics, and the Black Working Class* (New York: Free Press, 1994), 56.

14. Rawick, ed., *The American Slave,* ser. 1 and 2, vol. 2, South Carolina Narratives, parts 1 and 2, 235.

15. Berlin, Favreau, and Miller, eds., *Remembering Slavery,* 8.

16. Rawick, ed., *The American Slave,* sup. ser. 1, vol. 9, Mississippi Narratives, part 4, 1390.

17. Rawick, ed., *The American Slave,* ser. 1 and 2, vol. 5, Texas Narratives, parts 3 and 4, part 4, 167, 168–69.

18. Ibid., vol. 6, Alabama and Indiana Narratives, Alabama Narratives, 222.

19. Ibid., vol. 9, Arkansas Narratives, parts 3 and 4, part 3, 292–93.

20. Ibid., vol. 5, Texas Narratives, parts 3 and 4, part 3, 263.

21. Ibid., vol. 11, Arkansas and Missouri Narratives, Arkansas Narratives, part 7, 15–16.

22. Ibid., vol. 7, Oklahoma and Mississippi Narratives, Mississippi Narratives, 46. For an account of the dogs that slaves owned themselves, see John Campbell, " 'My Constant Companion': Slaves and Their Dogs in the Antebellum South," in *Working toward Freedom: Slave Society and Domestic Economy in the American South,* ed. Larry E. Hudson Jr. (Rochester, NY: University of Rochester Press, 1994), 53–76.

23. *New York Sun,* November 11, 1895, reprinted in Roger D. Abrahams, *Singing the Master: The Emergence of African American Culture in the Plantation South* (New York: Pantheon, 1992), 270.

24. Rawick, ed., *The American Slave,* ser. 1 and 2, vol. 13, Georgia Narratives, parts 3 and 4, part 4, 103–4.

25. Rawick, ed., *The American Slave*, sup. ser. 2, vol. 3, Texas Narratives, part 2, 575.

26. Ibid., sup. ser. 1, vol. 10, Mississippi Narratives, part 5, 2298–99.

27. Berlin, Favreau, and Miller, eds., *Remembering Slavery*, 346.

28. Rawick, ed., *The American Slave*, ser. 1 and 2, vol. 6, Alabama and Indiana Narratives, Indiana Narratives, 25.

29. Berlin, Favreau, and Miller, eds., *Remembering Slavery*, 287.

30. Rawick, ed., *The American Slave*, sup. ser. 2, vol. 4, Texas Narratives, part 3, 1215–16.

31. Moses Roper, *A Narrative of the Adventures and Escape of Moses Roper, from American Slavery* (Philadelphia: Merrihew & Gunn, 1838), reprinted in Yuval Taylor, ed., *I Was Born a Slave: An Anthology of Classic Slave Narratives*, vol. 1 (Chicago: Lawrence Hill, 1999), 497.

32. Berlin, Favreau, and Miller, eds., *Remembering Slavery*, 85.

33. Mark M. Smith, "Time, Slavery and Plantation Capitalism in the Ante-Bellum American South," *Past and Present* 150 (1996): 143, 152, 157, 158; Michael O'Malley, *Keeping Watch: A History of American Time* (New York: Viking, 1990), 47.

34. Rawick, ed., *The American Slave*, sup. ser. 1, vol. 10, Mississippi Narratives, part 5, 2148–49.

35. Rawick, ed., *The American Slave*, ser. 1 and 2, vol. 6, Alabama and Indiana Narratives, Alabama Narratives, p. 42.

36. On Pinkster, see Shane White, " 'It Was a Proud Day': African Americans, Festivals, and Parades in the North, 1741–1834," *Journal of American History* 81 (1994): 13–51. But also see Bradford Verter, "Interracial Festivity and Power in Antebellum New York: The Case of Pinkster," *Journal of Urban History* 28 (2002): 398–428.

37. *New-York Weekly Journal*, March 7, 1736.

38. Shane White, ed., "Pinkster in Albany, 1803: A Contemporary Description," *New York History* 70 (1989): 197.

39. Ibid., 198.

40. James Eights, "Pinkster Festivities in Albany Sixty Years Ago," in *Collections on the History of Albany, from Its Discovery to the Present Time*, ed. Joel Munsell, vol. 2 (Albany, NY: J. Munsell, 1865–71), 323–27.

41. Edward Warren, *A Doctor's Experiences in Three Continents* (Baltimore: Cushings & Bailey, 1885), 200–3. The best analysis of Jonkonnu remains Elizabeth A. Fenn, " 'A Perfect Equality Seemed to Reign': Slave Society and Jonkonnu," *North Carolina Historical Review* 65 (1988): 127–53.

42. Quoted in Abrahams, *Singing the Master*, 328. *Singing the Master* is the best analysis of corn shucking and has strongly influenced this account.

43. "Negro Minstrelsy—Ancient and Modern," *Putnam's Magazine* (January 1855): 77, reprinted in Abrahams, *Singing the Master*, 231–32.

44. James Battle Avirett, *The Old Plantation* (New York: F. T. Neely, 1901), reprinted in Abrahams, *Singing the Master*, 235–37.

45. William Wells Brown, M.D., *My Southern Home, or the South and Its People* (Boston: A. G. Brown, 1880), reprinted in Abrahams, *Singing the Master*, 246–49.

46. Elizabeth Ware Pearson, ed., *Letters From Port Royal Written at the Time of the Civil War* (Boston: W. B. Clark, 1906), 252–53.

47. Quoted in Sylvia R. Frey and Betty Wood, *Come Shouting to Zion: African American Protestantism in the American South and British Caribbean to 1830* (Chapel Hill: University of North Carolina Press, 1998), 24.

48. Rawick, ed., *The American Slave*, sup. ser. 2, vol. 2, Texas Narratives, part 1, 215.

49. Ibid., vol. 5, Texas Narratives, part 4, 1447.

50. Ibid., vol. 4, Texas Narratives, part 3, 1050.

51. Rawick, ed., *The American Slave*, ser. 1 and 2, vol. 12, Georgia Narratives, parts 1 and 2, part 2, 262.

52. Pearson, ed., *Letters from Port Royal*, 252–53.

53. Rawick, ed., *The American Slave*, sup. ser. 1, vol. 8, Mississippi Narratives, part 3, 1273.

54. Quoted in David R. Roediger, "And Die in Dixie: Funerals, Death, & Heaven in the Slave Community 1700–1865," *Massachusetts Review* 22 (1981): 170. This article was influential in shaping what we have written about funerals.

55. Rawick, ed., *The American Slave*, sup. ser. 1, vol. 7, Mississippi Narratives, part 2, 411.

56. Ibid., vol. 1, Alabama Narratives, part 1, 293.

57. Quoted in Roediger, "And Die in Dixie," 170.

58. Rawick, ed., *The American Slave*, sup. ser. 1, vol. 8, Mississippi Narratives, part 3, 1273.

59. For another use of the verb to "funeralize," see Rawick, ed., *The American Slave*, sup. ser. 2, vol. 6, Texas Narratives, part 5, 1950. For more recent use, see, for example, Karla F. C. Holloway, *Passed On: African American Mourning Stories* (Durham, NC: Duke University Press, 2002); chapter 4 is titled "Funeralized."

60. Rawick, ed., *The American Slave*, ser. 1 and 2, vol. 13, Georgia Narratives, parts 3 and 4, part 3, 43.

61. Ibid., vol. 12, Georgia Narratives, parts 1 and 2, part 1, 207.

62. Ibid., vol. 13, Georgia Narratives, parts 3 and 4, part 4, 20.

63. Rawick, ed., *The American Slave*, ser. 1 and 2, vol. 13, Georgia Narratives, parts 3 and 4, part 3, 300; vol. 12, Georgia Narratives, part 1, 207.

64. Rawick, ed., *The American Slave*, ser. 1 and 2, vol. 12, Georgia Narratives, part 2, 262; 5.

65. Ibid., vol. 6, Alabama and Indiana Narratives, part 1, 284.

66. Rawick, ed., *The American Slave*, sup. ser. 1, vol. 1, Alabama Narratives, part 1, 114.

67. Rawick, ed., *The American Slave*, ser. 1 and 2, vol. 12, Georgia Narratives, part 1, 77.

68. Rawick, ed., *The American Slave*, sup. ser. 2, vol. 9, Texas Narratives, part 8, 3757.

69. Rawick, ed., *The American Slave*, ser. 1 and 2, vol. 12, Georgia Narratives, part 2, 215.

70. Lucy Galloway told her interviewer that "I members once 'bout a African preacher tellin' us how dey burried folks in Africy. Dey always buried dem at night. Dey would dig de grave and when night would come dey all carried a torch and followed single file atter de ones totin' de corpse." Rawick, ed., *The American Slave*, sup. ser. 1, vol. 8, Mississippi Narratives, part 3, 810.

71. John Dixon Long, *Pictures of Slavery in Church and State* (Philadelphia: published by the author, 1857), quoted in Eileen Southern and Josephine Wright, *Images: Iconography of Music in African-American Culture, 1770s–1920s* (New York: Garland, 2000), 52.

72. Rawick, ed., *The American Slave*, sup. ser. 1, vol. 3, Georgia Narratives, part 1, 83.

73. Rawick, ed., *The American Slave*, ser. 1 and 2, vol. 12, Georgia Narratives, part 1, 208.

74. Long, *Pictures of Slavery*, quoted in Southern and Wright, *Images*, 52. On Africa, see Melville J. Herskovits, *The Myth of the Negro Past* (Boston: Beacon, 1958), 201–3; Roediger, "And Die in Dixie."

75. For eighteenth-century examples in what would become the United States, see Philip D. Morgan, *Slave Counterpoint: Black Culture in the Eighteenth-Century Chesapeake & Lowcountry* (Chapel Hill: University of North Carolina Press, 1998), 643–44.

76. Long, *Pictures of Slavery*, quoted in Southern and Wright, *Images*, 52.

77. Hamilton W. Pierson, *In the Brush; or, Old-Time Social, Political, and Religious Life in the Southwest* (New York: D. Appleton, 1881), quoted in Southern and Wright, *Images*, 53 (our emphasis).

78. Rawick, ed., *The American Slave*, ser. 1 and 2, vol. 12, Georgia Narratives, part 1, 208.

79. Viator, "The Night Funeral of a Slave," *Home Journal*, reprinted in *De*

Bow's Review 20 (1856): 218–21, reprinted in Paul F. Paskoff and Daniel J. Wilson, eds., *The Cause of the South: Selections From De Bow's Review, 1846–1867* (Baton Rouge: Louisiana State University Press, 1982), 54–57.

80. *Marion Harland's Autobiography: The Story of a Long Life* (New York: Harper & Brothers, 1910), quoted in Gregg D. Kimball, *American City, Southern Place: A Cultural History of Antebellum Richmond* (Athens: University of Georgia Press, 2000), 51.

CHAPTER 2 *"To translate everyday experiences into living sound"*

1. Frederick Law Olmsted, *The Slave States*, ed. Harvey Wish (New York: Capricorn, 1959 [orig. pub. 1856]), 114–15.
2. Samuel A. Floyd Jr., *The Power of Black Music: Interpreting Its History from Africa to the United States* (New York: Oxford University Press, 1995), 46.
3. Harold Courlander, *Negro Folk Music, U.S.A.* (New York: Columbia University Press, 1963), 85.
4. Ibid., 82.
5. Thomas J. Marshall, "Arwhoolie" cornfield holler, Edwards, Mississippi, 1939, Archive of Folk Culture, Library of Congress, AFS L8 (A6).
6. The Works Progress Administration interviews with ex-slaves were conducted in the 1930s and published in several series in the 1970s. The full citation is George P. Rawick, ed., *The American Slave: A Composite Autobiography*, Series 1 and 2 (ser. 1 and 2), 19 vols. (Westport, CT: Greenwood, 1972); Supplement, Series 1 (sup. ser. 1), 12 vols. (Westport, CT: Greenwood, 1977); Supplement, Series 2 (sup. ser. 2), 10 vols. (Westport, CT: Greenwood, 1979). If the reference is to the supplements it is stated in the note. In this case the reference is Rawick, ed., *The American Slave*, sup. ser. 2, vol. 9, Texas Narratives, part 8, 3752.
7. Rawick, ed., *The American Slave*, sup. ser. 1, vol. 1, Alabama Narratives, 273.
8. Olmsted, *The Slave States*, 115.
9. Rawick, ed., *The American Slave*, sup. ser. 2, vol. 4, Texas Narratives, part 3, 1022.
10. Rawick, ed., *The American Slave*, ser. 1 and 2, vol. 11, South Carolina Narratives, part 2, 146.
11. Rawick, ed., *The American Slave*, sup. ser. 2, vol. 3, Texas Narratives, part 2, 610.
12. Courlander, *Negro Folk Music*, 81.

13. Ashenafi Kebede, *Roots of Black Music: The Vocal, Instrumental, and Dance Heritage of Africa and Black America* (Englewood Cliffs, NJ: Prentice Hall, 1982), 47.

14. Thomas J. Marshall, "Arwhoolie" cornfield holler, Edwards, Mississippi, 1939, Archive of Folk Culture, Library of Congress, AFS L8 (A6).

15. Enoch Brown, holler, Livingston, Alabama, 1939, Archive of Folk Culture, Library of Congress, AFC 1939/001 2685b2.

16. Roosevelt "Giant" Hudson, field holler, Cummins State Farm, Varner, Arkansas, 1939, Archive of Folk Culture, Library of Congress, AFC 1939/001 2603b2.

17. Willie Henry Washington, "Oh If Your House Catches Fire," Cummins State Farm, Varner, Arkansas, 1939, Archive of Folk Culture, Library of Congress, AFC 1939/001 2663b1.

18. Willis Laurence James, "The Romance of the Negro Folk Cry in America," in *Mother Wit from the Laughing Barrel: Readings and Interpretation of Afro-American Folklore*, ed. Alan Dundes (Englewood Cliffs, NJ: Prentice Hall, 1973), 438.

19. Robert Farris Thompson, "The Song That Named the Land: The Visionary Presence of African-American Art," in *Black Art Ancestral Legacy: The African Impulse in African-American Art* (Dallas, TX: Dallas Museum of Art, 1989), 917.

20. Ibid.

21. Olly Wilson, "The Heterogeneous Sound Ideal in African-American Music," in *New Perspectives on Music: Essays in Honor of Eileen Southern*, ed. Josephine Wright (Warren, MI: Harmonie Park, 1992), 329.

22. Floyd, *The Power of Black Music*, 21.

23. Ibid., 8–9.

24. Willis Laurence James, *Stars in De Elements: A Study of Negro Folk Music*, ed. John Michael Spencer (Durham, NC: Duke University Press, 1995), 33.

25. Dena J. Epstein, *Sinful Tunes and Spirituals: Black Folk Music to the Civil War* (Urbana: University of Illinois Press, 1981 [orig. pub. 1977]), xiii–xv. See also Ronald Radano, *Lying Up a Nation: Race and Black Music* (Chicago: University of Chicago Press, 2003), 49–104.

26. Whitelaw Reid, *After the War: A Tour of the Southern States, 1865–1866*, ed. C. Vann Woodward (New York: Harper and Row, 1965), 100–103.

27. Ibid., 104–5.

28. Ibid., 108–11.

29. Ronald Radano, "Denoting Difference: The Writing of the Slave Spirituals," *Critical Inquiry* 22 (1996): 507.

30. William Francis Allen, Charles Pickard Ware, and Lucy McKim Garrison,

comps., *Slave Songs of the United States* (New York: Oak, 1965 [orig. pub. 1867]), 9–10.

31. Winthrop D. Jordan, *Tumult and Silence at Second Creek: An Inquiry into a Civil War Slave Conspiracy* (Baton Rouge: Louisiana State University Press, 1993), 20.

32. Laurence Oliphant, *Patriots and Filibusters; or, Incidents and Political & Exploratory Travel* (1860), quoted in Epstein, *Sinful Tunes*, 227–28.

33. Lucy McKim, "Songs of the Port Royal Contrabands," reprinted in Bruce Jackson, ed., *The Negro and His Folklore in Nineteenth-Century Periodicals* (Austin: University of Texas Press, 1967), 62.

34. Francis Bebey, *African Music: A People's Art* (London: Harrap, 1975 [orig. pub. 1969]), 2, 115.

35. Quoted in Bebey, *African Music*, 5.

36. Bebey, *African Music*, 115.

37. Frederick Law Olmsted, *The Cotton Kingdom: A Traveller's Observations on Cotton and Slavery in the American South*, ed. Arthur M. Schlesinger (New York: Knopf, 1953), 36.

38. Charles William Janson, *The Stranger in America 1793–1806* (1807), quoted in Epstein, *Sinful Tunes*, 72.

39. Reid, *After the War*, 523.

40. Janson, *The Stranger*, quoted in Epstein, *Sinful Tunes*, 84.

41. William Tallmadge, "Blue Notes and Blue Tonality," *Black Perspective in Music* 12 (1984): 155.

42. Allen, Ware, and Garrison, comps., *Slave Songs of the United States*, 10.

43. Sara Agnes Rice Pryor, *My Day: Reminiscences of a Long Life* (1909), quoted in Epstein, *Sinful Tunes*, 236.

44. Abbe Niles, introduction to William Christopher Handy, ed., *Blues: An Anthology* (1926), quoted in Tallmadge, "Blue Notes and Blue Tonality," 155.

45. Radano, "Denoting Difference," 534.

46. Lucy McKim [Garrison], "Songs of the Port Royal 'Contrabands,'" *Dwight's Journal of Music* 21 (1862): 254–55, quoted in Epstein, *Sinful Tunes*, 261.

47. Reid, *After the War*, 103.

48. Charles Colcock Jones, *Suggestions on the Religious Instruction of the Negroes in the Southern States* (n.d.), quoted in Epstein, *Sinful Tunes*, 201.

49. Thomas Wentworth Higginson, Diary MS, Houghton Library, Harvard University, quoted in Epstein, *Sinful Tunes*, 281.

50. Unsigned review of *Slave Songs of the United States*, in *Lippincott's Magazine* 1 (1868), 341–43, reprinted in Jackson, ed., *The Negro and His Folklore*, 107.

51. Elizabeth Kilham, "Sketches in Color," *Putnam's Magazine* 5 (1870): 309.

52. *Christian Watchman and Reflector*, July 18, 1867, 43.

53. Kilham, "Sketches in Color," 308.

54. *Western Freedman's Aid Commission, Second Annual Report* (1865), quoted in Epstein, *Sinful Tunes*, 276.

55. Thomas Wentworth Higginson, *Army Life in a Black Regiment* (New York: Norton, 1984 [orig. pub. 1864]), 136.

56. Shane White and Graham White, *Stylin': African American Expressive Culture from Its Beginnings to the Zoot Suit* (Ithaca, NY: Cornell University Press, 1998), 5–36.

57. Reid, *After the War*, 103–4.

58. Higginson, Diary MS, quoted in Epstein, *Sinful Tunes*, 281.

59. John Miller Chernoff, *African Rhythm and African Sensibility: Aesthetics and Social Action in African Musical Idioms* (Chicago: University of Chicago Press, 1979), 111.

60. Allen, *Slave Songs*, 75, 14.

61. George Pinckard, *Notes on the West Indies* (1816), quoted in Epstein, *Sinful Tunes*, 10.

62. Jeanette Robinson Murphy, "The Survival of African Folk Music in America," *Popular Science Monthly* 55 (1899): 660–672, reprinted in Jackson, ed., *The Negro and His Folklore*, 328, 331–33.

63. Wilson, "Heterogeneous Sound Ideal" in Wright, ed., *New Perspectives on Music*, 329.

64. Kilham, "Sketches in Color," 308.

CHAPTER 3   *"De music [of the slaves] make dese*
Cab Calloways of today git to de woods an' hide"

1. John Cabell Chenault, *Old Cane Springs: A Story of the War between the States in Madison county, Kentucky* (1937), reprinted in Roger D. Abrahams, *Singing the Master: The Emergence of African-American Culture in the Plantation South* (New York: Pantheon, 1992), 288–92.

2. Eugene L. Schwaab, ed., *Travels in the Old South, Selected from Periodicals of the Times*, 2 vols (Lexington: University of Kentucky Press, 1973), 491, quoted in Dena J. Epstein, *Sinful Tunes and Spirituals: Black Folk Music to the Civil War* (Urbana and Chicago: University of Illinois Press, 1977), 163.

3. "Songs of the Blacks," *Dwight's Journal of Music* 9 (1856): 660–72,

reprinted in *Dwight's Journal of Music* 15 (1859): 178–80, reprinted in Bruce Jackson, ed., *The Negro and His Folklore in Nineteenth-Century Periodicals* (Austin: University of Texas Press, 1967), 51–54.

4. Ira Berlin, Marc Favreau, and Steven F. Miller, eds., *Remembering Slavery: African Americans Talk about Their Personal Experiences of Slavery and Freedom* (New York: Free Press,1998), 176–77.

5. C. F. Sturgis, *Duties of Masters to Servants: Three Premium Essays* (1851), quoted in Epstein, *Sinful Tunes*, 224.

6. Daniel Robinson Hundley, *Social Relations in Our Southern States* (New York: Henry B. Price, 1860), 344–45.

7. Berlin, Favreau, and Miller, eds., *Remembering Slavery*, 185.

8. Glenn Hinson, essay and headnotes for *Virginia Work Songs* (Serrum, VA: BRI Records, 1983), 1.

9. Glenn Hinson, *Eight-Hand Sets and Holy Steps: Early Dance Tunes and Songs of Praise from North Carolina's Black Tradition* (Raleigh: North Carolina Museum of History and North Carolina Arts Council, 1988), 1; Eugene D. Genovese, *Roll Jordan, Roll: The World the Slaves Made* (New York: Vintage, 1976 [orig. pub. 1972]), 234; J. H. Kwabena Nketia, *The Music of Africa* (London: Gollancz, 1975), 206–8, 226.

10. Fredrika Bremer, *America of the Fifties: Letters of Fredrika Bremer*, ed. Adolph B. Benson (New York: American Scandinavian Foundation, 1924), 261–62.

11. Robin D. G. Kelley, *Race Rebels: Culture and Politics, and the Black Working Class* (New York: Free Press, 1994), 2.

12. Arthur Singleton, *Letters from the South and West* (Boston: Richardson and Lord, 1824), 77.

13. A group of convicts at the State Penitentiary, Parchman, Mississippi, 1939, Archive of Folk Culture, Library of Congress, AFC 1939/001 2685b2.

14. John Brown and a group of convicts, "New Buryin' Ground," State Penitentiary, Raiford, Florida, 1939, Archive of Folk Culture, Library of Congress, AFC 1939/001 AFC 2715a2.

15. Clyde Hill and a group of convicts, "Long Hot Summer Days," Clemens State Farm, Brazoria County, Texas, 1939, Archive of Folk Culture, Library of Congress, AFC 1939/001 2597b1.

16. Hinson, *Eight-Hand Sets and Holy Steps*, 1.

17. Edward C. Carter II, John C. Van Horne, and Lee W. Formwalt, eds., *The Journals of Benjamin Henry Latrobe, 1799–1820: From Philadelphia to New Orleans* (New Haven and London: Yale University Press, 1980), vol. 3, 203–4.

18. Nketia, *The Music of Africa*, 89.

19. Francis Bebey, *African Music: A People's Art* (London: Harrap, 1975 [orig. pub. 1969]), 92.

20. Nketia, *The Music of Africa*, 73–74.

21. James R. Creecy, *Scenes in the South, and Other Miscellaneous Pieces* (1860), quoted in Epstein, *Sinful Tunes*, 134.

22. Nketia, *The Music of Africa*, 137–38.

23. Olly Wilson, "The Heterogeneous Sound Ideal in African-American Music," in Josephine Wright, ed., *New Perspectives on Music: Essays in Honor of Eileen Southern* (Warren, MI: Harmonie Park, 1992), 329.

24. Robert Farris Thompson, "An Aesthetic of the Cool: West African Dance," *African Forum* 2, no. 2 (fall 1966): 87, 98.

25. Carter, Van Horne, and Formwalt, eds., *Journals of Benjamin Henry Latrobe*, vol. 3, 204.

26. Eileen Southern, *The Music of Black Americans: A History*, 2nd ed. (New York and London: Norton, 1983 [orig. pub. 1971]), 182; Cecelia Conway, *African Banjo Echoes in Appalachia: A Study of Folk Traditions* (Knoxville: University of Tennessee Press, 1995), 71–72.

27. The Works Progress Administration interviews with ex-slaves were conducted in the 1930s and published in several series in the 1970s. The full citation is George P. Rawick, ed., *The American Slave: A Composite Autobiography*, Series 1 and 2 (ser. 1 and 2), 19 vols. (Westport, CT: Greenwood, 1972); Supplement, Series 1 (sup. ser. 1), 12 vols. (Westport, CT: Greenwood, 1977); Supplement, Series 2 (sup. ser. 2), 10 vols. (Westport, CT: Greenwood, 1979). If the reference is to the supplements it is stated in the note. In this case the reference is Rawick, ed., *The American Slave*, ser. 1 and 2, vol. 5, Texas Narratives, parts 3 and 4, part 4, 198.

28. Rawick, *The American Slave*, ser. 1 and 2, vol. 12, Georgia Narratives, parts 1 and 2, part 1, 163.

29. Ibid., vol. 5, Texas Narratives, part 4, 228.

30. Ibid., vol. 7, Oklahoma and Mississippi Narratives, Oklahoma Narratives, 224.

31. Rawick, *The American Slave*, sup. ser. 1, vol. 11, North Carolina and South Carolina Narratives, South Carolina Narratives, 128.

32. Ibid., sup. ser. 2, vol. 2, Texas Narratives, part 1, 311–12. For an account of slave musical instruments with a different set of emphases from ours, see Richard Cullen Rath, *How Early America Sounded* (Ithaca, NY: Cornell University Press, 2003), 77–94.

33. Sue Eakin and Joseph Logsdon, eds., *Solomon Northup, Twelve Years a Slave* (Baton Rouge: Louisiana State University Press, 1968 [orig. pub. 1853]), 167.

34. Frederick Douglass, *My Bondage and My Freedom* (New York: Arno Press and *New York Times,* 1968 [orig. pub. 1855]), 252–53.

35. Sidney Lanier, *The Science of English Verse* (1880), quoted in Epstein, *Sinful Tunes,* 142–43.

36. Rawick, ed., *The American Slave,* ser. 1 and 2, vol. 13, Georgia Narratives, parts 3 and 4, part 3, 334.

37. Rawick, ed., *The American Slave,* sup. ser. 2, vol. 4, Texas Narratives, part 3, 1196.

38. Rawick, ed., *The American Slave,* ser. 1 and 2, , vol. 3, South Carolina Narratives, part 3, 244.

39. Charles Lanman, *Haw-Ho-Noo; or, Records of a Tourist* (Philadelphia: Lippincott, Grambo, 1850), 144–45.

40. Ibid.

41. Rawick, ed., *The American Slave,* ser. 1 and 2, vol. 12, Georgia Narratives, parts 1 and 2, part 2, 6.

42. Hinson, *Eight-Hand Sets and Holy Steps,* 12.

43. Kelley, *Race Rebels,* 71.

44. Abrahams, *Singing the Master,* 93.

45. Ibid., xxiii.

46. Ibid., xviii–xix.

47. Jeanette Robinson Murphy, "The Survival of African Folk Music in America," *Popular Science Monthly* 55 (1899): 660–72, reprinted in Bruce Jackson, ed., *The Negro and His Folklore in Nineteenth-Century Periodicals* (Austin: University of Texas Press), 328, 331–33.

48. Kilham, "Sketches in Color," *Putnam's Magazine* 5 (1870): 308.

49. Bebey, *African Music,* 40–41.

50. Nketia, *The Music of Africa,* 178.

51. Robert Farris Thompson, *Flash of the Spirit: African & Afro-American Art & Philosophy* (New York: Vintage, 1984), 208–10. The English explorer Thomas Edward Bowdich, who visited the Ashantee early in the nineteenth century, reported that the more important public officials wore garments made from "costly foreign silks which had been unravelled to weave them in all the varieties of colour, as well as pattern." Thomas Edward Bowdich, *Mission from Cape Coast to Ashantee* (1819), reprinted in Eileen Southern, ed., *Readings in Black American Music* (New York: Norton, 1971), 10.

52. Rawick, ed., *The American Slave,* ser. 1 and 2, vol. 3, South Carolina Narratives, parts 3 and 4, part 3, 180 (our italics).

53. Rawick, ed., *The American Slave,* sup. ser. 1, vol. 9, Mississippi Narratives, 1641–42.

54. Frances Ann Kemble, *Journal of a Residence on a Georgian Plantation in*

1838–1839, ed. John A. Scott (New York: New American Library, 1975 [orig. pub. 1863]), 93–94.

55. "The Fashions in Guinea," *Harper's New Monthly Magazine* 37 (July 1868): 166–67.

56. Kilham, "Sketches in Color," 308.

57. Thomas Wentworth Higginson, *Army Life in a Black Regiment* (New York and London: Norton, 1984 [orig. pub. 1869]), 136.

CHAPTER 4 *"Sing no hymns
of your own composing"*

1. Norman R. Yetman, ed., *Voices from Slavery* (New York: Holt, Rinehart and Winston, 1970), 262.

2. The Works Progress Administration interviews with ex-slaves were conducted in the 1930s and published in several series in the 1970s. The full citation is George P. Rawick, ed., *The American Slave: A Composite Autobiography,* Series 1 and 2 (ser. 1 and 2), 19 vols. (Westport, CT.: Greenwood, 1972); Supplement, Series 1 (sup. ser. 1), 12 vols. (Westport, CT: Greenwood, 1977); Supplement, Series 2 (sup. ser. 2), 10 vols. (Westport, CT: Greenwood, 1979). If the reference is to the supplements it is stated in the note. In this case the reference is Rawick, ed., *The American Slave,* sup. ser. 2, vol. 4, Texas Narratives, part 3, 1262.

3. Rawick, ed., *The American Slave,* sup. ser. 1, vol. 1, Alabama Narratives, 256.

4. John Watson, *Methodist Error; or, Friendly, Christian Advice to Those Methodists Who Indulge in Extravagant Emotions and Bodily Exercises* (Trenton, NJ: D. & E. Fenton, 1819), 28–30. Italics in original.

5. *The Doctrines and Discipline of the African Methodist Episcopal Church* (Philadelphia: John A. Cunningham, 1817), section 16, 94.

6. K. C., "Virginia," *Zion's Herald* 50 (1873): 133.

7. Jeanette Robinson Murphy, "The Survival of African Music in America," *Popular Science Monthly* 55 (1899): 660–72, reprinted in Bruce Jackson, ed., *The Negro and His Folklore in Nineteenth-Century Periodicals* (Austin: University of Texas Press, 1967), 329.

8. Rawick, ed., *The American Slave,* sup. ser. 2, Texas Narratives, vol. 4, part 3, 978.

9. Ira Berlin, Marc Favreau, and Steven F. Miller, eds., *Remembering Slavery: African Americans Talk about Their Personal Experiences of Slavery and Emancipation* (New York: New Press, 1998), 267.

10. J. Kinnard Jr., "Who Are Our National Poets?" *Knickerbocker Maga-*

zine 26 (1845): 331–41, reprinted in Jackson, *The Negro and His Folklore*, 32.

11. Glenn D. Hinson, *Eight-Hand Sets and Holy Steps: Early Dance Tunes and Songs of Praise from North Carolina's Black Tradition* (Raleigh: North Carolina Museum of History and North Carolina Arts Council, 1988), 6.

12. William Frances Allen, Charles Pickard Ware, and Lucy McKim Garrison, comps., *Slave Songs of the United States* (New York: A. Simpson, 1867), 9.

13. Kinnard, "Who Are Our National Poets?" in Jackson, ed., *The Negro and His Folklore*, 29.

14. Rawick, ed., *The American Slave*, ser. 1 and 2, vol. 4, Texas Narratives, parts 1 and 2, part 2, 26.

15. Hinson, *Eight-Hand Sets and Holy Steps*, 6.

16. Rawick, ed., *The American Slave*, ser. 1 and 2, vol. 6, Alabama and Indiana Narratives, Alabama Narratives, part 1, 228.

17. Rawick, *The American Slave*, sup. ser. 2, vol. 6, Texas Narratives, part 5, 2390–91.

18. Ibid., sup. ser. 1, vol. 1, Alabama Narratives, 235.

19. Hinson, *Eight-Hand Sets and Holy Steps*, 6.

20. Glenn D. Hinson, *Fire in My Bones: Transcendence and the Holy Spirit in African American Gospel Music* (Philadelphia: University of Pennsylvania Press, 2000), 194.

21. Henry Russell, *Cheer, Boys, Cheer: Memoirs of Men and Music* (London: John Macqueen, 1895), 85.

22. Charles Carleton Coffin, *Four Years of Fighting: A Volume of Personal Observation with the Army and Navy. From the First Battle of Bull Run to the Fall of Richmond* (Boston: Ticknor and Fields, 1866), 229.

23. Harvey Williams, "Go Preach My Gospel," New Zion Baptist Church, Clemson, South Carolina, 1939, Archive of Folk Culture, Library of Congress, AFC 1939/001 2663b1.

24. Willie Henry Washington, Arthur Bell, Robert Lee Roberston, Abraham Powell, "Jesus, My God, I Know His Name," Cummins State Farm, near Varner, Arkansas, 1939, Archive of Folk Culture, Library of Congress, AFC 1939/001 2668a1.

25. John Brown and a group of convicts, "New Buryin' Ground," State Penitentiary, Raiford, Florida, 1939, Archive of Folk Culture, Library of Congress, AFC 1939/001 2715a2.

26. Clyde Hill and a group of Negro convicts, Clemens State Farm, Brazoria County, Texas, Archive of Folk Culture, Library of Congress, AFC 1939/001 2597b1.

27. Hinson, *Eight-Hand Sets and Holy Steps*, 6.

28. Allen, Ware, and Garrison, comps., *Slave Songs of the United States*, 12.

29. W[illiam] Faux, *Memorable Days in America: Being a Journal of a Tour to the United States* (London: W. Simpkin and R. Marshall, 1823), 95.

30. Victoria Clay, *A Belle of the Fifties: Memoirs of Mrs. Clay of Alabama, Covering Social and Policital Life in Washington and the South, 1853–1866*, ed. Ada Sterling (New York: Doubleday, Page, 1905), 220.

31. Zora Neale Hurston, *The Sanctified Church: The Folklore Writings of Zora Neale Hurston* (Berkeley, CA: Turtle Island Press, 1981), 162–63.

32. Glenn D. Hinson, conversation with Graham White, March 1999.

33. Charles Lyell, *A Second Visit to the United States of North America* (1849), quoted in Lawrence W. Levine, *Black Culture and Black Consciousness: Afro-American Folk Thought from Slavery to Freedom* (New York: Oxford University Press, 1977), 31.

34. Mary Dickson Arrowood and Thomas Hoffman Hamilton, "Nine Negro Spirituals, 1850–1861," *Journal of American Folklore* 41 (1928): 582, 584, quoted in Levine, *Black Culture and Black Consciousness*, 31.

35. Glenn D. Hinson, essay and headnotes, *Virginia Work Songs* (Serrum, VA: BRI Records, 1983), 7–8.

36. Florida Hampton, "Go to Sleep," Livingston, Alabama, 1939, Archive of Folk Culture AFC 1939/001 2698b1.

37. Houston A. Baker Jr., *Blues, Ideology, and Afro-American Literature: A Vernacular Theory* (1984), quoted in Roger D. Abrahams, *Singing the Master: The Emergence of African-American Culture in the Plantation South* (New York: Pantheon, 1992), 121.

38. Albert Murray, "Improvisation and the Creative Process," in *The Jazz Cadence of American Culture*, ed. Robert G. O'Meally (New York: Columbia University Press, 1998), 112.

39. Karin Barber, "Interpreting Oriki as History and Literature," in *Discourse and Its Disguises: The Interpretation of African Oral Texts*, ed. Karin Barber and P. F. de Moraes Farias (Birmingham, UK: University of Birmingham Center of West African Studies, 1989), 16–18.

40. *The Family Magazine*, 1836, 42, quoted in Abrahams, *Singing the Master*, 209–10.

41. John Lambert, *Travels through Canada and the United States, in the Years 1806, 1807 and 1808* (1814), quoted in Dena J. Epstein, *Sinful Tunes and Spirituals: Black Folk Music to the Civil War* (Chicago: University of Illinois Press, 1981 [orig. pub. 1977], 167.

42. Brett Sutton and Pete Hartman, liner notes to *Primitive Baptist Hymns of the Blue Ridge* (Chapel Hill: American Folklore Recordings, University of North Carolina Press, 1982), 15.

43. Roger D. Abrahams, "Concerning African Performance Patterns," in *Neo-African Literature and Culture: Essays in Memory of Janheinz Jahn*, ed. Bernth Lindfors and Ulla Schild (Wiesbaden: B. Heymann, 1976), 34.

44. Lorenzo Dow Turner, *Africanisms in the Gullah Dialect* (Ann Arbor: University of Michigan Press, 1973 [orig. pub. 1949]), 265, 267.

45. Alex Bontemps, "Outlandishly Sensible: Surviving Acculturation: Self-Creativity/ Black Life in the American South Prior to 1920," unpublished MS, 359.

CHAPTER 5 *"He can invent a plausible Tale at a Moment's Warning"*

1. Christopher Looby, ed., *The Complete Civil War Journal and Selected Letters of Thomas Wentworth Higginson* (Chicago: University of Chicago Press, 2000), 48–50; Zora Neale Hurston, "Characteristics of Negro Expression," in *Zora Neale Hurston: Folklore, Memoirs, and Other Writings* (New York: Library of America, 1995), 830.

2. Ira Berlin, *Many Thousands Gone: The First Two Centuries of Slavery in North America* (Cambridge, MA: Harvard University Press, 1998); Samuel Dyssli, "Charlestown, 3 December 1737" *South Carolina Historical and Genealogical Magazine* 23 (1922): 90, quoted in Peter H. Wood, "'More Like a Negro Country': Demographic Patterns in Colonial South Carolina, 1700–1740," in *Race and Slavery in the Western Hemisphere: Quantitative Studies*, ed. Stanley L. Engerman and Eugene D. Genovese (Princeton, NJ: Princeton University Press, 1975), 131–32. Our account of eighteenth-century slave speech has drawn particularly from Alex Bontemps, *The Punished Self: Surviving Slavery in the Colonial South* (Ithaca, NY: Cornell University Press, 2001); Michael A. Gomez, *Exchanging Our Country Marks: The Transformation of African Identities in the Colonial and Antebellum South* (Chapel Hill: University of North Carolina Press, 1998), 170–85; and Philip D. Morgan, *Slave Counterpoint: Black Culture in the Eighteenth-Century Chesapeake and Lowcountry* (Chapel Hill: University of North Carolina Press, 1998), 560–80.

3. Morgan, *Slave Counterpoint*, 561; *South-Carolina and American General Gazette*, June 3, 1774, reprinted in Lathan A. Windley, comp., *Runaway Slave Advertisements: A Documentary History from the 1730s to 1790* (Wesport, CT: Greenwood Press, 1983), vol. 3, 455.

4. *Virginia Gazette*, February 7, 1771, reprinted in Windley, comp., *Runaway Slave Advertisements*, vol. 1, 310.

5. *State Gazette of South Carolina*, July 31, 1786, reprinted in Windley, comp., *Runaway Slave Advertisements*, vol. 3, 400.

6. Gomez, *Exchanging Our Country Marks*, 170–75.

7. *Virginia Gazette*, April 21, 1738, reprinted in Windley, comp., *Runaway Slave Advertisements*, vol. 1, 4; *Maryland Gazette*, August 20, 1761, reprinted in Windley, comp., *Runaway Slave Advertisements*, vol. 2, 41.

8. *Virginia Gazette*, August 10, 1769, reprinted in Windley, comp., *Runaway Slave Advertisements*, vol. 1, 300; *South Carolina Gazette*, August 30, 1773, reprinted in Windley, comp., *Runaway Slave Advertisements*, vol. 3, 328.

9. *South Carolina Gazette*, September 6, 1770, reprinted in Windley, comp., *Runaway Slave Advertisements*, vol. 3, 291.

10. Morgan, *Slave Counterpoint*, 587–89.

11. *South-Carolina and American General Gazette*, August 26, 1771, reprinted in Windley, comp., *Runaway Slave Advertisements*, vol. 3, 441; *Royal Gazette*, October 24, 1781, reprinted in Windley, comp., *Runaway Slave Advertisements*, vol. 3, 590.

12. *Maryland Gazette*, March 24, 1785, reprinted in Windley, comp., *Runaway Slave Advertisements*, vol. 4, 178–79; *Georgia Gazette*, August 5, 1790, reprinted in Windley, comp., *Runaway Slave Advertisements*, vol. 2, 151.

13. *Virginia Gazette*, March 30, 1776, reprinted in Windley, comp., *Runaway Slave Advertisements*, vol. 1, 175–76; *Virginia Gazette and Weekly Advertiser*, November 5, 1785, reprinted in Windley, comp., *Runaway Slave Advertisements*, vol. 1, 233–34.

14. *Virginia Gazette*, January 23, 1778, reprinted in Windley, comp., *Runaway Slave Advertisements*, vol. 1, 192.

15. Hurston, "Characteristics of Negro Expression," 831.

16. *Virginia Gazette*, March 19, 1772, reprinted in Windley, comp., *Runaway Slave Advertisements*, vol. 1, 111; *South Carolina Gazette*, August 4, 1733, reprinted in Windley, comp., *Runaway Slave Advertisements*, vol. 3, 7.

17. *New Jersey Journal*, May 7, 1780, reprinted in Graham Russell Hodges and Alan Edward Brown, eds., *"Pretends to Be Free": Runaway Slave Advertisements from Colonial and Revolutionary New York and New Jersey* (New York: Garland, 1994), 228; *New York Gazette*, October 15, 1753, reprinted in Hodges and Edwards, *Pretends to Be Free*, 47.

18. David Waldstreicher, "Reading the Runaways: Self-Fashioning, Print Culture, and Confidence in Slavery in the Eighteenth-Century Mid-Atlantic," *William and Mary Quarterly* 56 (1999): 261.

19. *Greenleaf's New York Journal*, May 3, 1794.

20. *South Carolina and American General Gazette*, January 29, 1768,

reprinted in Windley, comp., *Runaway Slave Advertisements*, vol. 3, 424–25; *Virginia Gazette*, March 30, 1776, reprinted in Windley, comp., *Runaway Slave Advertisements*, vol. 1, 175–76.

21. *Royal Gazette*, June 6, 1781, reprinted in Windley, comp., *Runaway Slave Advertisements*, vol. 3, 581; *South Carolina and American General Gazette*, August 21, 1776, reprinted in Windley, comp., *Runaway Slave Advertisements*, vol. 3, 485–86; *New York Daily Advertiser*, June 25, 1802; *Virginia Gazette*, August 14, 1752, reprinted in Windley, comp., *Runaway Slave Advertisements*, vol. 3, 29.

22. *Maryland Journal and Baltimore Advertiser*, May 25, 1779, reprinted in Windley, comp., *Runaway Slave Advertisements*, vol. 2, 223.

23. *New York Daily Advertiser*, July 21, 1792; *New Jersey Journal*, December 16, 1789; *Centinel of Freedom*, February 9, 1802.

24. *New York Daily Advertiser*, August 30, 1794; *New York Daily Advertiser*, May 19, 1789.

25. *South Carolina Gazette*, March 4, 1756, reprinted in Windley, comp., *Runaway Slave Advertisements*, vol. 3, 141; *South Carolina Gazette*, June 14, 1740, reprinted in Windley, comp., *Runaway Slave Advertisements*, vol. 3, 41.

26. Waldstreicher, "Reading the Runaways," 258. Some of the following argument was first rehearsed in a different context in Shane White, *Stories of Freedom in Black New York* (Cambridge, MA: Harvard University Press, 2002).

27. *Poulson's American Daily Advertiser*, January 2, 1813.

28. For the 1790s, see Shane White, *Somewhat More Independent: The End of Slavery in New York City, 1770–1810* (Athens: University of Georgia Press, 1991), 66–75.

29. On "Bobalition" and the African Grove Theater, see White, *Stories of Freedom*.

30. *New-York American*, May 24, 1828.

31. Mrs. Felton, *American Life: A Narrative of Two Years' City and Country Residence in the United States* (Boulton Percy, UK: privately printed, 1843), 56–57.

32. Ann Fripp Hampton, ed., *A Divided Heart: Letters of Sally Baxter Hampton, 1853–1862* (Spartanburg, SC: Reprint Company, 1980), 11–12. The assessment of Christy is taken from Edward Le Roy Rice, *Monarchs of Minstrelsy, From "Daddy" Rice to Date* (New York: Kenny, 1911), 20.

33. The Works Progress Administration interviews with ex-slaves were conducted in the 1930s and published in several series in the 1970s. The full citation is George P. Rawick, ed., *The American Slave: A Composite Autobiography*, Series 1 and 2 (ser. 1 and 2), 19 vols. (Westport, CT: Green-

wood, 1972); Supplement, Series 1 (sup. ser. 1), 12 vols. (Westport, CT: Greenwood, 1977); Supplement, Series 2 (sup. ser. 2), 10 vols. (Westport, CT: Greenwood, 1979). If the reference is to the supplement it is stated in the note. In this case the reference is Rawick, *The American Slave*, sup. ser. 2, vol. 3, Texas Narratives, part 2, 637.

34. Rawick, *The American Slave*, ser. 1 and 2, vol. 3, South Carolina Narratives, parts 3 and 4, part 3, 65.

35. For Gullah, see Lorenzo Dow Turner, *Africanisms in the Gullah Dialect* (Ann Arbor: University of Michigan Press, 1949); Charles Joyner, *Down By the Riverside: A South Carolina Slave Community* (Urbana: University of Illinois Press, 1984), 196–224; Samuel Gaillard Stoney and Gertrude Mathews, *Black Genesis: A Chronicle* (New York: Macmillan, 1930); Mason Crum, *Gullah: Negro Life in the Carolina Sea Islands* (Durham, NC: Duke University Press, 1940); Guy B. Johnson, *Folk Culture on St. Helena Island, South Carolina* (Chapel Hill: University of North Carolina Press, 1930).

36. Frances Ann Kemble, *Journal of a Residence on a Georgian Plantation in 1838–1839*, ed. John A. Scott (New York: Knopf, 1961 [orig. pub. 1863]), 251.

37. Quoted in Charles Joyner, " 'If You Ain't Got Education': Slave Language and Thought in Antebellum Charleston," in *Intellectual Life in Antebellum Charleston*, ed. Michael O'Brien and David Moltke Hansen (Knoxville: University of Tennessee Press, 1986), 258.

38. J[ames Miller] McKim, "Negro Songs," in *The Negro and His Folklore in Nineteenth-Century Periodicals*, ed. Bruce Jackson (Austin: University of Texas Press, 1967), 60.

39. Charles Nordhoff, *The Freemen of South Carolina: Some Account of their Appearance, Character, Condition, and Peculiar Customs* (New York: Charles T. Evans, 1863), 8.

40. Rawick, *The American Slave*, ser. 1 and 2, vol. 7, Oklahoma and Mississippi Narratives, Mississippi Narratives, 91.

41. Looby, *The Complete Civil War Journal and Selected Letters of Thomas Wentworth Higginson*, 253.

42. Ibid., 79.

43. Ibid., 156.

44. Ibid., 163.

45. William Francis Allen, Charles Pickard Ware, and Lucy McKim Garrison, comps., *Slave Songs of the United States* (New York: Oak, 1965 [orig. pub. 1867]), 14–17.

46. Looby, *The Complete Civil War Journal and Selected Letters of Thomas Wentworth Higginson*, 69.

47. Ibid., 174.

48. Alice D. Boyle, "Uh Yeddy Um, but Uh Ent Shum ... When They Gone, They Gone." This excellent paper, together with recordings of Demus Green's folktales, can be found in the Southern Folk Life Collection in the Wilson Library, University of North Carolina, Chapel Hill.

49. Frederick Law Olmsted, *The Cotton Kingdom: A Traveller's Observations on Cotton and Slavery in the American States*, ed. Arthur M. Schlesinger (New York: Knopf, 1953), 229.

50. Ronnie W. Clayton, *Mother Wit: The Ex-Slave Narratives of the Louisiana Writers' Project* (New York: Peter Lang, 1990), 104–5.

51. Lewis Clarke, "Leaves from a Slave's Journal of Life," reprinted in John W. Blassingame, ed., *Slave Testimony: Two Centuries of Letters, Speeches, Interviews and Autobiographies* (Baton Rouge: Louisiana State University Press, 1977), 163–64.

52. Ibid., 158.

53. Ibid., 151.

54. Ibid., 151–52.

55. Ibid., 152.

56. Ibid., 157.

57. Lester B. Shippe, ed., *Bishop Whipple's Southern Diary, 1843–1844* (Minneapolis; University of Minnesota Press, 1937), 112.

58. David McRae, *The American at Home: Pen-and-Ink Sketches of American Men, Manners and Institutions* (Edinburgh: Edmonston and Douglas, 1870), vol. 2, 73.

59. *New York Spectator*, February 19, 1822.

60. Quoted in Ruth Finnegan, *Oral Literature in Africa* (Oxford: Clarendon, 1970), 444.

61. Finnegan, *Oral Literature in Africa*, 444; Ruth Finnegan, *Limba Stories and Story-Telling* (Oxford: Clarendon, 1967), 42; Ethel M. Albert, "'Rhetoric,' 'Logic,' and 'Poetics,' in Burundi: Culture Patterning of Speech Behavior," *American Anthropologist* 66, no. 6, part 2 (December 1964): 35.

62. Virginia Ingraham Burr, ed., *The Secret Eye: The Journal of Gertrude Clanton Thomas, 1848–1889* (Chapel Hill: University of North Carolina Press, 1990), 194.

63. *New York Transcript*, July 23, 1834. Still one of the sharpest accounts of black eloquence is Hurston, "Characteristics of Negro Expression," 830–46.

64. Henri Herz, *My Travels in America*, trans. Henry Bertram Hill (Madison: State Historical Society of Wisconsin, 1963 [orig. pub. in French in 1866]), 75.

65. Frederick J. Jobson, *America and American Methodism* (London: J. S. Virtue, 1857), 65.

66. Peter Bailey, *Popular Culture and Performance in the Victorian City* (Cambridge, UK: Cambridge University Press, 1998), 197.

67. William Thomson, *A Tradesman's Travels, in the United States and Canada, in the Years 1840, 41, & 42* (Edinburgh: Oliver and Boyd, 1842), 192.

68. Lawrence W. Levine, *Black Culture and Black Consciousness: Afro-American Folk Thought from Slavery to Freedom* (New York: Oxford University Press, 1977), 298–366.

69. Mikhail Bakhtin, *Rabelais and His World*, trans. Hélène Iswolsky (Bloomington: Indiana University Press, 1984), 59–144.

70. Levine, *Black Culture and Black Consciousness*, 81–135.

71. Trying to collect contemporary evidence about slave storytelling is very difficult. Levine noted that very few of his tales were collected during the time of slavery, most coming from Reconstruction or even later in the century. See Levine, *Black Culture and Black Consciousness*, 81.

72. Lewis W. Paine, *Six Years in a Georgia Prison: Narrative of Lewis W. Paine* (Boston: Bela Marsh, 1852), quoted in Ronald Radano, *Lying Up a Nation: Race and Black Music* (Chicago: University of Chicago Press, 2003), 143.

73. J. K. Paulding, *Slavery in the United States* (New York: Harper and Brothers, 1836), 209.

74. James Weldon Johnson, *Along This Way: The Autobiography of James Weldon Johnson* (New York: Viking, 1968 [orig. pub. 1933]), 120.

75. Rhys Isaac, *Landon Carter's Uneasy Kingdom* (New York: Oxford University Press, 2004), 224. See p. xv for diary details.

76. John Davis, *Travels of Four Years and a Half in the United States of America* (1803), quoted in Morgan, *Slave Counterpoint*, 325.

77. Mark A. De Wolfe Howe, ed., "Journal of Josiah Quincy, Junior, 1773," Massachusetts Historical Society *Proceedings* 49 (1916): 456–57.

78. H. Roy Merrens, ed., "A View of Coastal Carolina in 1778: The Journal of Ebenezer Hazard," *South Carolina Historical Magazine* 73 (1972): 181.

79. Rawick, *The American Slave*, sup. ser. 2, vol. 4, Texas Narratives, part 3, 1319–20.

CHAPTER 6 *"Boots or no boots,
I gwine shout today!"*

1. Frederick Law Olmsted, *A Journey in the Back Country* (New York: Mason Brothers, 1860), 187–96.

2. The white churchman John Watson placed this text on the title page of his book *Methodist Error; or Friendly, Christian Advice, To those Methodists,*

Who indulge in extravagant emotions and bodily exercises (Trenton: D. & E. Fenton, 1819).

3. George H. Hepworth, *The Whip, Hoe, and Sword; or, the Gulf-Department in '63* (Boston: Walker, Wise, 1864), 163–65. Ex-slave Steve Weathersby described similar sounds to those heard by Hepworth. When slaves on Weathersby's plantation met on Sundays for worship in log cabins, they "would hum deep and low in long mournful tones swayin' to and fro. Uders would pray and sing soft while de 'Broder Preacher' wuz a deliverin' de humble message." The Works Progress Administration interviews with ex-slaves were conducted in the 1930s and published in several series in the 1970s. The full citation is George P. Rawick, ed., *The American Slave: A Composite Autobiography*, Series 1 and 2 (ser. 1 and 2), 19 vols. (Westport, CT: Greenwood, 1972); Supplement, Series 1 (sup. ser. 1), 12 vols. (Westport, CT: Greenwood, 1977); Supplement, Series 2 (sup. ser. 2), 10 vols. (Westport, CT: Greenwood, 1979). If the reference is to the supplements it is stated in the note. In this case the reference is Rawick, ed., *The American Slave*, sup. ser. 1, vol. 10, Mississippi Narratives, part 5, 2247.

4. Louisiana Writers' Project, *Gumbo Ya-Ya: A Collection of Louisiana Folk Tales* (1945), quoted in Lawrence W. Levine, *Black Culture and Black Consciousness: Afro-American Folk Thought from Slavery to Freedom* (New York: Oxford University Press, 1977), 41.

5. Henry Ward, Prayer, Johnson Place Baptist Church, near Livingston, Alabama, 1939, Archive of Folk Culture, Library of Congress, AFC 1939/001 2693a2.

6. W[illiam] Faux, *Memorable Days in America: Being a Journal of a Tour to the United States* (London: W. Simpkin and R. Marshall, 1823), 420.

7. Letter from Charles Mathews to his wife, Boston, January 7, 1823, quoted in Mrs. Charles Mathews, *Memoirs of Charles Mathews, Comedian* (London: Richard Bentley, 1839), vol. 3, 350.

8. Godfrey T. Vigne, *Six Months in America* (London: Whittaker, Treacher, 1832), vol. 2, 13–14.

9. Ebenezer Davies, *American Scenes, and Christian Slavery: A Recent Tour of Four Thousand Miles in the United States* (London: John Snow, 1849), 198–99.

10. Elizabeth Kilham, "Sketches in Color," *Putnam's Magazine*, March 15, 1870, 305–6, 310.

11. Charles Colcock Jones, *Suggestions on the Religious Instruction of the Negroes in the Southern States* (Philadelphia: Presbyterian Board of Publication, 1847), 15; Art Rosenbaum, *Shout Because You're Free: The Afri-*

can Ring Shout Tradition in Coastal Georgia (Athens: University of Georgia Press, 1998), 23.

12. Davies, *American Scenes*, 262–63.

13. Mechal Sobel, *Trabelin' On: The Slave Journey to an Afro-Baptist Faith* (Westport, CT: Greenwood, 1974), 194–95.

14. Kilham, "Sketches in Color," 306.

15. J. D. C., "Old Jenny's 'Woods Meeting,' " *Christian Watchman and Reflector* (July 18, 1867), 4.

16. John W. Blassingame, ed., *Slave Testimony: Two Centuries of Letters, Speeches, Interviews, and Autobiographies* (Baton Rouge: Louisiana State University Press, 1977), 643.

17. Rawick, ed., *The American Slave*, sup. ser. 1, vol. 8, Mississippi Narratives, part 3, 892–93.

18. Ibid., vol. 11, North Carolina and South Carolina Narratives, 113–14.

19. Francis Bebey, *African Music: A People's Art* (London, 1975 [orig. pub. 1969]) 2, 5, 115.

20. J. H. Kwabena Nketia, *The Music of Africa* (London: Victor Gollancz, Ltd., 1975), 178.

21. Eugene D. Genovese, *Roll, Jordan, Roll: The World the Slaves Made* (New York: Vintage Books, 1976 [orig. pub. 1974]), 189.

22. Yetman, ed., *Voices from Slavery*, 167.

23. Rawick, ed., *The American Slave*, ser. 1 and 2, vol. 6, Alabama and Indiana Narratives, Alabama Narratives, 22.

24. Yetman, ed., *Voices from Slavery*, 202.

25. Rawick, ed., *The American Slave*, ser. 1 and 2, vol. 3, South Carolina Narratives, part 3, 248.

26. Ibid., vol. 4, Texas Narratives, part 2, 170.

27. Rawick, ed., *The American Slave*, sup. ser. 1, Mississippi Narratives, vol. 7, part 2, 623.

28. Margaret Jackson, "Folklore in Slave Narratives before the Civil War," *New York Folklore Quarterly* 11 (1955): 5–6, 12, quoted in Levine, *Black Culture and Black Consciousness*, 41.

29. Rawick, ed., *The American Slave*, sup. ser. 1, vol. 7, Mississippi Narratives, part 2, 515.

30. Ibid., vol. 8, Mississippi Narratives, part 3, 940.

31. Ibid., vol. 11, North Carolina and South Carolina Narratives, 317.

32. Ibid., vol. 1, Alabama Narratives, 41.

33. Rawick, ed., *The American Slave*, ser. 1 and 2, vol. 5, Texas Narratives, part 3, 179.

34. Ibid., vol. 4, Texas Narratives, parts 1 and 2, part 2, 92.

35. Rawick, ed., *The American Slave*, sup. ser. 1, vol. 8, Mississippi Narratives, part 3, 1083.

36. Ibid., sup. ser. 2, vol. 10, Texas Narratives, part 9, 3953.

37. Ibid., vol. 8, Texas Narratives, part 7, 3371.

38. Rawick, ed., *The American Slave*, ser. 1 and 2, vol. 7, Texas Narratives, part 6, 2765–66.

39. Ibid., vol. 6, Alabama and Indiana Narratives, Alabama Narratives, 416.

40. Ibid., vol. 5, Texas Narratives, parts 3 and 4, part 3, 240.

41. Yetman, ed., *Voices of Slavery*, 177.

42. Rawick, ed., *The American Slave*, sup. ser. 1, vol. 10, Mississippi Narratives, part 5, 1926.

43. Rawick, ed., *The American Slave*, ser. 1 and 2, vol. 11, North Carolina and South Carolina Narratives, North Carolina Narratives, 5.

44. Rawick, ed., *The American Slave*, sup. ser. 2, vol. 3, Texas Narratives, part 2, 516.

45. Alan Lomax, liner notes to CD *Southern Journey*, vol. 12, Georgia Sea Islands, Rounder Records.

46. Rawick, ed., *The American Slave*, sup. ser. 2, vol. 6, Texas Narratives, part 5, 2235–36.

47. H. G. Spaulding, "Under the Palmetto," *Continental Monthly* 4 (1863): 188–203; excerpt reprinted in Bruce Jackson, ed., *The Negro and His Folklore in Nineteenth-Century Periodicals* (Austin: University of Texas Press, 1967), 67.

48. Quoted in Dena J. Epstein, *Sinful Tunes and Spirituals: Black Folk Music to the Civil War* (Urbana: University of Illinois Press, 1981 [orig. pub. 1977]), 281–82.

49. Laura Matilda Towne, *Letters and Diary of Laura M. Towne, Written from the Sea Islands of South Carolina, 1862–1884* (1912), quoted in Epstein, *Sinful Tunes*, 282.

50. Joe Washington Brown and Austin Coleman, "Run, Old Jeremiah," *Afro-American Spirituals, Work Songs, and Ballads*, Archive of Folk Song, Library of Congress, Recording Laboratory AFS L3.

51. William Francis Allen, [Marcel, pseud.], "Correspondence: The Negro Dialect," *Nation* 1, no. 24 (December 14, 1865): 745.

52. Our discussion of slave spirituals and their significance owes much to Lawrence Levine's pathbreaking study *Black Culture and Black Consciousness*.

53. James L. Smith, *Autobiography of James L. Smith* (1881), quoted in Albert J. Raboteau, *Slave Religion: The "Invisible Institution" in the Antebellum South* (New York: Oxford University Press, 1980), 243–44.

54. Rawick, ed., *The American Slave*, sup. ser. 1, vol. 1, Alabama Narratives, 20–21.

55. Rawick, ed., *The American Slave*, ser. 1 and 2, vol. 2, South Carolina Narratives, parts. 1 and 2, part 2, 63.

56. Alexander Dromgoole Sims, *A View of Slavery, Moral and Political* (Charleston, SC: A. E. Miller, 1834), quoted in Epstein, *Sinful Tunes*, 221.

57. Quoted in Levine, *Black Culture and Black Consciousness*, 50.

58. Newman I. White, *American Negro Folk-Songs* (Hatboro, PA: Folklore Associates, 1965), 121.

59. Allen, Ware, and Garrison, comps., *Slave Songs of the United States*, 39.

60. Lydia Parrish, *Slave Songs of the Georgia Sea Islands* (Athens: University of Georgia Press, 1992), 47.

61. Parrish, *Slave Songs*, 165.

62. Levine, *Black Culture and Black Consciousness*, 43.

63. Allen, Ware, and Garrison, comps., *Slave Songs of the United States*, 40–41.

64. Quoted in Levine, *Black Culture and Black Consciousness*, 50.

65. King James Version, 1 Peter 2:18.

66. Howard Thurman, *Deep River* (1945), quoted in Levine, *Black Culture and Black Consciousness*, 43–44.

67. Quoted in Levine, *Black Culture and Black Consciousness*, 33.

68. Ibid., 51.

69. Thomas Wentworth Higginson, *Army Life in a Black Regiment* (New York: Norton), 193.

70. Quoted in Levine, *Black Culture and Black Consciousness*, 40.

71. Higginson, *Army Life in a Black Regiment*, 191.

72. Ibid., 189.

73. *Southern Workman* 41 (1912): 241, quoted in Levine, *Black Culture and Black Consciousness*, 51.

74. Ibid.

75. Frederick Douglass, *My Bondage and My Freedom* (New York: Miller, Orton & Mulligan, 1855), reprinted in Eileen Southern, ed., *Readings in Black American Music* (New York: Norton, 1971), 87.

76. Rawick, ed., *The American Slave*, ser. 1 and 2, vol. 5, Texas Narratives, part 4, 198, reprinted in Raboteau, *Slave Religion*, 213.

77. Higginson, *Army Life in a Black Regiment*, 208–9.

78. *The Unwritten History of Slavery* (1941), quoted in Levine, *Black Culture and Black Consciousness*, 51.

79. Mandy Tartt, Sims Tartt, and Betty Atmore, "Job, Job," Livingston, Ala-

bama, 1939, Archive of Folk Culture, Library of Congress, AFC 1939/001 2704a1.

80. Clifford Reed, Johnny May Medlock, and Julia Griffin, "Sometimes I Feel Like a Motherless Child," State Farm, Raiford, Florida, 1939, Archive of Folk Culture, Library of Congress, AFC 1939/001 35556a1.

81. Mary Tollman and the Johnson Place Baptist Church Congregation, "Have Mercy, Lord," Livingston, Alabama, 1939, Archive of Folk Culture, Library of Congress, AFC 1939/001 2694a1.

CHAPTER 7 *"When we had a black preacher that was heaven"*

1. Philip D. Morgan, *Slave Counterpoint: Black Culture in the Eighteenth-Century Chesapeake and Lowcountry* (Chapel Hill: University of North Carolina Press, 1998), 646.

2. Mechal Sobel, *Trabelin' On: The Slave Journey to an Afro-Baptist Faith* (Westport, CT: Greenwood Press), 194.

3. Albert J. Raboteau, *Slave Religion: The "Invisible Institution" in the Antebellum South* (New York: Oxford University Press, 1978), 134.

4. Morgan, *Slave Counterpoint*, 653.

5. Ibid., 653.

6. Raboteau, *Slave Religion*, 103.

7. Ibid., 212.

8. William Thomson, *A Tradesman's Travels, in the United States and Canada, in the Years 1840, 41, & 42* (Edinburgh: Oliver and Boyd, 1842), 175.

9. Bruce Henry Clay, *The New Man. Twenty-Nine Years a Slave. Twenty-Nine Years a Free Man* (York, PA: P. Anstadt, 1895), 73.

10. Petition of James Spare et al., New Castle County to Delaware Assembly, 1831, in Loren Schweninger, ed., *The Southern Debate Over Slavery*, vol. 1, *Petitions to Southern Legislatures, 1778–1864* (Urbana: University of Illinois Press, 2001), 126–27; Petition of Commissioners of Raleigh to North Carolina Assembly, 1842, in Schweninger, ed., *Southern Debate over Slavery*, 184; Petition of Citizens of Hardeman County to Tennessee Assembly, 1857, in Schweninger, ed., *Southern Debate over Slavery*, 231–32.

11. Rawick, ed., *The American Slave*, ser. 1 and 2, vol. 8, Arkansas Narratives, parts. 1 and 2, part 1, 35.

12. Ibid., vol. 10, Arkansas Narratives, parts 5 and 6, part 6, 332.

13. Ibid., vol. 4, Texas Narratives, parts 1 and 2, part 2, 51.

14. Ibid., vol. 7, Oklahoma and Mississippi Narratives, Mississippi Narratives, 171–72.

15. Ibid., Oklahoma Narratives, 69.

16. John Stevens Cabot Abbott, *South or North; or, Impressions Received During a Trip to Cuba and the South* (New York: Abbey and Abbott, 1860), 75.

17. B. B. L. S. [Barbara Leigh Smith Bodichon], "Slave Preaching," *Littell's Living Age*, 65 (1860): 32–33.

18. George H. Hepworth, *The Whip, Hoe, and Sword; or, The Gulf-Department in '63* (Boston: Walker, Wise, and Company, 1864), 166–67.

19. Fredrika Bremer, *America of the Fifties: Letters of Fredrika Bremer*, ed. Adolph B. Benson (New York: American-Scandinavian Foundation, 1924), 132–34.

20. Frederick Law Olmsted, *A Journey in the Back Country* (New York: Mason Brothers, 1860), 193.

21. Godfrey T. Vigne, *Six Months in America* (London: Whittaker, Treacher and Company, 1832), vol. 2, 14.

22. Ebenezer Davies, *American Scenes, and Christian Slavery: A Recent Tour of Four Thousand Miles in the United States* (London: John Snow, 1849), 198–99.

23. Bremer, *America of the Fifties*, 149.

24. Elizabeth Kilham, "Sketches in Color," *Putnam's Magazine* 15 (1870): 304.

25. Charles Carleton Coffin, *Four Years of Fighting: A Volume of Personal Observation of the Army and Navy, from the First Battle of Bull Run to the Fall of Richmond* (Boston: Ticknor and Fields, 1866), 227.

26. Hepworth, *Whip, Hoe, and Sword*, 166–68; 165.

27. Charles A. Raymond, "The Religious Life of the Negro Slave," *Harper's New Monthly Magazine* 27, no. 161 (October 1863): 676–79.

28. C. Vann Woodward, ed., *Mary Chesnut's Civil War* (New Haven, CT: Yale University Press, 1981), 214.

29. Quoted in Dena J. Epstein, *Sinful Tunes and Spirituals: Black Folk Music to the Civil War* (Urbana: University of Illinois Press, 1981 [orig. pub. 1977]), 201, 281; unsigned review of William Francis Allen, Charles Pickard Ware, and Lucy McKim Garrison, comps., *Slave Songs of the United States* (New York: A Simpson, 1867), in *Lippincott's Magazine* (March 1868): 341–43, reprinted in Bruce Jackson, ed., *The Negro and His Folklore in Nineteenth Century Periodicals* (Austin: University of Texas Press, 1967), 107.

30. Bruce A. Rosenberg, *Can These Bones Live? The Art of the American Folk*

Preacher (Urbana: University of Illinois Press, 1988 [orig. pub. 1977]), 51.

31. Charles Colcock Jones, *Suggestions on the Religious Instruction of the Negroes in the Southern States* (Philadelphia: Presbyterian Board of Publication, 1847), 14.

32. James Weldon Johnson, *God's Trombones: Some Negro Sermons in Verse* (London: George Allen & Unwin, 1929), 14, 19–20, 15–16.

33. Charles A. Raymond, "The Religious Life of the Negro Slave," *Harper's New Monthly Magazine* 27, no. 160 (September 1863): 485; 479.

34. Charles A. Raymond, "The Religious Life of the Negro Slave," *Harper's New Monthly Magazine,* 27, no. 161 (October 1863): 679.

35. Charles A. Raymond, "The Religious Life of the Negro Slave," *Harper's New Monthly Magazine* 27, no. 160, 485.

36. Johnson, *God's Trombones,* 19.

37. Ibid., 19, 14, 20.

38. Walter J. Ong, *Interfaces of the Word: Studies in the Evolution of Consciousness and Culture* (Ithaca, NY: Cornell University Press, 1977), 105, 114–15.

39. Glenn Hinson, *Fire in My Bones: Transcendence and the Holy Spirit in African American Gospel* (Philadelphia: University of Pennsylvania Press, 2001), 71.

40. Rev. Harry Singleton, "The Unusual Task of the Gospel Preacher," Sandy Island, South Carolina, January 1972. Recorded by Charles Joyner. Reproduced here with the kind permission of Rev. Singleton.

41. Pete Welding, "Big Joe and Sonny Boy: The Shock of Recognition," record notes to Blues Classics, BC-21; quoted in Michael Ernest Taft, "The Lyrics of Race Record Blues, 1920–1942: A Semantic Approach to the Structural Analysis of a Formulaic System," Ph.D. diss., University of Newfoundland, 1977, 401; Taft, "Lyrics of Race Records Blues," 401–3.

42. Quoted in Patricia Jones-Jackson, "Let the Church Say 'Amen': The Language of Religious Rituals in Coastal South Carolina," in *The Crucible of Carolina: Essays in the Development of Gullah Language and Culture,* ed. Michael Montgomery (Athens: University of Georgia Press, 1994), 120.

43. Jones-Jackson, "Let the Church Say 'Amen,'" 116.

44. Arthur A. Raper, *Preface to Peasantry: A Tale of Two Black Belt Counties* (Chapel Hill: University of North Carolina Press, 1936), 368.

45. Lawrence W. Levine, *Black Culture and Black Consciousness: Afro-American Folk Thought from Slavery to Freedom* (New York: Oxford University Press, 1977), 36–37.

46. Jones-Jackson, "Let the Church Say 'Amen,'" 116.

47. The actual words of Matthew 5:13 in the King James Version are "Ye are the salt of the earth: but if the salt have lost his savour, wherewith shall it be salted? it is thenceforth good for nothing, but to be cast out, and to be trodden under foot of men."

48. Savannah Unit, Georgia Writers' Project, Works Progress Administration, *Drums and Shadows: Survival Studies among the Georgia Coastal Negroes* (Athens and London: University of Georgia Press, 1986 [orig. pub. 1940], 169–70.

49. A fuller version of the sermon can be found in John A. Lomax and Alan Lomax, *Our Singing Country: A Second Volume of American Ballads and Folk Songs* (New York: Macmillan, 1941), 9–13.

CHAPTER 8 *Soundtracks of the City: Charleston, New York, and New Orleans*

1. *South Carolina Gazette*, August 27, 1772; Carl Bridenbaugh, ed., "Patrick M'Robert's Tour through Parts of the North Provinces of America," *Pennsylvania Magazine of History and Biography* 59 (1935): 142. In this book we have used the modern spelling of "Charleston," other than in quotations from the eighteenth century. On eighteenth-century Charleston, see Philip D. Morgan, *Slave Counterpoint: Black Culture in the Eighteenth-Century Chesapeake & Lowcountry* (Chapel Hill: University of North Carolina Press, 1998); Robert Olwell, *Masters, Slaves, and Subjects: The Culture of Power in the South Carolina Low Country, 1740–1790* (Ithaca, NY: Cornell University Press, 1998); Peter H. Wood, *Black Majority: Negroes in Colonial South Carolina from 1670 through the Stono Rebellion* (New York: Knopf, 1974).

2. Philip D. Morgan, "Black Life in Eighteenth-Century Charleston," *Perspectives in American History* (new series) 1 (1984): 191.

3. Frederick Douglass, *Narrative of the Life of Frederick Douglass, An American Slave* (1845), reprinted in *Frederick Douglass: Autobiographies* (New York: Library of America, 1994), 38; Douglass, *My Bondage and My Freedom* (1855), reprinted in *Frederick Douglass: Autobiographies*, 218.

4. Quoted in Morgan, "Black Life in Charleston," 206.

5. Ibid., 206–7.

6. *South Carolina Gazette*, November 5, 1744; *South Carolina Gazette*, April 13, 1745.

7. Mark A. De Wolfe Howe, ed., "Journal of Josiah Quincy, Junior, 1773," *Massachusetts Historical Society Proceedings* 49 (1916): 453; quoted in Morgan, "Black Life In Charleston," 207.

8. *South Carolina Gazette,* May 9, 1768.

9. Ibid., September 5, 1768; June 1, 1769.

10. Ibid., September 24, 1772.

11. *South Carolina and American General Gazette,* February 19, 1778, quoted in Olwell, *Masters, Slaves, and Subjects,* 171; *South Carolina Gazette,* September 24, 1772.

12. Quoted in Olwell, *Masters, Slaves, and Subjects,* 176.

13. Ibid., 170.

14. *South Carolina Gazette,* October 22, 1763.

15. Ibid., September 24, 1772.

16. Ibid., September 17, 1772. The point about deference should not be over-emphasized. Examples of slaves behaving in a prickly, sometimes outrightly aggressive fashion are easy enough to find. See, for example, Morgan, "Black Life in Charleston," 227–28.

17. *Charleston Courier,* August 14, 1804, quoted in Morgan, *Slave Counterpoint,* 584.

18. Betty Wood, *Women's Work, Men's Work: The Informal Slave Economies of Lowcountry Georgia* (Athens: University of Georgia Press, 1995), 147–48.

19. Jon Butler has argued that those who created North American slavery effectively shattered slaves' African belief systems and that, as a result, in the period between the 1760s and the early years of the nineteenth century, "Afro-American Christianity paralleled its white counterpart far more closely than would ever be true again." In these years, Butler maintained, patterns of slave preaching remained close to European models, as also did the manner in which blacks rendered white hymns, whose transformation into something closer to African singing styles took place only slowly over time. The period stretching from the early nineteenth century until the Civil War, however, saw a strengthening of African influences. The outlawing of the slave trade in 1808 had failed to halt the importation of Africans, who brought with them fresh knowledge of the religious practices of their homeland. Increasingly too blacks took control of their own churches, providing blacks with opportunities to practice religion as they wished. In these years as well, Butler pointed out, slave spirituals began to be heard, and black preachers and exhorters crafted a theology that, likening the experiences of the slaves to those of the children of Israel, gave promise of ultimate deliverance. If Butler is right, his suggestions may go some way toward explaining why, in the eighteenth century, whites appear to have paid so little attention to slave music. See Jon Butler, *Awash in a Sea of Faith: Christianizing the American People* (Cambridge, MA: Harvard University Press, 1990), 248–52.

20. Ronald Radano, *Lying Up a Nation: Race and Black Music* (Chicago: University of Chicago Press, 2003), 67. Radano suggestively entitles his chapter "Resonances of Racial Absence." Rhys Isaac, *Landon Carter's Uneasy Kingdom* (New York, Oxford University Press, 2004). For a brilliant rumination on the broader issue of the representation of slaves in eighteenth-century America, both what was included and what was left out, see Alex Bontemps, *The Punished Self: Surviving Slavery in the Colonial South* (Ithaca, NY: Cornell University Press, 2001), 3–81.

21. *Centinel of Freedom*, May 1, 1798; September 26, 1809; October 3, 1809.

22. *The Trial of Amos Broad and His Wife, On Three Several Indictments for Assaulting and Beating Betty, a Slave, and Her Little Female Child Sarah, Aged Three Years* (New York: Henry C. Southwick, 1809); *The People v. Amos Broad,* filed February 25, 1809, District Attorney Indictment Papers, Municipal Archives of the City of New York; statement of Amos Broad, *The People v. Betty* (a Black), filed October 15, DAIP.

23. On the end of slavery in New York, see Shane White, *Somewhat More Independent: The End of Slavery in New York City, 1770–1810* (Athens: University of Georgia Press, 1991).

24. Shane White, *Stories of Freedom in Black New York* (Cambridge, MA: Harvard University Press, 2002), 46–48.

25. *The American,* October 2, 1820; *Commercial Advertiser,* April 17, 1832; *New York American,* July 23, 1830.

26. *The Cries of New York* (New York: Samuel Wood, 1809). For a fascinating account of the larger tradition of which this was a part, see Sean Shesgreen, *Images of the Outcast: The Urban Poor in the Cries of London* (New Brunswick, NJ: Rutgers University Press, 2002).

27. Bayard Still, "New York City in 1824: A Newly Discovered Description," *New-York Historical Society Quarterly* 46 (1962): 149.

28. Petition to the Corporation of the City of New York, August 12, 1817, reprinted in Paul A. Gilje and Howard B. Rock, eds., *Keepers of the Revolution: New Yorkers at Work in the Early Republic* (Ithaca, NY: Cornell University Press, 1992), 218–21.

29. *National Advocate,* August 3, 1821; May 18, 1815; *New York Evening Post,* September 22, 1826.

30. *New-York Enquirer,* March 28, 1827. On black parades, see also Shane White, " 'It was a Proud Day' ": African Americans, Festivals, and Parades in the North, 1741–1834," *Journal of American History* 81 (1994): 13–51.

31. *New York American,* July 6, 1827; *A Memorial Discourse by Reverend Henry Highland Garnet. With an Introduction by James McCune Smith, M.D.* (Philadelphia: Joseph M. Wilson, 1865), 24–26.

32. *National Advocate,* June 21, 1823.

33. *The Sun,* December 18, 1834. On dancing in New York City, see Shane White, "The Death of James Johnson," *American Quarterly* 51 (1999): 753–95.

34. Stuart M. Blumin, ed., *New York By Gas-Light and Other Urban Sketches by George G. Foster* (Berkeley: University of California Press, 1990), 142–43.

35. On use of "black dialect," see White, *Stories of Freedom,* 199–211.

36. *Morning Courier and New-York Enquirer,* February 12, 1833.

37. *New Orleans Daily Picayune,* July 16, 1858.

38. Henry Bradshaw Fearon, *Sketches of America: A Narrative of a Journey of Five Thousand Miles through the Eastern and Western States of America* (London: Longman, Hurst, Rees, Orme, and Brown, 1818), 277.

39. Leonard P. Curry, *The Free Black in Urban America, 1800–1850* (Chicago: University of Chicago Press, 1981), 245–51. On antebellum New Orleans, see John W. Blassingame, *Black New Orleans: 1860–1880* (Chicago: University of Chicago Press, 1973), 1–47.

40. Edward C. Carter II, John C. Van Horne, and Lee W. Formwalt, eds, *The Journals of Benjamin Henry Latrobe, 1799–1820: From Philadelphia to New Orleans* (New Haven, CT: Yale University Press, 1980), vol. 3, 301–2; Joseph R. Roach, "Deep Skin: Reconstructing Congo Square," in *African American Performance and Theater History,* ed. Harry J. Elam Jr. and David Krasner (New York: Oxford University Press, 2001), 101–13.

41. Quoted in Ira Berlin, *Slaves without Masters: The Free Negro in the Antebellum South* (New York: Pantheon, 1974), 307–8.

42. Frederick Law Olmsted, *The Cotton Kingdom: A Traveller's Observations on Cotton and Slavery in the American Slave States,* ed. Arthur M. Schlesinger (New York: Knopf, 1953), 34–35.

43. *Richmond Enquirer,* December 23, 1856.

44. Quoted in Richard C. Wade, *Slavery in the Cities: The South, 1820–1860* (New York: Oxford University Press, 1964), 84. The point about how late most African Americans converted to Christianity, with which we agree, has been emphasized of late by Ira Berlin. See, for example, Ira Berlin, *Generations of Captivity: A History of African-American Slaves* (Cambridge, MA: Harvard University Press, 2003), 161–244.

45. *New Orleans Bee,* October 13, 1835, quoted in Wade, *Slavery in the Cities,* 29.

46. Louisiana Writers' Project, *Gumbo Ya-Ya: A Collection of Louisiana Folk Tales,* compiled by Lyle Saxon, Edward Dreyer, and Robert Tallant (Boston: Houghton Mifflin, 1945), 27–49. The cala vendor's cry is at 32–33.

47. Henry A. Kmen, "Old Corn Meal: A Forgotten Urban Negro Folksinger," *Journal of American Folklore* 75 (1962): 29–34.

48. *New Orleans Bee,* October 13, 1835, quoted in Wade, *Slavery in the Cities,* 29.

49. [Joseph H. Ingraham], *The South-West. By a Yankee* (New York: Harper & Brothers, 1835), vol. 1, 99–102. Although she gives surprisingly little emphasis to the role of African Americans, on the larger role of markets in American society, see Helen Tangires, *Public Markets and Civic Culture in Nineteenth-Century America* (Baltimore: Johns Hopkins University Press, 2003).

50. Louisiana Writers' Project, *Gumbo Ya-Ya,* 30.

51. Quoted in Robin D. G. Kelley, *Freedom Dreams: The Black Radical Imagination* (Boston: Beacon, 2002), 183.

CHAPTER 9 *Soundtracks of the City: Richmond in the 1850s*

1. *Richmond Daily Dispatch,* November 10, 1852.

2. Ibid., November 13, 1852.

3. Ibid., August 12, 1852.

4. Peter Bailey, *Popular Culture and Performance in the Victorian City* (Cambridge, UK: Cambridge University Press, 1998), 195.

5. On Richmond generally see Gregg D. Kimball, *American City, Southern Place: A Cultural History of Antebellum Richmond* (Athens: University of Georgia Press, 2000); Joshua D. Rothman, *Notorious in the Neighborhood: Sex and Families across the Color Line in Virginia, 1787–1861* (Chapel Hill: University of North Carolina Press, 2003); James Sidbury, *Ploughshares into Swords: Race, Rebellion, and Identity in Gabriel's Virginia, 1730–1810* (Cambridge, UK, and New York: Cambridge University Press, 1997); Midori Takagi, *"Rearing Wolves to Our Own Destruction": Slavery in Richmond, Virginia, 1782–1865* (Charlottesville: University Press of Virginia, 1999). The population figures are taken from Kimball, *American City,* 31.

6. *Richmond Daily Dispatch,* December 22, 1852. The most recent study of slave hiring convincingly argues that the practice was in fact endemic to the South. We would still suggest that, in part because of the amount of industry, Richmond was still distinctive in the amount of slave hiring that occurred. See the excellent Jonathan D. Martin, *Divided Mastery: Slave Hiring in the American South* (Cambridge, MA: Harvard University Press, 2004).

7. *Richmond Daily Dispatch,* January 3, 1853.

8. Ibid., December 18, 1855.

9. Ibid., October 28, 1852. On the Winston murders, see Takagi, *"Rearing Wolves to Our Own Destruction,"* 112–15.

10. *Richmond Daily Dispatch*, August 5, 1852.

11. Ibid., September 14, 1852.

12. Ibid., March 9, 1852.

13. Ibid., January 22, 1852.

14. Quoted in Rothman, *Notorious in the Neighborhood,* 121. But see also *Richmond Daily Dispatch*, September 22, 1855, where the mayor explained that a gathering of more than five blacks in a grocery would be unlawful if they were there "for their *own purposes,*" whereas a similar gathering might occur *"for the purposes of the master and yet be lawful."*

15. *Richmond Daily Dispatch*, January 27, 1852.

16. Ibid., September 22, 1852; September 23, 1852. On the enforcement of the law about passes, see *Richmond Daily Dispatch*, January 15, 1852, for the mayor's instructions to have all blacks attending fires at night who did not "belong" to the engines to be "peremptorily" arrested, and *Richmond Daily Dispatch*, February 3, 1852, for a warning about giving slaves unendorsed passes. The mayor intended to carry out the law "to the very letter" and as he noted, "a sound thrashing will make the slaves more particular" about obeying the law exactly.

17. Quoted in Rothman, *Notorious in the Neighborhood,* 120.

18. *Richmond Daily Dispatch*, November 13, 1852.

19. Quoted in Rothman, *Notorious in the Neighborhood,* 120.

20. *Richmond Daily Dispatch*, June 2, 1852.

21. Frances Ann Kemble, *Journal of a Residence on a Georgian Plantation in 1838–1839,* ed. John A. Scott (New York: Meridian, 1975), 47–48; James Kirke Paulding, *Letters from the South, Written during an Excursion in the Summer of 1816 by the Author of John Bull & Brother Jonathan* (New York: James Eastburn, 1817), vol. 1, 117.

22. J. Alexander Patten, "Scenes in the Old Dominion. Number Two—A Tobacco Market," reprinted as "Scenes from Lynchburg," in *Travels in the Old South, Selected from Periodicals of the Times,* ed. Eugene L. Schwaab and Jacqueline Bull (Lexington: University Press of Kentucky, 1973), vol. 2, 541. For a penetrating few lines on whistling, see W. T. Lhamon Jr., *Raising Cain: Blackface Performance from Jim Crow to Hip Hop* (Cambridge, MA: Harvard University Press, 1998), 92–93.

23. *Daily Richmond Examiner*, September 28, 1861.

24. "Congregational Singing in Richmond, Virginia," *Dwight's Journal of Music* 18 (January 12, 1861), 333. On singing in the tobacco factories, see also Suzanne Gehring Schnittman, "Slavery in Virginia's Urban Tobacco

Industry—1840–1860," Ph.D. diss., University of Rochester, 1987, 174–78.

25. William Cullen Bryant, *The Prose Writings of William Cullen Bryant*, ed. Parke Godwin, vol. 2, *Travels, Addresses, and Comments* (New York: Russell & Russell, 1964 [orig. pub. 1884]), 25–26.

26. Quoted in Robert S. Starobin, *Industrial Slavery in the Old South* (New York: Oxford University Press, 1970), 18.

27. Extract from Samuel Mordecai, *Richmond in By-Gone Days* (1856), reprinted in Eileen Southern, comp. and ed., *Readings in Black American Music*, 2nd ed. (New York: Norton, 1983), 136–37.

28. "Congregational Singing in Richmond," 333.

29. "Congregational Singing in Richmond," 333; Bryant, *Travels, Addresses, and Comments*, 25–26.

30. Bryant, *Travels, Addresses, and Comments*, 25–26.

31. *Richmond Daily Dispatch*, July 28, 1852; July 30, 1852.

32. Ibid., July 19, 1855.

33. William Wells Brown, *My Southern Home: or, The South and Its People* (Boston: A. G. Brown, 1880), 211.

34. *Daily Richmond Examiner*, August 17, 1861.

35. *Richmond Daily Dispatch*, March 12, 1852; September 24, 1852. The historiography of the ministrel show is particularly rich. See Dale Cockrell, *Demons of Disorder: Early Blackface Minstrels and Their World* (Cambridge, UK: Cambridge University Press, 1997); W. T. Lhamon Jr, *Jump Jim Crow: Lost Plays, Lyrics, and Street Prose of the First Atlantic Popular Culture* (Cambridge, MA: Harvard University Press, 2003), 1–92; Lhamon, *Raising Cain*; Eric Lott, *Love and Theft: Blackface Minstrelsy and the American Working Class* (New York: Oxford University Press, 1993); William J. Mahar, *Behind the Burnt Cork Mask: Early Blackface Minstrelsy and Antebellum American Popular Culture* (Urbana: University of Illinois Press, 1999).

36. *Richmond Daily Dispatch*, September 24, 1852.

37. Ibid., March 12, 1852.

38. Ibid., September 25, 1852. Some minstrel performers may have paid particular attention to African American culture but at least some contemporaries were confident in their ability to differentiate between white and black. A story in the *Richmond Enquirer*, March 27, 1857, recounted that an "immense crowd" in South Carolina had watched "genuine plantation darkies" perform onstage. According to the writer, Christy's and other minstrel troupes "have never played 'plantation airs' as these little chaps do." He suggested that "if eloquence is essentially based on feeling the subject, the skill of these boys is more than usual eloquent music."

EPILOGUE   *The Sounds of Freedom*

1. Quoted in Leon F. Litwack's magisterial *Been in the Storm So Long: The Aftermath of Slavery* (New York: Knopf, 1980), 171–72.
2. On the way slavery ended, see Litwack, *Been in the Storm So Long*, 64–220.
3. The Works Progress Administration interviews with ex-slaves were conducted in the 1930s and published in several series in the 1970s. The full citation is George P. Rawick, ed., *The American Slave: A Composite Autobiography*, Series 1 and 2 (ser. 1 and 2), 19 vols. (Westport, CT: Greenwood, 1972); Supplement, Series 1 (sup. ser. 1), 12 vols. (Westport, CT: Greenwood, 1977); Supplement, Series 2 (sup. ser. 2), 10 vols. (Westport, CT: Greenwood, 1979). If the reference is to the supplements it is stated in the note. In this case the reference is Rawick, ed., *American Slave*, sup. ser. 1, vol. 10, Mississippi Narratives, 2077.
4. Norman R. Yetman, *Life under the "Peculiar Institution": Selections from the Slave Narrative Collection* (New York: Holt, Rinehart and Winston, 1970), 131.
5. Ibid., 54.
6. See Litwack, *Been in the Storm So Long*, 64–220.
7. T. Lindsay Baker and Julie P. Baker, eds., *The WPA Oklahoma Slave Narratives* (Norman: University of Oklahoma Press, 1996), 105.
8. Rawick, ed., *The American Slave*, ser. 1 and 2, vol. 9, Arkansas Narratives, parts 3 and 4, part 3, 67.
9. Ira Berlin, Marc Favreau, and Steven F. Miller, eds., *Remembering Slavery: African Americans Talk about Their Personal Experiences of Slavery and Emancipation* (New York: New Press, 1998), 265.
10. Rawick, ed., *The American Slave*, ser. 1 and 2, vol. 4, Texas Narratives, part 2, 117.
11. Quoted in Eric Foner, *Reconstruction: America's Unfinished Revolution, 1863–1877* (New York: Harper & Row, 1988), 10.
12. Quoted in Litwack, *Been in the Storm So Long*, 102.
13. Shane White and Graham White, *Stylin': African American Expressive Culture from Its Beginnings to the Zoot Suit* (Ithaca, NY: Cornell University Press, 1998), 130–38.
14. C. Vann Woodward, ed., *Mary Chesnut's Civil War* (New Haven, CT: Yale University Press, 1981), 834.

THE SOUNDS OF SLAVERY

*Recordings of African American field
calls, songs, prayers, and sermons*

Track 1: "Arwhoolie" (cornfield holler), performed by Thomas J. Marshall, at Edwards, Mississippi, in 1939. Recorded by John A. and Ruby T. Lomax.

Track 2: Levee holler, performed by Enoch Brown, at Livingston, Alabama, in 1939. Recorded by John A. and Ruby T. Lomax.

Track 3: Field holler, performed by Roosevelt "Giant" Hudson, at Cummins State Farm, Varner, Arkansas, in 1939. Recorded by John A. and Ruby T. Lomax.

Track 4: "Oh If Your House Catches Fire," levee camp holler, performed by Willie Henry Washington, at Cummins State Farm, Varner, Arkansas, in 1939. Recorded by John A. and Ruby T. Lomax.

Track 5: "Roxie" (work song), sung by a group of convicts at a penitentiary in Parchman, Mississippi, 1939. Recorded by John A. and Ruby T. Lomax.

Track 6: "New Buryin' Ground," sung by John Brown and a group of African American convicts, at the State Penitentiary, Railford, Florida, in 1939. Recorded by John A. and Ruby T. Lomax.

Track 7: "Long Hot Summer Day," sung by Clyde Hill and a group of African American convicts, at Clemens State Farm, Brazoria, Texas, in 1939. Recorded by John A. and Ruby T. Lomax.

Track 8: "Go Preach My Gospel," sung by Deacon Harvey Williams and the New Zion Baptist Church congregation, Clemson, South Carolina, in 1939. Recorded by John A. and Ruby T. Lomax.

Track 9: "Jesus, My God, I Know His Name," sung by Willie Henry Washington, Arthur Bell, Robert Lee Robertson, and Abraham Powell, at Cummins State Farm, near Varner, Arkansas, 1939. Recorded by John A. and Ruby T. Lomax.

Track 10: "Go to Sleep," sung by Florida Hampton, at Livingston, Alabama, in 1939. Recorded by John A. and Ruby T. Lomax.

Track 11: "The Buzzard and the Cooter," spoken by Demus Green at Charleston, South Carolina, in 1975. Recorded by Alice D. Boyle.

Track 12: "Prayer," spoken by Rev. Henry Ward, at Johnson Place Baptist Church, in Livingston, Alabama, in 1939. Recorded by John A. and Ruby T. Lomax.

Track 13: "Run, Old Jeremiah," sung by Joe Washington Brown and Austin Coleman, at Jennings, Louisiana, in 1934. Recorded by John A. and Alan Lomax.

Track 14: "Job, Job," sung by Mandy Tartt, Sims Tartt, and Betty Atmore, at Livingston, Alabama, in 1939. Recorded by John A. and Ruby T. Lomax.

Track 15: "Sometimes I Feel Like a Motherless Child," sung by Clifford Reed, Johnny Mae Medlock, and Julia Griffin, at the State Farm, Railford, Florida, in 1939. Recorded by John A. and Ruby T. Lomax.

Track 16: "Have Mercy, Lord" (spiritual), sung by Mary Tollman and the Reverend Henry Ward.

Track 17: "The Unusual Task of the Gospel Preacher," extracts from a sermon delivered by Rev. Harry Singleton, at Sandy Island, South Carolina, in 1972. Recorded by Charles Joyner.

Track 18: "The Man of Calvary," Easter sermon delivered by Sin-Killer Griffin, at Darrington State Farm, Sandy Point, Texas, in 1934. Recorded by John A. Lomax.

ACKNOWLEDGMENTS

Writing the history of African America from outside, indeed from halfway around the world, has many pleasures, and not the least of them in recent years has been trying to explain to the immigration officials at LAX or SFO, hypervigilantly guarding the United States, exactly what it is that an historian on a research trip does. Shane White has been the recipient of much gratuitous advice at American airports about how to write history. One immigration official, on being told that the Australian academic was flying on to New York, barked back, "There's history out *there*," pointing in the general direction of downtown Los Angeles or conceivably New York in the far distance. "Go and do it!" Shane White still occasionally wakes up in the middle of the night wondering about that little exchange. Distance creates a few logistical problems as well, but money helps overcome many of them. We are extremely grateful for the Australian Research Council's generous funding of our work through an ARC Small Grant for 1998–1999 and an ARC Large Grant for 2000–2002.

We also owe a very large debt to the various repositories, and their invariably helpful staff, who house the material that we have used in this book. These include the American Antiquarian Society; the Library Company of Philadelphia (especially Phil Lapsansky, still incomparable); the newspaper section of the Library of Congress; the Municipal Archives of the City of New York (where Ken Cobb has been most helpful); the National Library of Australia; the New York Historical Society; the New York Public Library; and the Davis Library and the Wilson Library (where Michael Taft was particularly helpful) at the University of North Carolina, Chapel Hill.

We are grateful to the staff of the Archive of Folk Culture of the Library of Congress for assisting us in our search for many of the tracks that finally appeared on our CD, and most particularly to Reference Specialist Ann Hoog, who so efficiently and pleasantly guided us over the various hurdles we needed to jump. Our warm thanks also to Alice Boyle, whose wonderful collection of folktales, as recounted to her by the Gullah speaker Demus Green, is held by the Southern Folklife Collection at the Wilson Library. With the kind assistance of her friend Kathy Schenek, Alice was able to put us in touch with Ben Green, Demus Green's only surviving relative, who kindly gave us permission to include one of Demus Green's animal trickster stories on our CD. And we would also like to thank the Reverend Harry Singleton for allowing us to use a lengthy extract from one of his sermons on the CD.

Our collaboration stems from the early 1980s, when we jointly taught a course in African American history at the University of Sydney. Lawrence Levine's *Black Culture and Black Consciousness: Afro-American Folk Thought from Slavery to Freedom* (1977) was the core of that course and the starting point for all that we have written since. Our intellectual debt to Larry Levine extends well beyond his published work: we thank him for his friendship, his advocacy of this project, and his incisive reading of the draft of most of this book.

This book is dedicated to two scholars who helped greatly in its creation. Glenn Hinson encouraged the project from the outset, giving generously of his time and pointing out to us all sorts of research material. To talk with Glenn is immediately to sense the excitement he brings to African American studies. *The Sounds of Slavery* bears the strong imprint of his rich insights into African American culture, especially in its musical dimensions. For nigh on two decades now, Charles Joyner has been a friend and ceaseless publicist of our work. Not only has he helped our understanding of black American music through countless hours of conversation and listening, but he also took Graham White to some of the Sea Islands of South Carolina and introduced him to Mrs. Genevieve Peterkin of Murrells Inlet, who as a very young child accompanied her mother as she conducted interviews with former slaves, and whose fascination with Gullah culture equals Charles's own. As well, over many years we have been deeply appreciative of Charles and Jean Joyner's matchless hospitality.

The Sounds of Slavery was conceived, mostly researched, and entirely written in Australia, and our debts in this country are substantial. We are both products of the History Department at the University of Sydney, a wonderful place at which to be educated and in which to work. We owe much to past and present colleagues for their support of our work. In particular, we would like to thank Frances Clarke, Clare Corbould, Andrew Fitzmaurice, Mike McDonnell, Stephen Robertson, and Glenda Sluga for countless hours of conversation and gallons of coffee. Elsewhere in the university, we would like to thank Charles Fairchild, whose careful commentary on the CD accompanying this book was particularly helpful, and Stephen Garton, a fine golfing companion until he became dean. Moira Gatens and Richard Waterhouse, in rather different ways, have also provided all manner of support. At various points in this project, Clare Corbould and Delwyn Elizabeth provided excellent research assistance. And elsewhere in Australia, Richard Bosworth, Greg Dening, David Goodman, Rhys Isaac, Donna Merwick, John Salmond, and Ian Tyrrell have all substantially contributed to the intellectual environment in which we work.

Outside of Australia, mostly in the United States, a number of colleagues and friends have given us, in person or through the modern miracle of e-mail, advice and references to various primary sources, or just talked with us about our project. We would like to thank Roger Abrahams, Peter Agree, Ira Berlin, Marybeth Hamilton, Deborah Kaplan, Robin Kelley, Rip Lhamon, Joe Opala, Marcus Rediker, Roy Rosenzweig, and David Waldstreicher. The staff at Beacon Press have been terrific—we particularly appreciated their help with the convoluted process of securing permissions for the tracks on the CD. Our editor, Gayatri Patnaik, has been a pleasure to work with. We especially appreciated her intelligent understanding of what we were trying to do, and her enthusiasm as our manuscript was transformed into this book.

A few hardy souls other than Larry Levine read chapters for us. We would like to thank Bruce Mansfield and Bernard Thorogood, who were kind enough to comment on early drafts of our material on slave religion, and Joan Mansfield, who read large sections of the manuscript and offered valuable advice about our analysis of slave music. We would also like to thank Leon Litwack. Leon did not read any of this material in draft, but he certainly heard enough about it, and a considerable amount of the research was done in his magnificent library. Alex Bontemps read the entire manuscript, some chapters many times. His sharp comments and suggestions had a considerable impact on the ultimate shape of this book. We would like to thank him for his help and friendship.

And lastly we come to our long-suffering families. Graham White would like to thank Sue White for her encouragement of this project and her perceptive comments on the tracks of our CD. We would both like to thank her for reading the book and using her fine editorial ear. Shane White would like to thank Lexie Macdonald for her patience, support, and her excellent judgment on all manner of things for near twenty-five years, and Mac simply for being Mac, and as good a kid as one could ever hope for. Finally, he would like to mention Scout Macdonald, who may be getting a bit long in the tooth but still enjoys seeing his name in print.

INDEX

CD TRACKS FOR
THE SOUNDS OF SLAVERY

TRACK 1 "Arwhoolie" holler / Thomas J. Marshall

TRACK 2 Levee holler / Enoch Brown

TRACK 3 Field holler / Roosevelt "Giant" Hudson

TRACK 4 "Oh If Your House Catches Fire"
levee camp holler / Willie Henry Washington

TRACK 5 "Roxie" / Convicts, Mississippi

TRACK 6 "New Buryin' Ground" / John Brown
and African American convicts

TRACK 7 "Long Hot Summer Day" / Clyde Hill
and African American convicts

TRACK 8 "Go Preach My Gospel" / Deacon Harvey Williams
and the New Zion Baptist Church congregation

TRACK 9 "Jesus, My God, I Know His Name" / Willie Henry Washington,
Arthur Bell, Robert Lee Robertson, and Abraham Powell

TRACK 10 "Go to Sleep" / Florida Hampton

TRACK 11 "The Buzzard and the Cooter" / Demus Green

TRACK 12 "Prayer" / Rev. Henry Ward

TRACK 13 "Run, Old Jeremiah" /
Joe Washington Brown and Austin Coleman

TRACK 14 "Job, Job" / Mandy Tartt, Sims Tartt, and Betty Atmore

TRACK 15 "Sometimes I Feel Like a Motherless Child" /
Clifford Reed, Johnny Mae Medlock, and Julia Griffin

TRACK 16 "Have Mercy, Lord" /
Mary Tollman and the Rev. Henry Ward

TRACK 17 "The Unusual Task of the
Gospel Preacher" / Rev. Harry Singleton

TRACK 18 "The Man of Calvary" / Sin-Killer Griffin